FIONA HAMILTON-FAIRLEY

I CAN'T COOK:
ENTERTAINING

BLOOMSBURY

To
Tilman, Sebastian and Melinda

I would like to thank: Tilman, Geoff, Sarah, Tessa, Karen, Chey, Ulla, Robert and Tracy, plus numerous other guinea pigs for their support and encouragement in preparing this book. It is due to the success of the *I Can't Cook Book* and the constant nagging from students and friends that I have written *I Can't Cook: Entertaining*.

First published 1995
by Bloomsbury Publishing Plc,
2 Soho Square, London, W1V 6HB

Copyright © 1995 Fiona Hamilton-Fairley
The moral right of the author has been asserted.

A copy of the CIP entry for this book is available from the British Library.

ISBN 0 7475 2299 5

10 9 8 7 6 5 4 3 2 1

Typeset by Hewer Text Composition Services, Edinburgh
Printed in England by Clays Ltd, St Ives plc

Contents

1. Fast all-season supper
Fresh melon boats
Fresh pasta with pesto sauce
Crisp side salad with French dressing
Maple syrup and sour cream waffles

2. Two-course weekend supper from the store cupboard
Bacon and onion rosti with frozen peas
Hot banana split

3. Lacto-vegetarian menu (winter or spring)
Chilled sliced tomatoes with mozzarella cheese and basil
Baked pasta and vegetables in a creamy sauce
Brown bread and apricot ice-cream

4. Casual lunch or dinner party menu
Egg and mushroom ramekins
Vegetable and seafood risotto
Mixed leaf salad with walnut dressing
Banana and chocolate cream

5. Quick pre-theatre or cinema dinner
Hummus dip with crudités or pitta bread
Home-made savoury quiche
Tomato, avocado and chicory salad with sour cream dressing
Chilled ginger and lemon terrine

6. Mediterranean menu
Greek salad with ciabatta bread
Stuffed aubergines with mushroom and sun-dried tomatoes
Fresh pasta
Fresh figs with Greek yoghurt and honey

7. Summer picnic hamper
Home-made tuna fish dip or cottage cheese and cucumber dip with crudités, pitta bread or tortilla chips
Home-made savoury pizza
Mixed pasta salad
Spicy chicken drumsticks
Smoked salmon and cream cheese or roast beef, mustard and cress croissants
Fresh fruit kebabs or vanilla custard tarts

8. Vegan menu (spring/summer) (This menu would suit vegetarians who don't eat eggs or dairy products)
Fresh asparagus with vinaigrette and French bread
TVP and tomato meatloaf
Baked potatoes
French beans
Pears in red wine

9. Chinese stir-fry menu
Hot and sour soup
Lemon chicken with cashew nuts
Egg fried rice
Quick-fried bean sprouts and bamboo shoots
Frozen mango crunch

10. Summer or winter menu
Artichoke hearts with croûtons and lemon vinaigrette
Pork chop casserole with apple and sage
Oven-fried potatoes
Red or white buttered cabbage
Lemon or orange pancakes

11. Barbecue menu
Herb and garlic bread
Lamb, fish or vegetarian kebabs
Marinated chicken legs or spare ribs
Baked potatoes or rice
Mixed green salad and coleslaw
Home-made chocolate cheesecake

12. Curry menu
Dahl soup with nan bread
Lamb rogan josh with cucumber raita
Almond sag
Saffron or pilau rice with poppadoms
Lemon and lime sorbet

13. Winter or spring dinner party menu
Tomato and orange soup with croûtons or French bread
Chicken casserole with peanut and ginger sauce
Spiced mixed vegetables with yoghurt
Plain or saffron rice
Mousse au chocolat

14. All-season menu
Mixed cheese and croûton salad
Boeuf bourguignonne
Potato and spinach layer
Vichy carrots
Crème brûlée

15. Summer lunch or dinner menu
Chilled ratatouille with French bread
Fillet of sole véronique
New potatoes
Avocado and fresh spinach salad
Summer pudding with crème fraîche

16. Smart winter dinner party menu
Seafood vol-au-vents
Noisettes of lamb cooked with orange and rosemary
Brussels sprouts, buttered carrots and duchesse potatoes
Hazelnut meringue gâteau

17. Cocktail or drinks party menu
Dips: Guacamole dip or smoked mackerel dip, served with crudités and tortillla chips
Cold canapés: Smoked salmon turn-ups with fresh lime
Parma ham and asparagus rolls
Grape and melon cheese sticks
Hot canapés: Mushroom and coriander meatballs with mustard sauce
Choux buns stuffed with Gruyère cheese
Scampi with tartare sauce
Pizza bits

18. Summer lunch or dinner buffet menu
Spinach and Gruyère roulade
Cold chicken in a tomato and basil sauce
Cold roast beef with horseradish cream
Cold new potatoes with fresh chives
Mixed bean salad with walnut dressing
Watercress and pepper salad
Fresh fruit salad with cream
Mixed cheese platter with biscuits

19. Christmas roast menu
Roast turkey
Sausage-meat and apple stuffing
Sage and onion stuffing
Chipolata sausages and bacon rolls
Roast potatoes, parsnips, carrots and onions
Brussels sprouts with chestnuts
Bread sauce, cranberry sauce and gravy
Christmas pudding with brandy butter
Mince pies with fresh cream
Christmas cake

20. Crème de la crème menu
Lambs liver terrine with melba toast
Crispy duck à l'orange with a red wine sauce
Roast baby new potatoes
Mange-tout or French beans
Hot mocha soufflé with wafer biscuits and cream

Introduction

This book is aimed at people who would love to entertain but are fed up of buying ready-made meals and pretending that they are home-made. You know you can cook but you have never plucked up the courage to do so. Well, here is your chance!

This book, a sequel to the *I Can't Cook Book*, is designed to make cooking and entertaining as simple and enjoyable as possible. All you have to do is follow the step-by-step countdown method used in the recipes and you will surprise your guests – and yourself – with a delicious three-course meal. The menu planning and timing are done for you, while the equipment and shopping lists ensure you won't forget anything. If you want, you can mix and match courses from different menus, as equipment and shopping lists are provided for each individual course. As you try out more recipes, you will acquire the basic skills necessary to be a successful cook.

This book does not assume that you aready know a lot about cooking, yet you can pick up and prepare a three-course meal without any trouble. I have endeavoured to explain every step required for preparing the individual menus, and I have also tried to cover all the basic skills needed to make a nutritious and delicious meal whatever the occasion. The recipes avoid using difficult cookery terms and special equipment that you might not have.

In my view there are far too many cookery books that frighten people off by assuming an in-depth knowledge of cookery. In fact, all you need to become a proficient cook is time and effort. While writing this book, I constantly asked myself such questions as 'Why should someone know how to make a soufflé or what a bain-marie is?' I am not trying to turn you into a gourmet chef, but to make you feel comfortable and confident in the kitchen. I have tried to show that cooking need not be a chore, but that it can be enormous fun. Once you get used to the countdown method, you will soon be having dinners, buffets and cocktail parties, and will be entertaining for pleasure.

There are 20 different three-course menus in the book, including summer, winter and vegetarian meals, as well as picnics, cocktail parties and a buffet. Just choose or mix the menus to suit the occasion and your guests. You also have the option of leaving out a course if time or expense are against you: replace a dessert with cheese and biscuits, for example, or just make a main course for a few friends. The recipes serve four people, so it is easy to double the quantity for a party of eight or halve them for a romantic dinner for two.

The layout of the book is easy to follow. All quantities are given in both imperial and metric measurements. Remember to stick to one system: do not mix them. Don't forget to check your store cupboard against the shopping list so that you don't buy ingredients twice.

As you work through the menus you will find that I have not always stuck to the same method of cooking a certain meat, vegetable or pasta, as there is a multitude of ways to prepare food. This means you can decide which method suits you and adapt it to your own recipes. Check the Handy Tip column while you are cooking; it might get you out of a sticky situation.

Throughout the book, there are plenty of opportunities to make sauces, gravies, stews and casseroles. Conquer the art of sauce-making and the kitchen is yours. Sauces are particularly important if you want to cook meat and vegetables in the oven. They stop the food from drying out and allow the goodness and delicious flavours to be retained in the dish. As you progress, you will find that sauce-making becomes easier and easier. Soon you will be creating your own varieties of gravies, stews and casseroles.

Why are there no photographs in this book? For the good reason that without pictures you won't feel obliged to recreate a meal exactly as it looks in a glossy photograph. You are bound to be disappointed if a finished dish doesn't remotely resemble its picture, even if it tastes delicious. So never mind the photographs – make your own mental pictures. It's more creative and much more fun.

I wish you luck and enjoyment and hope that this book helps you to break through your fear of entertaining. Happy cooking!

Fiona Hamilton-Fairley
March 1995

Healthy eating habits

Over the last few years we have all become more health conscious as there is an abundance of information about health, diet and lifestyle. Supermarkets are now full of products which aim to help us cut down on the things known to be bad for us, such as fat, sugar and salt. Products such as skimmed milk, low-fat yoghurt, sugar-free baked beans and leaner meat are readily available and encourage healthier eating habits wihout sacrificing flavour or variety.

All the menus in this book have been carefully compiled. They are well balanced in terms of fat, fibre, protein and calories, yet they also take account of cost and time available. Given current information on a healthy diet, try to minimize the following items in your cooking:

Animal fats, such as butter and lard, should be avoided. Replace them with sunflower cooking margarine or oil (see Handy Tip 14, page xix). When a recipe requires milk, cheese or any other fatty ingredient, use the low-fat varieties now widely available. Serve crème fraîche, fromage frais or half-fat cream instead of full-fat cream, and always serve cream separately so that your guests can choose whether to eat it or not. And why not place butter *and* margarine on the table for your guests to choose the one they prefer?

Salt is the most over-used flavouring of all and can be harmful to health if used in large quantities. Use the minimum amount possible in your cooking, or cut it out altogether. Remember that it is always possible to add more salt if necessary, but it cannot be taken away once a dish is made. As we all have different tolerances, place a salt and pepper mill on the table and invite your guests to help themselves – this way they will be able to season the dish to their liking. Experiment with different spices and seasonings as they will reduce the need to flavour dishes with salt.

Sugar is another flavouring that is often over-used. Try to cut down on the amount you add to desserts. Instead, place a sugar bowl on the table for your guests to help themselves. The same rule applies to sugar as to salt: it can be easily added to a dish but it cannot be taken away, so do not be heavy-handed.

Don't be shy of telling your guests that you have tried to keep the menu healthy. Many people are trying to cut down on fat, salt and sugar in their day-to-day lives, so you may be helping them by making your dinner party more health conscious.

Entertaining vegetarians

There are growing numbers of people who prefer to eat little or no meat, whether for taste, health or ethical reasons. Although most vegetarians are used to making do with side dishes, salads, pasta and bread, it is polite when entertaining to check beforehand whether your guests are vegetarians and to provide options for them, including a vegetarian main course. This will avoid embarrassment on all sides. There are several types of vegetarians; the following guidelines may be helpful when planning a meal for those in the two main groups.

Lacto vegetarians
Those who eat no meat, meat products, fish or shellfish but do eat eggs and dairy products are called lacto vegetarians. Note that cheese must be rennet-free. Products suitable for vegetarian consumption frequently have a symbol on the packaging.

Vegans
Those who eat no meat, meat products, fish, shellfish, eggs or dairy products are called vegans. Their diet tends to consist of vegetables, nuts, grains, seeds and fruit. Take care to check your cooking fats and oils when preparing food for vegans, as some are blended and may contain animal fat. Also be careful of any prepared foods as they may contain animal fats or stocks.

Fortunately, vegetarian cookery has progressed beyond tofu. There are a wide variety of meatless dishes you can buy and make. This book contains two lacto-vegetarian menus (4 and 10) and one vegan menu (7). There are also many vegetarian starters and side dishes, and meat dishes which can be made with meat substitutes such as chick peas, lentils or buckwheat, or with a variety of minced nuts and grated root vegetables. Alternatively, use one of the modern meat substitutes which are both nutritious and versatile. These are:

Quorn – a high-protein food made from mushrooms.
Tofu (bean curd) – a high-protein food made from soya beans.
Textured vegetable protein (TVP) – soya mince or chunks.
Tempeh – fermented tofu.

These ingredients tend to be rather bland, so make sure you use them in conjuction with a well-seasoned sauce.

There are also many ready-made vegetarian dishes widely available in supermarkets and health food shops; these include complete meals, as well as bean burgers, vege-bangers and vegetable grills.

Most importantly, do not limit these options to vegetarians. Non-meat dishes can be savoury and satisfying to everyone; they are also low in fat and economical.

Planning a party

1. When planning a dinner, buffet or cocktail party there are several important things to consider before you start. How many guests will you invite? What is your budget? (This must include drink as well as food.) How much time do you have for preparation and cooking? Don't forget you can always make one or two dishes in advance, and some can even be frozen. Find out if any of your guests have special dietary requirements: remember, there's more than one kind of vegetarian. Even among meat-eaters there are many people who prefer not to eat red meat. If you are unsure of your guests' likes and dislikes, it is a good idea to vary the menu to cover all the options. Choose a menu suitable for the season. In winter-time have at least one hot course; a summer menu can be cold, but you will need plenty of space in the fridge for all the dishes to be chilled.

2. The menus in this book are designed to cover all occasions and every season. They also cater for different budgets, so you can plan in advance how much you want to spend. If you decide to mix the courses from different menus, make sure you have the right equipment and that there is enough room in the oven for all the courses.

3. Check that you have enough cutlery for each course so that you do not have to wash up between courses. Also make sure you have enough serving dishes for all the courses. See page xx for detailed advice on laying the table for different occasions. Choose a menu that won't involve extra washing up so that you can spend more time with your guests.

4. Check the equipment list carefully, especially if you are making something very elaborate which you have not made before. Remember to check your store cupboard before you go shopping so you don't buy ingredients you already have. For a special occasion, add some pretty napkins, candles and a bunch of flowers to your shopping list. Small touches like these create a good impression, brighten up a party and show that you have really made an effort.

Deep-freeze stores

Most people have a deep freeze nowadays, even if it is only a tiny one at the top of the fridge. If this is the case, you will have to choose carefully what to keep in the compartment as space will be limited. If you do a lot of entertaining and have only a small freezer compartment, it might be a good idea to think about getting a larger freezer: you will find it immensely useful and cost effective. There is less wastage because leftovers can be frozen for some time; kept in the fridge, they would have to be eaten very quickly or thrown away. When you are preparing a meal, you can always make extra quantities to freeze and use on a separate occasion. This is especially important if you are cooking for one or two people. You will also have the option of making a few dishes in advance of a dinner party, leaving less to prepare at the last minute. You will end up saving yourself time and effort.

F* I have used this symbol to indicate which dishes in each menu can be frozen. It also lets you know which dishes can be prepared in advance for a party.

Freezing home-made food

Make the dish as instructed in the countdown method. If preparing meat or vegetables, it is a good idea to stop cooking them approximately 20–30 minutes before the given time. This will prevent them deteriorating: they will be re-heated and therefore cooked completely before being served. Allow the food to cool to room temperature, then place in a freezer container and cover with cling film and a lid. Label clearly with the date, contents and number of servings, then place in the deep freeze.

Never put hot food into a fridge or freezer; always wait until it has cooled to room temperature.

Frozen food can remain in the freezer for 2–3 months if it is a three-star (***) freezer. All frozen food must be defrosted thoroughly before use. The time will vary depending on the type of food. Meat dishes are best defrosted very slowly, preferably overnight in the fridge.

Desserts take less time to defrost and will need 4–6 hours. If you are unsure about defrosting times, take the food out of the freezer and leave it at room temperature for 4–5 hours. Then transfer it to the fridge where it can continue to defrost for a few more hours.

Remember, all dishes which are going to be served hot must be cooked thoroughly before being served.

Basic deep-freeze stores

brown or white sliced bread
1 packet (8oz/225g) shortcrust pastry
ice-cream
frozen vegetables (such as peas, corn, beans and spinach)
frozen chopped parsley
1 packet butter or margarine

If you have a separate deep freeze with lots of space, it is a good idea to stock a few items which can be made quickly when you get home from work, or if you have unexpected guests. Such items include:

Vol-au-vent cases (medium or large). These cases are cooked from frozen and can be filled with a variety of delicious fillings.
Mini pizzas (individual meat or vegetarian pizzas). These are cooked from frozen and are made even better by adding tomato purée, cheese, salami, onions, herbs, olives or whatever you fancy. Place the pizzas under a hot grill first to crispen them up and then add all the extra toppings. The whole process should take no longer than 20–25 minutes. Serve with a fresh salad or some cooked frozen vegetables.
Chicken nuggets or pieces (cooked from frozen). These can be served with pasta and a green salad or vegetables.
Meat or vegetable pasties (cooked from frozen). These can be served with potatoes, rice, salad or vegetables.

Don't let shop-bought prepared foods dominate your freezer space; remember to leave enough room for your home-made meals.

Equipment

Below is a comprehensive list of cooking equipment. It is not necessary to have everything listed, but as you use the book you might want to buy a few extra gadgets which will save you time and energy. All the essentials are marked with an asterisk (*).

1* **Kitchen scale.** This is essential for measuring ingredients accurately. It doesn't have to be expensive or modern. You can also use tablespoons to measure quantities although that method is not as accurate.

1* **Measuring jug,** with both metric and imperial mesurements.

1* **Chopping board,** savoury (see Handy Tip 15, page xix).

1* **Chopping board,** sweet (see Handy Tip 15, page xix).

1* **Large chopping knife** (all purpose).

2(1*) **Wooden spoons,** savoury, used for onions, vegetables, etc. (see Handy Tip 15, page xix).

2(1*) **Wooden spoons,** sweet, used for fruits, chocolate, etc. (see Handy Tip 15, page xix).

1* **Small chopping knife** (all purpose).

1* **Potato peeler,** swivel-bladed, all-purpose.

2* **Medium saucepans** with lids.

1* **Medium frying pan.**

1* **Non-stick spatula** (savoury) for turning food when frying.

1* **Large roasting tin.**

1* **Flat baking tray** (non-stick makes washing up easier).

1* **Medium ovenproof casserole dish** with lid.

6–8(4*) **Ramekins.** These are individual ovenproof dishes which are useful for starters and desserts. They can go straight from the oven or fridge to the table. They are also very useful for serving dips, sauces, mustard and peanuts.

2(1*) **Plastic or glass mixing bowls.** Plastic bowls make less noise when whisking egg whites, cream, etc. with a hand-held electrical mixer or a balloon whisk. Glass bowls can also be used for serving if necessary.

1* **Balloon whisk.** This is made from thin metal wires formed into a balloon shape. It is excellent for whisking eggs and cream and for beating lumps out of sauces and gravy. A balloon whisk is essential if you don't have a hand-held electrical mixer or a food processor.

2* **Tablespoons** for cooking. They should be the same size, especially if you use them to measure with.

1* **Dessertspoon**

1* **Teaspoon.** If used for measuring, it must have a 5ml capacity.

1* **All-purpose grater** with four grating surfaces on it.

1* **Medium fine sieve.**

1* **Colander** for washing and draining vegetables, fruit, rice and pasta.

1* **Lemon squeezer** (large enough to hold the juice of at least one whole lemon or orange).

1* **Garlic crusher** or round-ended knife (see Handy Tip 1, page xvii).

1* **Tin opener.**

1* **Corkscrew and bottle opener.**

2* **Oven gloves.**

1 **Medium serrated-edge knife** for bread and certain vegetables.

1 **Large saucepan** with lid.

1 **Small saucepan** with lid.

1 **Double saucepan** or 1 heatproof mixing bowl that fits snugly over one of your saucepans without touching the bottom. It can be used to melt chocolate or whisk egg yolks, neither of which should be done over a direct heat.

1 **Large frying pan** with tight-fitting lid.

1	Medium roasting tin.	1	Freezer-proof container with lid, 2 pint/1.2 litre capacity.
1	Grill and grill pan.		
1	Loaf tin, 2lb/900g capacity (8 × 4 inch/20 × 10cm).	1	Flexible spatula (sweet) for folding.
		1	Ladle.
1	12-hole bun tin, preferably non-stick for Yorkshire puddings or fairy cakes.	1	Small fine sieve.
		1	Rolling pin with solid ends (these are useful for crushing biscuits and nuts). You can also use a clean wine bottle to roll out pastry if you don't have a rolling pin.
1	Flan tin, 8 inch/20cm plain or fluted loose-bottomed, or 1 ceramic oven-proof dish (for quiches, cheesecakes, etc.).		
2	Cake tins, non-stick 8-inch/20-cm.	1	Pastry brush.
1	Cooling rack.	1	Hand-held electric mixer.
1	Large ovenproof casserole dish with lid.	1	Pair of kitchen scissors.
		1	Potato masher.
1	Medium ovenproof glass dish with lid for vegetables and desserts.	1	Salad shaker or spinner. This is useful if you have to dry a lettuce quickly. A wet salad will be heavy and not mix easily with a French dressing.
1	Pudding basin, 2 pint/1.2 litre capacity.		

I have tried to make all the recipes adaptable to the equipment you will have in your kitchen. If you are working from the basic essential equipment list, always check the equipment list before starting to prepare the recipes; this will ensure that you don't get halfway through the menu before discovering that you haven't got a vital piece of equipment. The more you cook and enjoy it, the more likely you are to collect useful utensils and machinery. It is a good idea to borrow equipment from a friend before buying your own to see if it helps you and suits your style of cooking.

Dishes needed for serving

This is a detailed list and you are not expected to have everything on it; essentials are marked with an asterisk (*). It is assumed that you have a set of china and cutlery to serve a least 4 people, so the list below is what you will need in the way of extra serving dishes once the food has been cooked.

1*	Large salad bowl (wooden or glass).	1	Serving ladle.
1*	Pair of salad servers.	1	Flat fish slice for serving fish, meats, cheesecakes and cakes.
3(2*)	Vegetable dishes with lids. The lids will help to keep food hot.	1	Soufflé dish (7 × 3½ inch/18 × 8 cm).
3(2*)	Pairs of serving spoons for vegetables.	1	Round or oval bread basket. (This could also be used for baked potatoes or cheese biscuits.)
2(1*)	Casserole dishes (see equipment list). Try to buy a nice-looking casserole dish which can be used straight from the oven to the table.		
		1	Butter dish (or you can use an extra ramekin).
1*	Flat oval plate for serving meat, fish, pasta, or even a dessert.	1	Butter knife.
		1	Cheeseboard.
1*	Large all-purpose glass bowl for fruit salads, mousses, etc.	1	Cheese knife.
		1	Picnic hamper with 4 place settings and plastic containers for transporting food.
6–8(4*)	Ramekins (see Equipment list, page xiii, for details).		
1	Soup tureen (or a large bowl or a saucepan).		

Food processors, liquidizers and blenders

There is a wide range of food processors, liquidizers and blenders on the market, and it is hard to say which are the best as they all perform different tasks to varying degrees of precision. I have always maintained that it is possible to manage without any of them if the recipes are simple and suggest alternative equipment, as in this book. On the other hand, there is a lot to be said for these machines if you cook and entertain a lot: they do save you time and energy, and their speed and precision are excellent. Many people are intimidated by food processors as they look complicated, but once you conquer your fear, the processor will become a firm friend and ease the workload in the kitchen significantly.

If you are tempted to buy a food processor, liquidizer or blender, make sure you research it well to see if it will perform the tasks you require. Ideally, try to borrow a similar machine from a friend to see if it meets your needs. Hand-held electric mixers are particularly useful for whisking egg whites and beating cream and cake mixtures. They are a good investment if you cook and entertain a lot, and they have the added advantage of being inexpensive. Hand-held blenders and liquidizers are excellent for making soups and purées.

Store cupboard stock list

Dry ingredients

Plain flour
Self-raising flour
Cornflour (the best thickening agent)
Stock cubes (chicken, beef, vegetable)
Granulated sugar
Caster sugar
Demerara sugar
Chocolate Flakes
Cocoa powder
Dried breadcrumbs
Sultanas
Gelatine or Agar (vegetarian setting agent)
White long-rain rice (easy cook)
Pasta (white or green)
Salted peanuts or crisps
Flaked almonds
Parmesan cheese
Plain chocolate
Vanilla essence
Cheese biscuits (keep in an airtight tin)
Boudoir or Langues de chat biscuits (to serve with a dessert)
Croûtons
Kitchen paper
Cling film
Aluminium foil

Dry herbs and seasonings

Cooking salt
Black peppercorns (if you have a pepper mill)
Ground black pepper
Ground white pepper (it is only necessary to have white pepper if you don't want black speckles in a white sauce)
Cayenne pepper
Dried mustard powder
Ground nutmeg
Cinnamon
Oregano
Mixed herbs
Bay leaves
Bouquet garni
Curry powder (hot, medium or mild)
Chilli powder

Packet mixes

Don't feel embarrassed about using packet mixes – they will save you time and effort, especially if you get home late and want to cook something quickly.
Instant custard powder
Instant hollandaise sauce
Stuffing (sage and onion)
Instant bread sauce

Instant savoury sauce
Instant soups (mushroom, French onion)
Instant potato granules
Vacuum-packed pizza base

Tins and bottles

Worcestershire sauce
Soya sauce
Tabasco sauce
Tomato ketchup
Tomato purée
Garlic purée
Lemon juice
Vegetable and/or sunflower oil
Olive oil
Dry sherry
White wine vinegar
Chopped tomatoes
Plum tomatoes
Sweetcorn
Tuna fish
Peach halves
Mandarin oranges
Condensed milk
Olives
Thick honey
Chutney (mango or peach)
Orange marmalade

Peanut butter
Carton UHT milk (in case you run out of fresh milk)

Fridge stores

Butter
Garlic and herb butter
Cooking margarine (see Handy Tip 14, page xix)
Table margarine (sunflower)
Bacon
Eggs (size 1 or 2)
Mayonnaise
Milk
Cheddar cheese
Mustard (whole grain, French, English)

Fresh stores

Onions
Garlic
Root ginger (see Handy Tip 6, page xviii)
Potatoes
Lemon
Apples
Bananas
Small loaf, brown or white (or see Deep-freeze Stores)

Handy tips

1. How to crush garlic without a garlic crusher

Peel the garlic clove and place it on a savoury chopping board (see Handy Tip 15). Place a teaspoon of cooking salt near the edge of the board and hold the garlic firmly next to it. Take a round-edged knife in your other hand, dip the blade into the salt and start pressing the garlic, working the flat of the blade up and down and using more salt as necessary. You should be left with a fine paste of garlic which is ready to use. Discard any excess salt and take care when seasoning the dish as you will have used a lot of salt with the garlic.

2. How to separate eggs

There are two easy and foolproof ways of separating eggs. Use whichever you find easiest.
Method 1. First wash your hands well. Take 2 bowls which are large enough to hold the separated egg and any other ingredients you may add to them later. (This saves time and washing up.) Take an egg and make a crack in the middle of the shell by knocking it sharply on the side of a bowl. Slowly prise the eggshell apart and empty the whole egg into your cupped hand. Allow the egg white to run between your fingers into the bowl underneath. You will have to open your fingers a few times to do this. You should be left with a yolk sitting in the palm of your hand. Transfer it to a clean bowl and repeat the process with any remaining eggs.
Method 2. Take an egg and carefully crack it on the side of a saucer. Prise the shell apart and let the whole egg fall gently into the saucer. Place an egg cup upside-down over the yolk, hold it firmly in place, then tip the egg white off the saucer into a separate bowl. Once all the egg white has drained away, remove the egg cup and place the yolk in a separate bowl.

3. Fresh breadcrumbs from frozen bread

Take the required amount of bread out of the deep freeze: 1 slice will make 1oz/25g of breadcrumbs. Grate it on to a plate using a medium-hole grater. If the last little piece of bread starts to defrost from the heat of your hand, crumble it with your fingers.

4. How to get rid of lumps in a sauce or gravy

Sauces and gravies tend to become lumpy if the margarine and flour mixture (the 'roux') is too thick or overheated. You should add the liquid to the roux away from the heat, as slowly as possible, stirring all the time. If the mixture starts to 'clump', stop adding the liquid at once. Take a balloon whisk or savoury wooden spoon and beat the sauce or gravy as hard as possible. Within a few minutes you should be left with a smooth mixture. Once the sauce is smooth again, you can continue to add the liquid slowly, stirring all the time. However, if you still have a very lumpy sauce, the best thing to do is sieve it into another saucepan or bowl, make sure you get as much of the roux through the sieve as possible. Add the remaining liquid, if you have any, put the sauce back over a medium heat and bring to the boil stirring constantly. Cook for 2–3 minutes to remove the starch. If the sauce is too thin, you can use some cornflour to thicken it up later (see Handy Tip 13).

5. Squeezing oranges and lemons

Before squeezing the juice from oranges or lemons, it is a good idea to roll the fruit under the palm of your hand on a flat surface. This will release the flesh inside the fruit and make squeezing it more efficient.

6. Using fresh root ginger

Fresh root ginger is a knobbly root wih a thin grey-brown skin. Avoid the very large roots as a little goes a long way.

To use fresh ginger, peel off the skin with a sharp vegetable peeler or knife, then grate it using a fine grater. Most recipes ask you to cook ginger before you eat it as it can be very strong. It is delicious with casseroles and fresh vegetables, and in cakes and desserts.

Store fresh ginger in a cool dry place (perhaps with your onions and garlic). Remember that the longer you keep root ginger, the stronger and more woody in texture it will become. You might have to reduce the amount you use if you have kept it for quite some time.

7. Frozen chopped parsley

Buy a large bunch of fresh parsley, wash it well, shake off any excess water, then pat dry with kitchen paper. Place on a savoury chopping board and chop finely using a very sharp knife. Place in a small freezer container, cover with a lid or cling film, then freeze until required.

When needed, take the parsley out of the freezer and use a sharp knife to crumble off as much as you need. The remaining parsley can be returned to the freezer and used for other dishes.

This technique can also be used with other fresh herbs such as coriander, chives, sage and mint.

8. Removing fat from sauces, gravies and casseroles

The easy way to remove unwanted fat from a dish is to place a double thickness of kitchen paper on top of it. Allow the paper to absorb as much grease as possible, then carefully lift it off. Discard the paper and repeat the process until there is no more fat to be seen. This technique can also be used with cheese-topped dishes.

9. Tear-free onions

If you find that chopping onions irritates your eyes, move the chopping board over to the sink and gently run some cold water. Continue to chop the onion as close to the running water as possible. This should ease the problem.

10. How to ripen an avocado

Remember to buy avocados 3 to 4 days before you need to use them so that they have time to ripen. If you are having a dinner party for 4 guests, buy 3 hard avocados and make sure their skins are unblemished. It is always best to buy more avocados than you actually need so that you can choose the ripest ones.

Place the avocados in one or more brown paper bags and put them in a warm place, such as an airing cupboard. Check how well they are ripening after 2–3 days and turn them over in the bag. By day 3 or 4 they should be ripe and ready to eat: the narrow end should be soft to the touch. Always cut an avocado lengthways, not around the middle. If the avocado is ripe, the stone should fall out and the skin will peel off easily.

11. Cooking vegetables

Stick to one general rule when cooking vegetables, and you can't go wrong.
- Vegetables that grow under the ground, such as carrots, potatoes and parsnips, should be put into cold water and brought slowly to the boil. They should then simmer until cooked with a lid half on.

- Vegetables that grow above the ground, such as broccoli, beans and peas, should be plunged into boiling water, or have boiling water poured over them. Bring the pan swiftly to the boil, then simmer until cooked.

Always cook vegetables in as little water as possible but with enough to cover them. Much of the vitamin content is lost in the cooking water.

Most of us have become very salt conscious these days, so use only a pinch of salt in the cooking water. Guests can add more seasoning at the table if they wish.

12. Toasting almonds

If you do a lot of entertaining and enjoy desserts, it is a good idea to have some toasted almonds ready for decoration. They are simple to make but need to be watched carefully as they can burn very easily. Preheat the oven to 180°C/350°F/Gas mark 4. Take 4oz/100g of flaked almonds and spread them out evenly on a baking tray. Place in the preheated oven for 5–8 minutes to brown, turning them over with a fish slice, half-way through cooking time. As soon as they are golden brown all over, take them out of the oven and leave to cool. Store in an airtight container and use as required.

13. How to use cornflour

Place 1 level tablespoon of cornflour in a small mixing bowl and add enough water to make a thin paste. Stir well and add to the sauce or gravy, off the heat. Put the saucepan back over a low heat and slowly bring back to the boil, stirring constantly. The sauce thickens as it boils. It is very important to cook it for several minutes after thickening to remove the starchy taste. If the sauce is still not thick enough, repeat until you reach the correct consistency.

14. Why use cooking margarine rather than table margarine?

Cooking margarine can withstand higher temperatures than table margarine so it is less likely to burn. Some recipes call for cooking margarine and oil to be used together. This is to increase the heat resistance and prevent burning. Look in your local supermarket for cooking margarine (it will be clearly labelled). As a general rule, use a cooking margarine or oil for dishes cooked in the oven or on the hob. For delicate dishes use butter or a good margarine.

15. Chopping boards and wooden spoons

Wooden utensils are prone to absorb strong flavours, so use two chopping boards – one for savoury things like onions, garlic, fish or meat and another for sweet things such as strawberries, peaches and chocolate. The same rule applies to wooden spoons.

16. Boiling eggs

However you want to cook your eggs, there are a few general rules to follow for the best results.
- Always check that eggs are not cracked or broken before starting to cook them.
- Always boil the water in the saucepan first before adding the eggs. This means you can time them more accurately as you will know exactly when they start to cook.
- If possible, use an egg hole-puncher to pierce a small hole in the eggshell. This releases the air inside the egg and stops it from cracking while cooking. If you do not have a hole-puncher, make a hole with a clean needle or pin. Another way to stop eggs cracking is to add a teaspoon of salt or vinegar to the water.
- Plunge all the eggs into the saucepan at the same time so that they cook evenly; start the timer at once. Cook a hard-boiled egg for 8–10 minutes.
- Cook a soft-boiled egg for 4–6 minutes. The time will vary depending on the size of the egg.

Setting the table

While it's not a complicated affair, setting the table needs planning and common sense. The most important issue is to judge the nature of your meal. The more formal the event, the more careful you should be in laying the table to suit the occasion.

The basic rule about cutlery is that there is a set of cutlery for every course. Those furthest from the plate (the starter cutlery) are used first, and you work inwards with each course until you reach the dessert cutlery. The only exception to this rule is that the dessert cutlery can sometimes be placed above the plate for an informal supper or if there is not enough room at the side of the plate.

The standard rule applied to cutlery also applies to glasses – provide a glass for each 'course' of drinks. There should be a glass for each type of wine you are going to serve so that the flavours will not be mixed; also include a water glass and place a jug of iced water on the table for your guests to help themselves. If it is a very smart occasion, you might want to include a port or liqueur glass for an after-dinner drink.

If serving bread, put a small side plate with a butter knife on top to the left of the large plate. If serving soup, place the bowl on top of the main course plate.

The napkins can be placed on the main or side plate, or prettily pushed into a wine glass. Extra touches include candlesticks and flowers.

See below for diagrams of possible place settings and the menus they would suit.

Easy, 2-course meal
Suitable for: Menu 2

wine glass

dessertspoon and fork

main course knife and fork

Easy, informal 3-course meal
Suitable for: Menus 1, 3, 4 , 5, 6

wine glass
water tumbler
dessertspoon and fork

starter spoon
(sometimes knife and fork)

bread plate and knife

main course fork and knife

Moderate 3-course meal
Suitable for: Menus 8, 10, 11

red wine glass
white wine glass
water tumbler

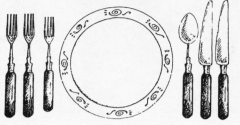

dessertspoon and fork
main course knife and fork
starter knife and fork

Moderate 3-course meal with soup
Suitable for: Menus 12, 13

red wine glass
white wine glas
water tumbler

soup spoon
main course knife and fork
dessert spoon and fork
bread plate and knife

Difficult, 3- or more course meal
Suitable for: Menus 14, 15, 16, 18, 19, 20

port glass
red wine glass
water tumbler
white wine glass

dessertspoon and fork
main course knife and fork
starter knife and fork

bread plate and knife

Measurements

Ounces	Grams
	(Recommended conversion to the nearest unit of 25 grams.)
1oz	25g
2oz	50g
3oz	75g
4oz (¼lb)	100g
5oz	125g
6oz	175g
7oz	200g
8oz (½lb)	225g
9oz	250g (¼Kg)
10oz	275g
11oz	300g
12oz	350g
13oz	375g
14oz	400g
15oz	425g
16oz (1lb)	450g
17oz	475g
18oz	500g (½Kg)
19oz	550g
20oz (1¼lb)	575g
2lb 3oz	1000g (1Kg)

For the best results you should measure things out accurately with kitchen scales. If you do not have any scales then the general rule is: 1oz/25g=1 tablespoon.

If you measure out small amounts with a tablespoon always use the same tablespoon for all the ingredients, this will ensure relative accuracy.

Liquid measurements

Imperial measure	Imperial measure floz	Metric measure nearest ml. (millilitre)
¼ pint	5 fl oz	150 ml
½ pint	10 fl oz	300 ml
¾ pint	15 fl oz	450 ml
1 pint	20 fl oz	600 ml
1½ pints	30 fl oz	900 ml
1¾ pints	35 fl oz	1000 ml (1 litre)

Oven settings

	°C	°F	Gas Mark
Very Cool	110	225	¼
	120	250	½
Cool	140	275	1
	150	300	2
Moderate	160	325	3
	180	350	4
Moderately Hot	190	375	5
	200	400	6
Hot	220	425	7
	230	450	8
Very Hot	240	475	9

Ovens can vary tremendously – from modern fan-assisted ovens to conventional ovens or Agas. I have always had an electric oven and a gas hob, so I have enjoyed the best of both worlds. I believe that gas is easier to work with as it is far easier to control the temperature and keep things simmering, rather than boiling.

Experiment with your oven. You will soon discover how best to control your oven and hob, but don't forget it might take a little time before you feel confident and happy using it.

Fast all-season supper

Easy to prepare and cook
Cost level: inexpensive
Serves: 4

1

There is no break incorporated in this menu.

<u>Starter</u>	Fresh melon boats	*Preparation time = 15 minutes* *Cooking time = None*
<u>Main course</u>	Fresh pasta with pesto sauce Crisp side salad with French dressing	*Preparation time = 35 minutes* *Cooking time = 10 minutes*
<u>Dessert</u>	Maple syrup and sour cream waffles	*Preparation time = 10 minutes* *Cooking time = 5–6 minutes*
<u>Drink</u>	Light and fruity white wine, chilled	

The menu is quick and easy to prepare. The starter should be prepared at the last minute to make sure the melon doesn't dry out. It is a good idea to buy the melon a few days in advance so that it has time to ripen. Keep the melon at room temperature on the day itself so that it becomes aromatic.

The main course is prepared and cooked on the night and served at once. The salad can be made with any combination of salad ingredients, but remember to keep it simple. You will need a French dressing so turn to page 201 for instructions or, if time is short, buy a ready-made dressing.

The dessert is simple and fun and can be topped with any seasonal soft fruit of your choice. If time is short, or if you haven't managed to get hold of any waffles, you can always serve a cheese platter and/or fresh fruit.

MENU 1

Equipment needed – Menu 1

Starter

1 sweet chopping board
1 sharp knife
1 teaspoon or dessertspoon

Main course

1 large saucepan with lid
1 savoury chopping board
1 sharp knife
1 frying pan
1 savoury wooden spoon
1 tablespoon
1 colander
Side salad
  1 sharp knife
  1 savoury chopping board
  1 colander
  1 potato peeler
  1 measuring jug

Dessert

1 grill pan
1 small mixing bowl
1 fork
1 tablespoon
1 round-ended knife

Shopping list – Menu 1

Starter

1 honeydew or cantaloupe melon (ripe – soft
  with a pleasant aroma)
*2 teaspoons demarara sugar

Main course

14–16oz/400–500g fresh pasta of your choice,
  e.g. tagliatelle
*2 tablespoons olive oil
*salt and pepper
*1 onion
1 jar pesto sauce (7oz/200g)
2oz/50g (2 tablespoons) finely grated Parmesan
  cheese to serve
1–2 tablespoons pine kernels to serve
Side salad
  2 little gem lettuces
  4 tomatoes
  ¼ cucumber
  1 bunch radishes
  ¼ pint/150ml French dressing (see page 201)

Dessert

4 egg waffles (fresh **or** frozen)
seasonal soft fruits for topping, e.g. 1 ripe
  banana, 6 strawberries, 1 peach
4oz/100g sour cream
4 tablespoons maple syrup

Check store cupboard

Countdown – Menu 1

If you want to prepare and cook the whole menu, you will need 65 minutes (1 hour and 5 minutes). As this is such a fast and flexible menu, there is no break incorporated. However, if you would like a break, the starter can be made 1–2 hours before serving and placed in the fridge to chill. If you are a slow cook, add 5–10 minutes to each course to ensure you do not run out of time. Remember, the times given are only a guide as each cook will take different lengths of time to complete each task. The main course must be made fresh and served piping hot straight to the table. The dessert is very quick and should be served hot so that it remains crisp.

Starter

PROBLEMS AND HANDY TIPS

Preparation time: 15 minutes
Cooking time: None

About 1–2 hours before serving assemble all the ingredients and equipment you need for the starter. Set your timer for 15 minutes.

15 mins Take the ripe melon and cut it in half from top to bottom, not through the middle. Remove all the seeds using a teaspoon or dessert-spoon. Slice the melon in half again lengthways to make four melon boats.

Leave as much juice as possible in the melon as this will keep it moist and stop it from drying out.

10 mins Take a sharp knife and carefully slice underneath the flesh of the melon as close to the skin as possible. You should end up with the melon flesh detached from the skin but still lying on top.

Try not to cut through the skin – keeping it whole makes a better boat. If you do happen to cut through it, don't worry; you can hide the damage underneath the melon pieces.

5 mins Using a sharp knife, cut the flesh of each melon into bite-size pieces by cutting through the centre of the flesh and then across several times, loosening the pieces. You should end up with a neat patchwork of melon pieces lying on the boat-shaped skin. Sprinkle each boat with a small amount of demerara sugar and chill until required.

Use only a small amount of sugar. Your guests can always add more themselves if it is not sweet enough.

0 mins Wash up and clear away.

MENU 1

Main course

Preparation time: 35 minutes
Cooking time: 10 minutes

Assemble all the ingredients and equipment you need for the main course. Set your timer for 35 minutes.

35 mins Fill the kettle and put it on to boil. Place the fresh pasta in a large saucepan, add 1 tablespoon of olive oil and a pinch of salt. Pour enough boiling water over the pasta to cover and come ½inch/1cm above it. Put over a medium heat and bring to the boil; cook for approximately 3–4 minutes. Check packet for cooking times as different brands will vary.

A drop of olive oil in the cooking water prevents the pasta from sticking together.

Dried pasta takes longer to cook than fresh pasta. Check the packet and cooking instructions carefully.

30 mins While the pasta is cooking, peel and chop 1 onion and place it in a frying pan. Add 1 tablespoon of olive oil and place over a medium to high heat. Cook the onion until it is golden brown.

Add extra olive oil if the onion becomes dry. Do not allow the onion to burn: it should be golden brown.

25 mins While the onion is cooking, check the pasta and if it is cooked, drain it through a colander. Put it back into the saucepan and cover with warm water to stop it from sticking together. Set aside.

20 mins Check the onion and make sure it is not burning, stir well and add a jar of pesto sauce to the onion. Check the seasoning and add a little salt and pepper if required. Continue to cook slowly until the pesto is heated right through.

The pesto sauce should be cooked over a low heat so that it does not curdle.

Side salad

16 mins Take the little gem lettuces and using either a sharp knife or your fingers, cut or tear them up. Place in a colander, wash under cold running water and leave to drain.

Always wash your lettuce and salad ingredients really well, as so many chemicals are used in their cultivation.

10 mins Take 4 tomatoes, discard the stalks, then wash well. Cut into thin slices or quarters. Wash the cucumber and radishes, if using. Peel the cucumber if you like, then slice it thinly or dice it. Top and tail the radishes, then slice or cut into quarters.

2 mins Put all the salad ingredients into a bowl but do not dress until just before serving.

Always dress the salad at the last minute otherwise it will become soggy.

0 mins Wash up and clear away.

Dessert

PROBLEMS AND HANDY TIPS

Preparation time: 10 minutes
Cooking time: 5–6 minutes

Assemble all the ingredients and equipment you need for the dessert. You can prepare the waffles in advance and cook them once you have eaten the main course. Preheat the grill to a high setting. Set your timer for 10 minutes.

The grill must be very hot before placing the waffles under it. You could use a toaster at this stage, but you will need a grill later on.

10 mins Place the waffles, either fresh or frozen, under a hot grill and toast on both sides so that they become golden brown and crisp. Watch them carefully as they burn very easily.

8 mins If you are using seasonal fruit, place in a mixing bowl and mash with a fork to form a textured paste. Add 2–3 tablespoons of sour cream and stir well.

You will need to peel certain soft fruits.

5 mins Pour 1 tablespoon of maple syrup on to each waffle, then add 1 tablespoon of the fruit mixture or sour cream to each one. Spread out evenly. Set aside if you are going to cook the waffles after the main course.

The waffles can be adapted to suit your taste, adding more or less maple syrup or sour cream, or even adding a favourite chocolate spread.

0 mins Wash up and clear away.

Last-minute tasks

PROBLEMS AND HANDY TIPS

Set your timer for 5 minutes; this is how long you have before serving the starter.

5 mins Drain the pasta, which has been sitting in warm water. Return it to the saucepan and pour in the pesto mixture from the frying pan. Mix well so that all the pasta is covered by the pesto sauce. Put

Make sure you heat the pasta and sauce thoroughly before serving. Keep the lid on the saucepan while it is heating.

MENU 1

back over a low to medium heat and allow the pasta to warm gradually.

0 mins Wash up and clear away.

Watch points

Once the meal has started, it is difficult to predict how long each course will take. The following instructions are given only as a guide.

Turn the pasta off so that it doesn't burn. Serve the melon boats.

Turn the pasta back on and heat gently while you dress the salad.

Shake the French dressing well and pour it all over the salad; toss thoroughly and place on the table.

Serve the pasta immediately with grated Parmesan cheese and a handful of pine kernels scattered over the top as a garnish.

Serve the grated Parmesan cheese separately in a bowl. Place it on the table for your guests to help themselves.

Preheat the grill. Put the waffles under it and cook for a further 3–4 minutes. Once the mixture is bubbling turn the grill off. Serve piping hot with extra topping if desired.

Watch the waffles because they can burn very easily as they have so much butter in them.

Two-course weekend supper from the store cupboard

2

Easy to prepare and cook
Cost level: inexpensive
Serves: 4

There is no break incorporated in this menu.

Main course	Bacon and onion rosti with frozen peas	*Preparation time = 30 minutes* *Cooking time = 25–30 minutes*
Dessert	Hot banana split	*Preparation time = 10 minutes* *Cooking time = 15 minutes*
Drink	Medium-bodied red wine	

This menu is useful when you find that you are down to the bare essentials. Most of the ingredients should already be in your store cupboard and fridge, but the local corner shop can always assist if there are a few items missing. This menu can be adapted to suit your taste: if, for example, you prefer not to use bacon in the rosti, you can add some fresh or tinned mushrooms instead. A rosti is a savoury Swiss 'cake' consisting of potato, onion and cheese, traditionally cooked in a heavy frying pan. It looks similar to an omelette, but contains no eggs. If you don't have a good-quality non-stick frying pan, it might be easier to cook the rosti in a non-stick cake tin in the oven: this will enable you to have a break.

The dessert is simple and fun. Don't forget, you can always leave out this course if you don't have the ingredients or the time. Alternatively, you could serve some fresh fruit or cheese, if available.

MENU 2

Equipment needed – Menu 2

Main course

1 potato peeler
1 large saucepan
1 savoury chopping board
1 sharp knife
1 cheese grater **or** food processor with grater blade
1 large mixing bowl
1 non-stick frying pan with lid **or** 1 non-stick 8inch/20 cm cake tin
1 non-stick fish slice
1 plate large enough to fit over the rim of the frying pan
1 small saucepan

Dessert

1 sweet chopping board
1 sharp knife
2 or 4 sheets aluminium foil
1 baking tray
1 serving plate **or** 4 individual bowls or plates
1 tablespoon **or** ice-cream scoop

Shopping list – Menu 2

Main course

6–8 medium-sized old potatoes
1 onion
8oz/225g rindless bacon **or** 8oz/225g fresh or tinned mushrooms
2oz/50g (2 tablespoons) mature Cheddar cheese
1oz/25g (1 tablespoon) cooking margarine or butter
salt and ground black pepper
nutmeg, mustard powder
8oz/225g frozen peas or other frozen vegetable
pinch sugar

Dessert

2 large or 4 small bananas, not too ripe or bruised
2 teaspoons lemon juice
2 milk chocolate Flakes
1 tub vanilla ice-cream, approx. 1 tablespoon or scoop per person
grated chocolate **or** packet of hundreds and thousands for decoration

All these items should be in your store cupboard.

Countdown – Menu 2

If you want to prepare the whole menu, you will need 50 minutes. If you would like a break, use the oven instead of the hob to cook the rosti. If you are a slow cook, add 5–10 minutes to each course to ensure you do not run out of time. Remember, the times given are only a guide as each cook will take different lengths of time to complete each task. If you take a break while the main course is cooking make sure that everything else is ready. Once the rosti is cooked, you will need to serve it right away. The dessert can be made in advance and cooked while you are eating the main course.

Dessert

PROBLEMS AND HANDY TIPS

Preparation time: 10 minutes
Cooking time: 15 minutes

Assemble all the ingredients and equipment you need for the dessert. Set your timer for 10 minutes. If you are going to cook the bananas straight away, preheat the oven to 200°C/400°F/Gas mark 6.

10 mins Take either 2 large or 4 small bananas, peel them and discard the skin. Carefully cut a V-shaped wedge out of each banana from top to bottom. Discard the wedges. Try to keep the remaining part of banana in one piece and not falling into two halves.

5 mins Sprinkle a small amount of lemon juice over each banana. Take 2 chocolate Flakes and crumble half a Flake into each V-shape opening. Take 2 or 4 lengths of aluminium foil and wrap the bananas individually, ensuring they are well covered. Place the bananas on a baking sheet and cook in the oven for 15 minutes, or set aside until you are ready to cook them.

0 mins Wash up and clear away.

It is important not to cut rght through the banana; cut the wedge three-quarters of the way through so that there is a large enough opening for the Flake to sit in.

Lemon juice prevents the banana turning brown.

Make sure the bananas are well wrapped in the foil so that the chocolate does not escape.

If you are using 2 large bananas rather than 4 small, you will cut them in half before serving them.

9

MENU 2

Main course

Preparation time: 30 minutes
Cooking time: 25–30 minutes

Assemble all the ingredients and equipment you need for the main course. If you have a food processor with a large hole grater blade, use it for the potatoes and cheese; this will save you time and energy. Set your timer for 30 minutes.

30 mins Take the potatoes, peel and cut them in half and place them in a large saucepan of cold, salted water. Put over a medium to high heat and bring to the boil.

Make sure you use old potatoes as they have a high starch content and are much better for this dish.

25 mins While the potatoes are cooking, peel and chop 1 onion and set aside. Take 8oz/225g of rindless bacon and slice into bite-size pieces. If you are not using the bacon, substitute 8oz/225g freshly chopped mushrooms or tinned mushrooms with the liquid drained off.

If the bacon has rind, you will need to remove it before chopping the bacon up.

18 mins Take 2oz/50g (2 tablespoons) of mature Cheddar and grate it on the largest hole into a large mixing bowl. Set aside.

13 mins After the potatoes have been boiling for approximately 5 minutes, remove from the heat and drain them. Put the potatoes back in the saucepan and run some cold water over them; this stops them from continuing to cook and makes them easier to handle. When the potatoes are cool, grate them into the bowl with the cheese, taking care not to grate your fingers. Mix the cheese and potato together well.

If the potatoes are still too hot to handle, run them under cold water again.

6 mins Put 1oz/25g (1 tablespoon) of margarine or butter in a frying pan and place over a medium heat. Add the chopped onion and cook until slightly coloured. Add the chopped bacon or mushrooms and cook for a further 4 minutes.

A non-stick frying pan makes it easier to turn the rosti over, but if using an uncoated pan, add an extra 1oz/25g of margarine to prevent the mixture sticking to the bottom.

4 mins Once all the ingredients are lightly coloured, turn off and pour the onion and bacon into the bowl containing the potato and cheese mixture. Make sure you mix all the ingredients very well as the potato will be very sticky. Season with a very small amount of salt and ground black pepper, add a pinch of nutmeg and mustard powder and mix well. If you have used mushrooms rather than bacon, you can use a little extra salt.

Only use a small amount of salt if you are using bacon, as it is already very salty.
The mushrooms will not need to cook for as long as the bacon, so watch them – they will need approximately 2–3 minutes.

Cooking the rosti

If you want to have a break from the cooker, you can bake the rosti in a large cake tin. Remember to preheat the oven to 200°C/400°F/Gas mark 6. The rosti will need 15 minutes on one side, before being turned over and cooked for a further 10–15 minutes on the other side. Set your timer for 25 minutes: this is how long the rosti will take to cook.
25 mins Place the potato mixture in the frying pan and pat it down evenly with a fish slice. Place it over a medium heat and cook, covered, for 10–15 minutes. Do not allow it to burn.
10 mins While the rosti is cooking, wash up and clear away. Turn the rosti over after 10–15 minutes. To do this place a large plate over the top of the frying pan using a thick oven glove to hold the plate in position, quickly invert the pan and on to the plate. Carefully remove the frying pan, then slide the rosti, uncooked side down, back into the pan, with the assistance of a fish slice. Cook for a further 5–10 minutes. It should be brown on both sides before serving.

If you are going to cook the rosti in the oven instead of a frying pan, use a large cake tin, either greased or non-stick. Pat the rosti down to form an even circle and cook in a preheated oven at 200°C/400°F/Gas mark 6, for 15 minutes. Turn the rosti over as explained in the method, and continue to cook on the other side for a further 15 minutes.

If you don't have a large enough plate, use a large chopping board for manoeuvring the rosti in and out of the pan.

Last-minute tasks

PROBLEMS AND HANDY TIPS

Set your timer for 10 minutes.
10 mins Fill the kettle and put it on to boil. Place the frozen peas or vegetable of your choice in a small saucepan, add a teaspoon of sugar and a pinch of salt, pour the boiling water over and cook over a medium to high heat for approximately 5 minutes.
7 mins Place the tray of wrapped bananas in the preheated oven at 200°C/400°F/Gas mark 6 (if not

The teaspoon of sugar brings out the flavour of the peas.

MENU 2

already cooked) while you eat the main course. Set your timer for 15 minutes so that you do not forget the bananas.

4 mins Take the pan of rosti off the stove or out of the oven ready to serve. Drain the peas through a colander or sieve.

0 mins Serve the main course, piping hot.

The peas are cooked after approximately 4 minutes, once they turn bright green.

Watch points

Once the meal has started, it is difficult to predict how long each course will take. The following instructions are given only as a guide.

Serve the main course.

Take the bananas out of the oven and unwrap them. Place each banana on a plate, or if you have used 2 large bananas, cut them in half. Add a scoop of soft vanilla ice-cream to each banana split. Decorate with some grated chocolate or hundreds and thousands.

Serve at once as the ice-cream will start to melt on the hot bananas.

Remember that the foil and bananas will be very hot, so use oven gloves to unwrap them. Be careful of the steam inside the foil as this will be very hot as well.

Lacto-vegetarian menu
(winter or spring)

Easy to prepare and cook
Cost level: inexpensive
Serves: 4

3

A 30-minute break is incorporated in this menu.

Starter	Chilled sliced tomatoes with mozzarella cheese and basil	*Preparation time = 20 minutes* *Cooking time = None*
Main course	Baked pasta and vegetables in a creamy sauce F*	*Preparation time = 40 minutes* *Cooking time = 60 minutes*
Dessert	Brown bread and apricot ice-cream F*	*Preparation time = 35 minutes* *Cooking time = None* *Freezing time = 12 hours*
Drink	Full-bodied white wine, chilled	

This menu would suit those vegetarians who eat eggs and dairy products. The starter is light and delicious, and the fresh basil gives it a refreshing lift. It must be made on the night so that it doesn't dry out.

The main course is straightforward and cooked in the oven, which allows you to leave the kitchen and have a break while it is cooking. The ingredients can be varied to suit your taste.

The ice-cream is easy to prepare and does not need any fancy equipment, but it must be made at least the night before to ensure it is frozen properly. Make sure you have a freezer container big enough to hold the ice-cream and that it will fit into your deep freeze or ice-making compartment at the top of your fridge. A food processor or blender allows the brown bread and apricots to be chopped finely to make a smoother mixture. The ice-cream should be taken out of the freezer 10 minutes before required to ensure it is soft enough for serving.

MENU 3

Equipment needed – Menu 3

Starter

1 sharp knife
1 savoury chopping board
1 measuring jug
1 tablespoon

Main course

1 large saucepan with lid
1 teaspoon
1 savoury wooden spoon
1 savoury chopping board
1 sharp knife
1 medium saucepan
1 colander
1 measuring jug
1 ovenproof dish or casserole
1 cheese grater
1 tablespoon

Dessert

1 food processor with fine chopping blade or 1
  sharp knife or rolling pin
3 medium mixing bowls
1 sweet wooden spoon
1 double saucepan or 1 large saucepan with 1
  heatproof bowl that fits tightly inside it
1 large mixing bowl
1 balloon whisk or hand-held electric mixer
1 teaspoon
1 flexible spatula
2 pint/1.2 litre freezer container with tight-
  fitting lid

Shopping list – Menu 3

Starter

2 large tomatoes
4oz/100g mozzarella cheese
1 large handful fresh basil
*¼ pint/150ml pint French dressing
1 long French loaf
4oz/100g butter or table margarine

Main course

1 packet fresh or dried vari-coloured pasta
  shells, approx. 16–18oz/450–500g
*2oz/50g (2 tablespoons) cooking margarine
*salt and pepper
*1 large onion
2 peppers, either green or red, yellow or mixed
8oz/225g button mushrooms
4oz/100g mange-tout
2 carrots
4oz/100g baby corn
*2oz/50g (2 tablespoons) plain flour
1 pint/600g fresh vegetable stock or 1 vegetable
  stock cube
*mustard
*nutmeg
*1 teaspoon lemon juice
*6oz/175g Cheddar cheese
4oz/100g sour cream
1 tablespoon fresh coriander

Dessert

1oz/25g fresh brown bread (approximately 1
  slice)
2oz/50g (2 tablespoons) ready-to-use dried
  apricots
*2 large eggs
*3oz/75g caster sugar
*2 teaspoons vanilla essence
½ pint/300ml whipping or double cream
1 packet wafer biscuits of your choice
½ pint/300ml single cream (optional)

*Check store cupboard

14

Countdown – Menu 3

If you want to prepare the whole menu, you will need 135 minutes (2 hours and 15 minutes), which includes a 30-minute break. If you are a slow cook, add 5–10 minutes to each course to ensure that you do not run out of time. Remember, the times are only a guide as each cook will take different lengths of time to complete each task. This menu is quite flexible and the main course can sit in a warm oven without spoiling. The ice-cream must be made in advance – at least the night before the dinner party – to allow it time to freeze.

Dessert

PROBLEMS AND HANDY TIPS

Preparation time: 35 minutes
Cooking time: None
Freezing time: 12 hours

Assemble all the ingredients and equipment you need for the dessert. Use a food processor or blender and hand-held electric mixer to save time and energy. Set your timer for 35 minutes.

A food processor will give a finer mix, but doing it by hand will still give a good finish.

35 mins Take 1oz/25g (1 slice) of fresh brown bread, including the crusts, and toast until golden brown. If you have a food processor, break the toast up with your hands, place it in the processor bowl and whiz until it becomes fine crumbs. Otherwise, break up the bread with your fingers and chop it into fine breadcrumbs with a sharp knife, or place it in a mixing bowl and crush with one end of a rolling pin.

The toast should be only lightly toasted, not dark brown or burnt.

An alternative way of making the crumbs is to place the toast in a plastic bag tied up at the top and then crush it with a rolling pin or meat hammer.

30 mins Take a large saucepan, fill it half full with water, put it over the heat and bring to the boil. Take 2oz/50g (2 tablespoons) of dried apricots, place them in the processor with the toasted bread and process. They should be quite fine but not mixed to a pulp. If you are using a knife, chop the apricots into fine pieces, add them to the breadcrumbs and mix well with a wooden spoon. Set aside.

MENU 3

25 mins Take 2 eggs and carefully separate them. Make sure that the yolks go into a heatproof mixing bowl which is the right size to fit inside a large saucepan of boiling water. The egg whites should go into a large mixing bowl as they increase in bulk when whisked.

See Handy Tip 2, page xvii for an easy way to separate eggs.

20 mins Measure out 3oz/75g of caster sugar and add it to the egg yolks in the heatproof bowl. Turn the heat right down under the saucepan of boiling water and place the bowl inside it. Take a balloon whisk or hand-held electric mixer and beat the mixture until the egg yolks become thick, creamy and a pale yellow colour. Once they have reached this stage, remove the bowl from the saucepan and allow to cool. Add 2 teaspoons of vanilla essence and stir well.

Do not have the water boiling too hard in case some of it splashes into the bowl of egg yolk and sugar. Be very careful not to burn yourself when you remove the bowl from the saucepan as it and the steam will be very hot.

Do not worry if some of the sugar is stuck to the bottom of the bowl.

15 mins Take ½ pint/300ml pint of whipping cream, place it in a mixing bowl and beat until thick using either a balloon whisk or electric mixer. Be careful not to overbeat or it will curdle: you want the cream to hold its shape but not be too stiff. Set aside.

Do not overbeat the cream. If you are unsure whether it is stiff enough, stop beating. It is always better to have cream that is too thin than too thick or even curdled.

11 mins Wash and dry the balloon whisk or beaters well. Take the egg whites and beat until they hold their shape and stand in peaks.

If you are whisking the egg whites by hand, it will take a little longer than 4 minutes for them to reach the point where they will hold their shape.

7 mins Now it is time to put the ice-cream together. You should have 4 bowls: 1 with the beaten egg yolks and sugar, 1 with the whipped cream, 1 with the beaten egg whites, and 1 with the brown bread and apricots.

6 mins Using a flexible spatula, pour the egg yolks and sugar into the whipped cream bowl and mix well. Now add the breadcrumb and apricot mixture to the cream and fold together carefully. Lastly, fold in the egg whites. Make sure you go right to the bottom of the bowl to ensure the mixture is well combined. Once you can't see any lumps of cream, egg white or yolk, pour the mixture into a 2 pint/1.2 litre plastic freezer container, put the lid on tightly and freeze immediately.

It is important that the ingredients are really well mixed. Use a tablespoon or flexible spatula to lift the mixture to incorporate as much air as possible. This makes a lighter ice-cream.

0 mins Wash up and clear away.

Note: It should not be necessary to stir the ice-cream halfway through freezing, but if your mixture was rather runny, you might need to check it to see if the breadcrumbs and apricots have started to sink. If so, take a fork and mix the ice-cream up again. Replace the lid and put it back into the freezer to complete the freeezing process.

It is unlikely that the ice-cream will need stirring as the consistency should be stiff enough to keep the fruit and crumbs from sinking.

Main course

PROBLEMS AND HANDY TIPS

Preparation time: 40 minutes
Cooking time: 60 minutes

Assemble all the ingredients and equipment you need for the main course. Set your timer for 40 minutes.

40 mins Fill the kettle with water and bring to the boil. Place the pasta shells in a large saucepan. Add 1 teaspoon of margarine and a pinch of salt. Pour the boiling water over the pasta and stir well. Cook over a low to medium heat for approximately 15 minutes. While the pasta is cooking, peel and finely chop 1 large onion. Place the chopped onion in a medium-sized saucepan.

You will need to check the instructions on the pasta packet as different varieties take different lengths of time to cook. The margarine in the saucepan helps to stop the pasta from sticking together while it is cooking. The pasta should boil for only a few minutes as it will continue to cook in the oven with the vegetables.

35 mins Stir the pasta, then drain it through a colander. Return it to the saucepan and pour lukewarm water over it to stop it cooking. Leave the pasta in the warm water and set aside.

30 mins Add 2oz/50g (2 tablespoons) of cooking margarine to the onions and place over a low heat to soften. Meanwhile, take your mixed peppers, cut them in half, then discard the stalks and seeds. Wash the peppers under cold running water to remove any stray seeds, then slice into thin strips and set aside. Check the onions and stir well.

It is important to remove all the seeds in the pepper as it is unpleasant to come across seeds while eating the bake.

25 mins Add the peppers to the onion and cook for a further 5 minutes, stirring from time to time. Meanwhile, wash the button mushrooms under cold running water and leave to drain. Take the mangetout, carrots and baby corn and cut them into even-sized pieces approximately 1½inch/4 cm long.

Try to keep all the vegetables roughly the same size so that they cook evenly and will all be ready at the same time.

MENU 3

16 mins Stir the peppers and onions, then turn off the heat. Take 2oz/50g (2 tablespoons) of plain flour and stir into the peppers and onion; mix well to make a roux. Make sure the roux is the correct consistency, neither too thick or dry, nor too thin. Put the roux over a low heat and cook for 2 minutes, before turning the heat off. Preheat the oven to 200°C/400°F/Gas mark 6.

A roux is a mixture of margarine and flour. It is the basis for all sauces and gravies.

12 mins If you are using fresh vegetable stock, pour 1 pint/600ml into a measuring jug then slowly add to the roux off the heat, stirring all the time. If you are using a stock cube, crumble it into the roux and carefully add 1 pint/600ml of cold water off the heat until the mixture is smooth. Place the pan over a medium heat and allow to thicken, stirring all the time. Once it has thickened, cook for a further 2 minutes to remove the starchy flavour. Season well with salt and pepper, a pinch of mustard powder and nutmeg, and 1 teaspoon of lemon juice. Taste the sauce and adjust.

Make sure you season the sauce really well as this dish can be rather bland if not properly seasoned.

8 mins Take the mushrooms and cut them into halves or quarters. Add them, together with the carrots, mange-tout and baby corn, to the sauce and cook on a low heat for a further 5 minutes. While the sauce is cooking, drain the pasta through a colander and place in an ovenproof dish.

If you like your mange-tout and corn to be slightly crunchy, don't add them to the casserole now. Put them in 20 minutes before serving.

5 mins Grate 6oz/175g of Cheddar cheese. Add half to the pasta in the dish and mix well with a wooden spoon.

2 mins Stir the vegetable sauce, then turn the heat off. Pour the sauce over the pasta in the casserole dish. Finally, pour 4oz/100g sour cream over the top of the pasta and sprinkle with the remaining grated cheese. Place in the preheated oven for 60 minutes.

0 mins Wash up and clear away.

Starter

Preparation time: 20 minutes
Cooking time: None

Assemble all the ingredients and equipment you need for the starter. Set your timer for 20 minutes.
20 mins Take 2 large tomatoes. Wash them under cold running water and dry well. Using a very sharp knife, cut the tomatoes in half, then slice thinly. Set aside.
15 mins Take 4oz/100g of mozzarella cheese and slice it thinly. Arrange the tomato and cheese slices on a large serving platter or individual plates. Chill until required. (Do not prepare more than one hour in advance or the ingredients will dry out.)
10 mins Take the fresh basil leaves and wash well under cold running water. Separate half the leaves and chop them finely; the other half should be kept for decorating the salad just before serving.
5 mins You will need a French dressing. Turn to page 201 if you want to make it yourself, or use a ready-made one. Add the chopped basil leaves to the French dressing and mix well. The starter should be dressed and decorated just before serving.
0 mins Wash up and clear away.

It is best to use a very sharp knife for cutting tomatoes so that they slice evenly and thinly without tearing.

If the mozzarella you buy is already cubed, you should sprinkle it over the tomatoes. The basil in the French dressing complements the flavour of the tomatoes.

Home-made French dressing is best made in advance so that all the flavours can merge together.

Relax

Have a break. Take your timer with you and set it for 30 minutes. When you return you will only have to check the pasta bake and then dress and decorate your salad before serving.

Welcome back

Feeling better after your break? Now you only have the last-minute tasks to prepare. Finish off the starter, check the main course and then serve.

MENU 3

Last-minute tasks

Set your timer for 10 minutes. This is how long you have before you serve the starter.

10 mins Put your French bread in the oven to warm. Check the pasta bake and if it is looking very brown and almost cooked, turn the oven down to 110°C/225°F/Gas mark 2. The pasta will not spoil if you leave it in a warm oven.

If you have left the mange-tout and corn out of the pasta bake, add them now so that they will have enough time to cook but still remain crisp.

7 mins Take the tomatoes and mozzarella cheese out of the fridge and decorate with the whole basil leaves. Mix the French dressing well and pour it over the salad.

Always stir a French dressing well before using it as the oil floats to the top very quickly.

5 mins Take the fresh coriander and wash it well. Shake off the excess water, chop finely, then place in a small bowl and set aside.

0 mins Wash up and clear away.

Watch points

Once the meal has started, it is difficult to predict how long each course will take. The following instructions are given only as a guide.

Take the bread out of the oven. Place it on the table with the salad and butter for your guests to help themselves.

Take the baked pasta and vegetables out of the oven. Sprinkle with fresh coriander and then serve.

The dessert should be served with some wafer biscuits and single cream for those who really want to indulge.

Casual lunch or dinner party menu

4

Easy to prepare and cook
Cost level: good value
Serves: 4

A 30-minute break is incorporated in this menu.

Starter	Egg and mushroom ramekins	*Preparation time = 20 minutes* *Cooking time = 15 minutes*
Main course	Vegetable and seafood risotto ^{F*} Mixed leaf salad with walnut dressing	*Preparation time = 55 minutes* *Cooking time = 20 minutes*
Dessert	Banana and chocolate cream ^{F*}	*Preparation time = 20 minutes* *Cooking time = None* *Chilling time = 2 hours* *minimum*
Drink	Crisp, dry white wine, chilled	

You should manage to find quite a few of the ingredients you need for this menu in your store cupboard and fridge.

This is a good menu if time is short and you want to prepare a few things in advance. The starter is unusual and must only be cooked once all your guests have arrived and you know how much time you have left. Otherwise the egg will overcook and become hard. The main course is quite happy to sit while you finish other tasks; add the fish at the last minute or it will spoil by overcooking and falling apart. The salad should be prepared just before serving. The walnut dressing can be made in advance and kept in a cool place; alternatively, buy a ready-made dressing. To keep the salad crisp, add the dressing just before serving. The dessert can be made in advance and chilled. It is easy to prepare, and the combination of banana and chocolate is delicious.

MENU 4

Equipment needed – Menu 4

Starter

1 savoury chopping board
1 sharp knife
1 small saucepan
1 savoury wooden spoon
1 garlic crusher (or see Handy Tip 1, page xvii)
1 teaspoon
1 tablespoon
1 cheese grater
4 ovenproof ramekins

Main course

1 colander
1 tablespoon
1 small mixing bowl or jam jar wih lid
1 teaspoon
1 salad bowl
1 savoury chopping board
1 sharp knife
1 large saucepan with lid
1 savoury wooden spoon
1 garlic crusher (or see page xvii)
1 measuring jug
1 wine glass
1 tin opener

Dessert

1 double saucepan or 1 heatproof bowl that fits
   tightly inside a large saucepan
2 mixing bowls
1 fork
1 teaspoon
1 tablespoon
1 balloon whisk or hand-held electric mixer
1 flexible spatula
1 serving dish

*Check store cupboard

Shopping list – Menu 4

Starter

8oz/225g button mushrooms
*1oz/25g (1 tablespoon) cooking margarine
*1 clove garlic (optional)
*salt, pepper, nutmeg, mustard powder
*1 teaspoon lemon juice
2 tablespoons sour cream
*2oz/50g Cheddar cheese
*4 eggs
*4 teaspoons dried breadcrumbs
4 brown rolls, butter (optional)

Main course

2 medium-sized leeks
2 peppers (red, green, yellow, or mixed)
*2oz/50g (2 tablespoons) margarine or butter
*1–2 cloves garlic (optional)
*salt, pepper, mustard powder, nutmeg
*1 tablespoon Worcestershire sauce
12oz/350g easy-cook brown or white rice
¾ pint/450ml fresh vegetable or fish stock, or
   *1 fish or vegetable stock cube
1 glass white wine (optional)
8oz/225g fresh cod fillet
8oz/225g fresh trout fillet
4oz/100g fresh scallops
8oz/225g fresh or tinned baby corn
*4oz/100g frozen peas

Garnish
watercress leaves or chopped parsley
*1 lemon to make lemon wedges

Mixed leaf salad
selection of salad leaves, eg. rocket, frisee, cos,
   little gem, Chinese leaves, iceberg
6 tablespoons walnut oil
3 tablespoons cider vinegar
*salt, pepper, sugar, French mustard
1 packet plain croûtons

Dessert

*6oz/175g plain chocolate
2 bananas
*1oz/25g (1 tablespoon) caster sugar
*1 teaspoon vanilla essence
½ pint/300ml whipping cream
*flaked chocolate or chopped almonds to decorate
½ pint/300ml single cream, dessert biscuits
   (optional)

22

Countdown – Menu 4

If you want to prepare the whole menu, you will need 135 minutes (2 hours 15 minutes), which includes a 30-minute break. If you are a slow cook, add 5–10 minutes to each course to ensure that you do not run out of time. Remember, the times given are only a guide as each cook will take different lengths of time to complete each task. The starter and main course can be made and cooked in advance, then reheated, or cooked just before serving. The dessert must definitely be made in advance to give it time to chill and set before serving.

Dessert

PROBLEMS AND HANDY TIPS

Preparation time: 20 minutes
Cooking time: None
Chilling time: 2 hours minimum

Assemble all the ingredients and equipment you need for the dessert. Set your timer for 20 minutes.
20 mins Place 6oz/175g plain chocolate in the top of a double saucepan or in a heatproof bowl over a saucepan of boiling water. Leave the chocolate to melt over a low to medium heat.

Do not allow the chocolate to get too hot or it will become lumpy.

17 mins Peel two bananas and place them in a mixing bowl. Add 1oz/25g (1 tablespoon) caster sugar, then mash the bananas and sugar to form a paste. Add 1 teaspoon of vanilla essence and mix well.

Don't worry if the banana starts to discolour a little; added to the chocolate and cream, the discoloration will stop and will not be noticeable.

13 mins Stir the chocolate and make sure that the water isn't boiling too rapidly. Once the chocolate is melted, add it to the banana mixture and stir well. You will notice that the mixture thickens slightly. Leave to stand. Using a balloon whisk or hand-held electric mixer, whisk ½ pint/300ml of whipping cream. Beat until it is thick and will hold its shape. Do not overbeat or the cream will curdle.

The banana mixture can be slightly textured.

Take care not to spill any water into the chocolate while it is melting as it will make the chocolate lumpy and difficult to use.

Stop whipping the cream as soon as it starts to leave a trail and hold its shape.

5 mins Using a tablespoon or flexible spatula, fold the cream into the chocolate and banana mixture;

It is important to use a metal spoon or spatula for folding to

be careful not to beat it in case the mixture starts to curdle. Once well combined, transfer the mixture to a serving dish. Chill until required.
0 mins Wash up and clear away.

Main course
Mixed leaf salad with walnut dressing

Preparation time: 15 minutes
Cooking time: None

Assemble all the ingredients and equipment you need for the salad. Set your timer for 15 minutes.
15 mins Take the various salad leaves and wash them well under cold running water. Shake off any excess water and leave to drain in a colander.
10 mins Place 6 tablespoons of walnut oil in a small mixing bowl or jam jar with a tight-fitting lid. Add 3 tablespoons of cider vinegar, 1 teaspoon of French mustard, a good pinch of salt and sugar and some freshly ground pepper. Mix well, check the seasoning and add any extra herbs you feel might improve the taste and set aside.
5 mins Take the drained salad leaves and if they are very large, tear them into bite-sized pieces. Place in a salad bowl, cover with a clean tea towel or cling film and set aside.
0 mins Wash up and clear away.

Relax

Have a 30-minute break. When you return you will need to prepare and cook the starter and main course.

Welcome back

Feeling better after your break?

keep the mixture light and to prevent it from curdling.

Decorate the dessert just before serving or the chocolate will melt and the nuts will become soft.

PROBLEMS AND HANDY TIPS

Make sure the leaves are really well washed. Try to remove as much excess water from them as possible to keep the salad crisp.

Always well mix the dressing before using as the oil floats to the top when left standing.

Add a little lemon juice or some herbs to make a different dressing.

Vegetable and seafood risotto

Preparation time: 40 minutes
Cooking time: 20 minutes

Assemble all the ingredients and equipment you need for the main course. Set your timer for 40 minutes.

40 mins Take two leeks, trim the ends, then slice from top to bottom, down the centre. Slice the leeks thinly, transfer to a colander, wash well under cold running water and leave to drain.

Make sure you wash the leeks well as they always have a lot of sand and grit in them.

35 mins Cut the peppers in half and remove the stalks and seeds; any excess seeds can be removed under cold running water. Wash the peppers and cut them into long, thin slices 2inch/5 cm wide.

The strips of peppers should be sliced to roughly the same size so that they cook evenly.

30 mins Take a large saucepan and add 2oz/50g (2 tablespoons) cooking margarine. Place over a low heat and allow the margarine to melt. Add the sliced peppers and cook over a low to medium heat. If including the garlic, peel and crush it while the peppers are cooking. Add the crushed garlic to the peppers and continue to cook.

See Handy Tip 1, page xvii, for an easy way to crush garlic if you don't have a garlic crusher.

25 mins Add the drained leeks, then season with salt, freshly ground pepper, a pinch of mustard powder and nutmeg. Add 1 tablespoon of Worcestershire sauce. Put over a very low heat and cook for 5–6 minutes.

You will need to check the seasoning again before serving the dish.

22 mins Fill the kettle with water and put it on to boil. Measure out 12oz/350g of brown or white rice. Take a measuring jug and crumble one vegetable or fish stock cube into it. (If using fresh stock, you will not need to do this.) Once the water has boiled, pour ¾pint/450ml of it into the measuring jug and stir well to dissolve the stock cube.

If the rice is well stirred and coated with the fat in the saucepan, it will not stick together while cooking.

18 mins Turn off the leek and pepper mixture. Pour the weighed rice into the saucepan and stir well so that everything is well combined. Add the stock (either fresh or prepared with a stock cube) and stir well. Add a glass of white wine if you like, then place the mixture over a low heat, cover the pan and cook for approximately 15–20 minutes. (If

Risotto rice will absorb much more liquid than easy-cook rice, so keep an eye on it if you have used this type.

Brown rice and wild rice will take much longer to cook than easy-cook rice. Check the packet timings and do not add the fish or vegetables until the rice is just 10

25

using brown rice, check the instructions on the packet as cooking times can vary.)

14 mins While the risotto is cooking, prepare the fish. Remove any bones or skin, then cut into small, even-sized chunks. (You can use the scallops as a guide to the size required.)

8 mins Stir the risotto and make sure that it is not bubbling too fast – it must only simmer.

4 mins Check the rice and the amount of liquid: you may need to add a little more, depending on the type of rice you have used. Once all the liquid has been absorbed and the rice is soft, you can add the baby corn, 4oz/100g frozen peas, the scallops and all the fish, but do this only if you are 10 minutes away from serving; any longer and those ingredients will be overcooked.

0 mins Wash up and clear away.

Starter

Preparation time: 20 minutes
Cooking time: 15 minutes

Assemble all the ingredients and equipment you need for the starter. Set your timer for 20 minutes. Preheat the oven to 200°C/400°F/Gas mark 6.

20 mins Take 8oz/225g of button mushrooms and wash them well under cold running water. Cut off the stalks and slice the mushrooms thinly. Place in a small saucepan.

15 mins Place 1oz/25g (1 tablespoon) of cooking margarine in the saucepan with the mushrooms, put over a low to medium heat and allow the mushrooms to cook. Meanwhile, if including the garlic, peel and crush it. Once the mushrooms have softened a little, add the garlic and season the mixture with salt and pepper, a pinch of nutmeg and mustard and 1 teaspoon of lemon.

10 mins Take the mushrooms off the heat, add 2 tablespoons of sour cream and stir well. Grate 2oz/ 50g (2 tablespoons) of cheese on to a plate. Add

minutes away from being cooked.

Take care to remove all the fish bones as they can be hazardous to the unsuspecting eater.

If the risotto is cooking too fast, the liquid will evaporate and the rice might start to burn on the bottom of the pan.

To check that the rice and fish are cooked take out a small amount and taste it. The rice should be soft but still have some texture, not too soft. The fish should be able to hold its shape, firm and not falling apart.

Make sure you season the risotto well, but taste it again before serving.

PROBLEMS AND HANDY TIPS

If the mushrooms are very large, cut them in half or quarters before slicing them – they must be able to fit into the ramekins.

Do not let the mushrooms burn.

See Handy Tip 1, page xvii for an easy way to crush garlic if you do not have a garlic crusher.

Nutmeg enhances the flavour of the mushrooms.

half the cheese to the mushroom mixture and stir well. Divide the mixture between the four ramekin dishes. Carefully crack 1 egg into each ramekin. Season the top of each egg with a pinch of salt and pepper, then sprinkle the remaining cheese on top. Finally, add a small amount of dried breadcrumbs to each ramekin. Bake in the preheated oven for 15 minutes or until the egg white has set but the yolk is still soft.

0 mins Wash up and clear away.

See Handy Tip 2, page xvii, for an easy way of cracking eggs without breaking the yolk.

Last-minute tasks

PROBLEMS AND HANDY TIPS

Set your timer for 10 minutes. This is how long you have before serving the starter.

10 mins Add the baby corn, 4oz/100g of frozen peas, the scallops and all the fish to the rice if you have not done so already, and cook for 10 minutes.

7 mins If you are serving bread rolls with the starter, put them into the oven to warm. Decorate the banana and chocolate cream with crumbled chocolate flake or chopped almonds, then put it back into the fridge until you are ready to serve.

3 mins Check the ramekins: if the white looks firm but the yolks are soft, take them out of the oven ready to serve.

0 mins Wash up and clear away.

The dessert can be topped with any decoration you might have in store. It can also be served without decoration.

Try not to overcook the eggs. If you are worried that this might happen take them out of the oven, then continue to cook them once you are only a few minutes away from serving.

Watch points

Once the meal has started, it is difficult to predict how long each course will take. The following instructions are given only as a guide.

Serve the egg and mushroom ramekins. If you are serving bread rolls, don't forget to put some butter on the table for your guests to help themselves.

The mixed leaf salad should be dressed with the walnut dressing and served with croûtons sprinkled

Remember to mix the dressing well before pouring it over the salad.

over the top. Garnish the vegetable and seafood risotto with watercress or chopped parsley, and serve piping hot with lemon wedges.

Serve the dessert, but offer the biscuits and single cream separately for your guests to help themselves.

Quick pre-theatre or cinema dinner

5

Easy to prepare and cook
Cost level: inexpensive
Serves: 4

A 30-minute break is incorporated in this menu.

Starter	Hummus dip ^{F*} with crudités or pitta bread	*Preparation time = 20 minutes* *Cooking time = None*
Main course	Home-made savoury quiche ^{F*} Tomato, avocado and chicory salad with sour cream dressing	*Preparation time = 50 minutes* *Cooking time = 50–55 minutes*
Dessert	Chilled ginger and lemon terrine	*Preparation time = 10 minutes* *Cooking time = None* *Setting time = 2 hours*
Drink	Light red wine	

This menu is easy to prepare and cook. The starter can be bought ready-to-serve, or made in advance to allow the flavours to combine. It is served with crudités (raw vegetables) or pitta bread.

The main course can be made in advance and frozen. Don't forget to defrost the quiche 12 hours before needed. The pastry can be bought ready-made, or turn to page 203 if you want to make it yourself. If the pastry is frozen, it will need to defrost at room temperature for one hour before being used. The salad should be put together at the last minute and dressed just before serving. If you would like to make your own dressing, turn to page 201; otherwise you can buy a bottle of ready-made dressing. The dessert must be made in advance to allow it time to set.

MENU 5

Equipment needed – Menu 5

Starter

1 tin opener
1 fine sieve
1 mixing bowl
1 food processor, potato masher or fork
1 garlic crusher (or see page xvii)
1 savoury chopping board
1 sharp knife
1 tablespoon
1 teaspoon

Main course

1 rolling pin or clean wine bottle
1 loose-bottomed quiche tin or ovenproof flan
   dish, 8inches/20 cm in diameter
1 sharp knife
1 baking tray
1 savoury chopping board
1 large frying pan
1 teaspoon
1 non-stick fish slice
1 pair kitchen scissors
1 large mixing bowl
1 fork or balloon whisk
1 measuring jug
1 cheese grater
Side salad
1 savoury chopping board
1 sharp knife
1 colander
1 teaspoon
1 measuring jug or jam jar with lid

Dessert

1 loaf tin 8 × 5inch/20 × 12.5cm
1 measuring jug
1 tablespoon
1 tin opener
1 fine sieve
1 mixing bowl
1 balloon whisk or hand-held electric mixer
1 large serving plate
1 flexible spatula

Shopping list – Menu 5

Starter

8oz/225g ready-made hummus dip or
1lb/450g tinned cooked chick peas
*1 clove garlic (optional)
*2 tablespoons olive oil
*3 teaspoons lemon juice
*salt, paprika, pepper
Vegetables for crudités
4 carrots, 2 celery sticks, 1 red or green pepper
   or 4 pieces of pitta bread

Main course

8oz/225g (1 packet) shortcrust pastry
*1 onion
*1 teaspoon cooking margarine
*¼ pint/150ml French dressing
2 tablespoons sour cream
*nutmeg, salt, black pepper
*3 eggs
*mustard powder
*½ pint/300ml full fat or half fat milk
*4oz/100g Cheddar cheese
2 tablespoons chopped parsley, fresh or *frozen
   (see page xviii)
Side salad
4 tomatoes
2 heads chicory
1 ripe avocado
*¼ pint/150ml French dressing
2 tablespoons sour cream

Dessert

1 packet (7oz/200g) ginger biscuits
1 packet (approx. 5oz/125g) lemon jelly
1 small tin (7oz/200g) mandarin or orange
   segments
½ pint/300ml whipping cream
1 tablespoon chopped almonds to decorate

*Check store cupboard

Countdown – Menu 5

If you want to prepare the whole menu, you will need 130 minutes (2 hours 10 minutes), which includes a 30-minute break. If you are a slow cook, add 5–10 minutes to each course to ensure that you do not run out of time. Remember, the times given are only a guide as each cook will take different lengths of time to complete each task. Start with the dessert, which must be made at least 2 hours before serving to allow it time to set and chill. You will only have to turn it out and decorate it with cream before serving. The quiche can also be made in advance (with home-made or shop-bought pastry) and frozen. Don't forget it must be defrosted at least 12 hours before serving. The hummus can also be shop-bought or home-made. If you are going to cook the chick peas yourself, you must soak them for a minimum of 12 hours. They then need to be cooked for 1½ to 2 hours.

Dessert

Preparation time: 10 minutes
Cooking time: None
Setting time: 2 hours minimum

Assemble all the ingredients and equipment you need for the dessert. Set your timer for 10 minutes.
10 mins Unwrap the packet of ginger biscuits and place them on their sides in the middle of a loaf tin.
8 mins Fill the kettle and put it on to boil. Tear the jelly apart and place the cubes in a measuring jug. Pour in ½ pint/300ml of boiling water and stir well until the jelly has dissolved completely.
5 mins Open the tin of mandarin segments and strain the juice into the jug with the jelly. Place the fruit in the loaf tin over the ginger biscuits. Top up the jelly mixture with enough cold water to bring the liquid up to 1 pint/600ml; add less water for a stiffer set jelly.

PROBLEMS AND HANDY TIPS

Don't forget that this dessert needs to chill and set before being served.

Check the instructions on the packet as different brands will vary in the quantity of liquid used for the jelly.

Adding cold water helps the jelly to set more quickly.

MENU 5

2 mins Now pour the jelly all over the biscuits and fruit in the loaf tin and place in the fridge to set. Don't worry if the biscuits and fruit start to float to the top of the jelly – once it is turned out and decorated, nobody will notice.

0 mins Wash up and clear away.

If you have made the dessert at the last minute and need it to set quickly, place it in the deep freeze for aproximately 1 hour, or until it has set. Transfer to the fridge until required.

Starter

PROBLEMS AND HANDY TIPS

Preparation time: 20 minutes
Cooking time: None

Assemble all the ingredients and equipment you need for the starter. Using a food processor will save time and energy and also make a smoother paste. Prepare the starter at least 2–3 hours before serving. Set your timer for 20 minutes.

20 mins Open the tin of pre-cooked chick peas and drain them through a fine sieve. Discard the liquid and place in a mixing bowl.

18 mins Peel 1 clove of garlic, if using. Place in a food processor and blend, or crush it by hand. Add it to the bowl with the chick peas.

15 mins Process the chick peas and garlic, or mash with a potato masher or fork until the mixture starts to form a thick paste. Add 2 tablespsoons of olive oil, 2–3 teaspoons of lemon juice and mix again until the mixture is quite smooth and well combined. If the consistency is too thick, add 1–2 tablespoons of cold water. Taste the hummus and season with a pinch of salt and a pinch of paprika or pepper. Add extra lemon juice if you like.

7 mins Place the hummus in a serving bowl and chill until required. If serving with vegetables, rather than pitta bread, prepare them now. Wash them well, then put through a food processor on a medium to fine cutting blade. Alternatively, slice the vegetables into thin 2 inch/5 cm strips. Cover and chill until required.

0 mins Wash up and clear away.

If you are going to cook the chick peas youself, note that different brands take different lengths of time to cook, so check the instructions. Once the chick peas are cooked, run them under cold water to stop them cooking, then set aside to cool.

See Handy Tip 1, page xvii, for an easy way to crush garlic if you don't have a garlic crusher or food processor.

The hummus should be thick and smooth. Season it well as the vegetables or pitta bread accompanying it are quite bland.

To keep the prepared vegetables fresh, immerse them in a bowl of cold water with some ice cubes. Cover and set aside.

Main course

Preparation time: 40 minutes
Cooking time: 50–55 minutes

Assemble all the ingredients and equipment you need for the main course. Set your timer for 40 minutes. Preheat the oven to 200°C/400°F/Gas mark 6. See page 203 if you are going to make the shortcrust pastry yourself.

40 mins Roll out the pastry on a clean, dry work surface dusted with flour. Make sure you also dust the rolling pin. Roll the pastry as thinly as possible, trying not to make any holes or tears in it. Once the pastry is slightly larger than the quiche tin, roll the pastry around the rolling pin and lift it carefully over the top of the tin. Ease the pastry into the tin, ensuring that it comes all the way up the sides. If you have areas where pastry is missing, it will be necessary to patch them. When correctly positioned, trim the pastry around the edges. Place the quiche tin on a baking tray before putting it in the fridge to chill.

> It is essential to dust the work surface with flour or the pastry will sick to it and tear.

> To transfer the pastry to the quiche tin, place the rolling pin in the centre of the pastry, fold the pastry over the rolling pin and carefully lift.

> If you do have to patch your pastry case, wet the pastry with a little cold water to help the patches stick.

30 mins Peel 1 onion and chop it as finely as possible. Place it in a large frying pan and put over a medium heat. Add 1 teaspoon of cooking margarine and allow the onion to soften. Meanwhile, trim the rind (if necessary) from 4 rashers of bacon. Cut the bacon up roughly and set aside. Stir the onions.

> It is much quicker to use kitchen scissors than a knife for removing the bacon rind and chopping the bacon.

23 mins Take 8oz/225g of mushrooms, wash them well, discard the stalks and slice thinly. Once the onion is cooked, add the bacon to the pan and cook until it begins to curl.

> The onion should be soft and golden but not brown.

15 mins Add the sliced mushrooms to the pan and season with a pinch of nutmeg and black pepper. Once the mushrooms start to change colour, turn the heat off and leave to stand.

12 mins Take 3 eggs, break them into a large mixing bowl and whisk with a fork or balloon whisk. Season with pepper, a little salt and a good pinch of mustard powder. Measure out ½ pint/

> Do not use any salt, or very little, if using bacon as it is already very salty.

> Half fat milk can be used in the filling to cut down on the fat content.

MENU 5

300ml of milk and add it to the egg mixture.

8 mins Grate 4oz/100g of cheese straight into the bowl with the egg and milk mixture. Add all the fried ingredients and mix well. If using parsley, wash and chop it, then stir into the mixture.

4 mins Take the lined quiche out of the fridge and pour all the ingredients into it. Transfer the tin on its baking tray to the preheated oven and bake for 15 minutes. Reduce the heat to 160°C/325°F/Gas mark 3 and cook for a further 40 minutes.

0 mins Wash up and clear away.

Placing the quiche tin on a baking tray makes it easier to transport, especially if it is a loose-bottomed tin. It is also useful in case the filling seeps out of the pastry.

Side salad

Set your timer for 10 minutes.

10 mins Wash the tomatoes under cold running water, then slice them thinly with a sharp knife. Set aside. Take the chicory, slice very thinly, wash well under cold running water and leave in a colander to drain.

4 mins Check the quiche, if it has been cooking for 15 minutes, and turn the oven down to 160°C/325°F/Gas mark 3. Continue to cook for a further 40 minutes.

1 min Place the tomato and chicory in a salad bowl and set aside. The avocado will be added just before serving, otherwise it will discolour.

0 mins Wash up and clear away.

The base or root end of chicory can be very bitter and unpleasant to eat, so it is a good idea to remove this part of the stalk so that it doesn't spoil the taste of the salad.

Relax

Have a 30-minute break. Take your timer with you. When you return you will only need to put out your starter, dress your salad and decorate the dessert.

Welcome back

Feeling better after your break?

Last-minute tasks

Set your timer for 20 minutes. This is how long you have before sitting down to eat the starter.

20 mins Check the quiche. If it is golden brown and almost cooked, move it to a lower part of the oven or turn the oven right down.

18 mins Place ½ pint/300ml whipping cream in a bowl and whip it using a balloon whisk or a hand-held electric mixer. Be careful not to overbeat it or it will curdle. Once the cream starts to thicken and hold its shape, stop whisking.

> It is better to underwhip the cream than overwhip it, as it will be very difficult to spread over the jelly if it is too thick.

12 mins To turn out the terrine, fill the sink with a small amount of hot water and place the loaf tin in it for 20 seconds. Remove and dry the bottom of the tin. Place a large plate over the top of the loaf tin and quickly turn the whole thing upside-down. Give the tin a sharp shake and the jelly should fall out. If it doesn't turn out the first time, repeat the process with the hot water and try again.

> Don't keep the jelly in the hot water for more than the recommended time or it will fall apart when turned out.

10 mins Using a flexible spatula, cover the top and sides of the dessert with a thin layer of whipped cream. Decorate the top with 1 tablespoon of chopped almonds, then chill until required.

5 mins Cut the avocado in half, remove the stone and peel the flesh. If this is not possible, scoop the flesh out of the skin with a teaspoon. Place the avocado in the salad bowl with the tomato and chicory. Sprinkle a teaspoon of lemon juice over the avocado to prevent it from discolouring.

> If your avocado is unripe, it is better to leave it out. If it is very ripe, remove any bruised parts before adding it to the salad. The lemon juice prevents the avocado from discolouring.

0 mins Wash up and clear away.

Watch points

Once the meal has started, it is difficult to predict how long each course will take. The following instructions are given only as a guide.

Take the hummus out of the fridge. Drain the vegetables or slice the pitta bread into thin pieces and arrange on a platter. Serve the starter.

MENU 5

Make the French dressing in a measuring jug, add 2 tablespoons of sour cream and mix well before pouring it over the salad. Toss just before serving and make sure that all the ingredients are covered with the dressing. Serve immediately.

Take the quiche out of the oven and remove the outside ring of the tin, if possible, before serving. Alternatively, serve the quiche straight from the dish.

Serve the dessert, which has already been decorated.

A good way to mix French dressing is to place it in a jam jar with a tight-fitting lid. Add the correct quantity of sour cream, screw the lid on firmly and shake really well.

If you cannot remove the quiche from the tin without it falling apart, serve the quiche out of the tin.

Mediterranean menu

Easy to prepare and cook
Cost level: inexpensive
Serves: 4

6

A 30-minute break is incorporated in this menu.

Starter	Greek salad with ciabatta bread	*Preparation time = 15 minutes* *Cooking time = None*
Main course	Stuffed aubergines with mushrooms and sun-dried tomatoes F* Fresh pasta	*Preparation time = 50 minutes* *Cooking time = 35–40 minutes*
Dessert	Fresh figs with Greek yoghurt and honey	*Preparation time = 15 minutes* *Cooking time = None*
Drink	Aromatic white wine, chilled (Retsina would add an authentic Greek touch)	

This menu uses lots of ingredients that come from the Mediterranean and would also be suitable for vegetarians who eat eggs and dairy products.

All the dishes are easy to prepare and cook. The Greek salad can be made in advance, but the dressing should be added just before serving. The main course can also be made in advance, then stored in the fridge until you are ready to cook it on the night. The stuffing for the aubergines can be adapted to suit your taste: once you are happy with the basic mixture, you can add all your favourite ingredients. The pasta is cooked at the last minute and served with the stuffed aubergines.

The fresh figs are delicious with the Greek yoghurt and honey. If you cannot get hold of fresh ones, use tinned figs instead.

MENU 6

Equipment needed – Menu 6

Starter

1 colander
1 savoury chopping board
1 sharp knife
5 small bowls or saucers
1 salad bowl
1 tablespoon
1 teaspoon

Main course

1 savoury chopping board
1 sharp knife
1 teaspoon
2 mixing bowls
1 large plate
1 medium saucepan
1 garlic crusher (see page xvii)
1 colander
1 cheese grater
kitchen paper or clean tea towel
1 frying pan
1 baking tray
1 tablespoon

Dessert

1 fine sieve
1 tin opener
1 sweet chopping board
1 sharp knife
1 teaspoon
1 serving plate

Shopping list – Menu 6

Starter

2 large tomatoes
1 small cucumber
12 pitted olives, green or black
*1 small onion
4oz/100g feta cheese
*6 tablespoons of olive oil
*2 tablespoons wine vinegar
*salt, pepper, mustard powder
*chopped parsley to garnish (see page xviii)
1 ciabatta loaf
*4oz/100g butter or margarine

Main course

2 aubergines
*salt, pepper, nutmeg
*1 onion
*2oz/50g (2 tablespoons) cooking margarine
*1 clove garlic (optional)
8oz/225g button mushrooms
*4oz/100g fresh breadcrumbs (see page xvii)
1 teaspoon lemon juice
*1 egg
*4oz/100g Cheddar cheese
*2–4 tablespoons olive oil
2oz/50g (2 tablespoons) sun-dried tomatoes in oil
*2oz/50g (2 tablespoons) dried breadcrumbs
8oz/225g fresh pasta of your choice
*1 teaspoon margarine or oil

Dessert

8 fresh figs or 1 tin (8oz/225g)
*½ teaspoon lemon juice
*8 teaspoons clear honey
4oz/100g plain Greek yoghurt
*toasted flaked almonds to decorate

*Check store cupboard

Countdown – Menu 6

If you want to prepare the whole menu, you will need 125 minutes (2 hours 5 minutes). This includes a 30-minute break. If you are a slow cook, add 5–10 minutes to each course to ensure you don't run out of time. Remember, the times given are only a guide as each cook will take different lengths of time to complete each task. You can leave out any course if time is short. The dessert and starter can be made in advance, but the Greek salad must not be dressed until you are ready to serve it. The aubergines can also be made in advance, then chilled and cooked on the night. The dessert is simple and refreshingly different. Serve it chilled, decorated with flaked almonds.

Dessert

PROBLEMS AND HANDY TIPS

Preparation time: 15 minutes
Cooking time: None

Assemble all the ingredients and equipment you need for the dessert. Set your timer for 15 minutes.
15 mins Take 8 fresh figs and wash them well under cold running water. If using tinned figs, drain off the liquid through a fine sieve. Trim the stalk top from each fig, then cut down almost through to the base of each fig, dividing it in quarters. Carefully open out the sections to form petals, then add a small drop of lemon juice to each fig.

Tinned figs are not as firm as fresh ones, but they can be prepared in the same way.

8 mins Pour 1 teaspoon of clear honey over each fig, then place a large teaspoon of yoghurt on top of the honey, and carefully press the petals back together again.

Don't worry if the yoghurt and honey ooze out a bit from the figs – any excess can be spooned over the top of them before serving.

2 mins Place the figs on a serving plate and chill until required. Decorate with some toasted flaked almonds before serving.
0 mins Wash up and clear away.

MENU 6

Starter

Preparation time: 15 minutes
Cooking time: None

Assemble all the ingredients and equipment you need for the starter. Set your timer for 15 minutes.
15 mins Wash the tomatoes and cucumber under cold running water. Leave them to dry in a colander.
12 mins Take the olives and cut them in half if they are very large. Place them in a bowl and set aside. Peel 1 small onion, chop it finely and place it in a separate bowl.
8 mins Take 4oz/100g of feta cheese, cut it into bite-size cubes and place it in another bowl.
4 mins Remove the tomato stalks and eyes with a sharp knife, then cut the tomatoes into quarters or thin slices. Place them in a bowl. Peel the cucumber with a potato peeler. Cut it in half lengthways and then into quarters, then slice into small dice. Place in a bowl and chill with the other bowls of salad ingredients until required.
0 mins Wash up and clear away.

Make sure you wash the tomatoes well as there are so many chemicals used on vegetables these days.

Keep all the ingredients in separate bowls until the last minute. This will keep the flavours fresh and aromatic.

The cucumber skin can be left on if it is tender and without any blemishes. To create a frilly edge to the slices, run a fork down through the skin.

Main course

Preparation time: 50 minutes
Cooking time: 35–40 minutes

Assemble all the ingredients and equipment you need for the main course. Set your timer for 50 minutes.
50 mins Take 2 aubergines and cut them in half lengthwise down the middle. Keep the green stalk on if possible as this keeps the aubergine together and also adds colour and garnish to the dish. Using a sharp knife, cut around the skin of the aubergine to release the flesh, run the knife underneath the flesh to loosen it. Scoop out all the flesh with a teaspoon into a mixing bowl. You should be left with 4 smooth, hollowed-out halves.

Be careful not to cut through the skin of the aubergines. If you do, the hole can be hidden with the stuffing.

45 mins Hold each aubergine shell under cold running water, then place them on a large plate and sprinkle lightly with enough salt to cover the inside. This process, called degorging, draws out the sometimes bitter flavour of aubergines. Leave to stand.

The hollowed-out skin should be approximately ¼ inch/1 cm thick.

Degorging the aubergines is very important as it removes the bitter flavour and extracts any excess moisture.

42 mins Place the aubergine flesh on a chopping board and chop it roughly. Return it to the mixing bowl, sprinkle lightly with salt and mix it so that the salt covers all the flesh. Leave it to degorge.

37 mins Peel 1 onion and chop it as finely as possible. Place it in a saucepan, add 1oz/25g (1 tablespoon) of cooking margarine and put over a low heat to soften. Meanwhile, peel and crush 1 clove of garlic, if using. Stir the onion well, then add the garlic. Do not allow it to burn. Turn the heat off after 2 minutes.

Keep the onion on a low heat so that it doesn't burn.

See Handy Tip 1, page xvii for an easy way to crush garlic if you do not have a garlic crusher.

32 mins Take 8oz/225g of button mushrooms and wash them well under cold running water.

29 mins Make 4oz/100g of fresh breadcrumbs by crumbling 4 slices of fresh bread into a bowl. Set aside.

See Handy Tip 3, page xvii for an easy way to make fresh breadcrumbs from frozen bread.

25 mins Take the drained mushrooms and chop them up into small pieces. Add them to the onion and garlic and cook over a medium heat. Add a teaspoon of lemon juice and season well with a pinch of salt, freshly ground pepper and a generous pinch of nutmeg. Stir well again.

Nutmeg enhances the flavour of the mushrooms and gives them a delicious taste.

20 mins Take the saucepan off the heat and pour the mushroom mixture into the bowl with the breadcrumbs. Break 1 egg into the mixture and stir well. Grate 4oz/100g of Cheddar cheese on to a plate, then add half to the mushroom mixture and stir well.

Do not use all the grated cheese at this stage: it is important to have enough to sprinkle over the top of each aubergine to prevent drying out.

15 mins Transfer the aubergine flesh to a colander and wash well to remove all the salt. Pat dry with kitchen paper or clean tea towel. Place the flesh in a frying pan, add 2 tablespoons of olive oil and cook for a few minutes on a high heat. Stir well. If there is too much flesh to fit in the pan, you will have to cook it in batches. When the flesh has browned a little, add it to the mixing bowl and stir well. Preheat the oven to 200°C/400°F/Gas mark 6.

The aubergine flesh might need a little extra olive oil while it is cooking as it tends to be very absorbent. Do not exceed 4 tablespoons or the dish will become very greasy.

MENU 6

10 mins Take the aubergine shells and wash them under cold running water to remove all the salt. Pat dry with some kitchen paper or a clean tea towel. Place the shells on a baking tray.

8 mins Remove the sun-dried tomatoes from their oil, chop them roughly and stir into the aubergine mixture. The stuffing is now finished.

5 mins Carefully divide the stuffing between the 4 hollowed-out aubergines. Place the stuffed aubergines on a baking tray and sprinkle with the remaining grated cheese and a small amount of dried breadcrumbs. Place them in the preheated oven and bake for 40 minutes, until the aubergine is soft and the cheese is golden brown and crispy.

0 mins Wash up and clear away.

Note If you would like to take a longer break, or if you have made the stuffed aubergines in advance, cover them in the fridge until you are ready to cook them.

Relax

Have a 30-minute break. Take your timer with you and when you return you will only have to cook the pasta and dress the salad.

Welcome back

Feeling better after your break? If you have not cooked the aubergines yet, preheat the oven to 200°C/400°F/Gas mark 6 and bake them for 40 minutes.

Last-minute tasks

Set your timer for 15 minutes. This is how long you will have before serving the starter.

15 mins Fill the kettle and put it on to boil.

Make sure you wash all the salt off the aubergines or the flavour of the finished dish will be spoilt.

Make sure there is plenty of stuffing in each shell before adding the cheese.

The cheese on top of the aubergines stops them from drying out, and the dried breadcrumbs absorb some of the fat from the cheese and stop them becoming greasy.

PROBLEMS AND HANDY TIPS

14 mins Check the aubergines in the oven; if you feel that they are browning too quickly, either move them down in the oven or lower the heat. Put the ciabatta bread into the oven to warm.

12 mins Empty the pasta into a medium saucepan, add 1 teaspoon of margarine and a pinch of salt. Read the instructions on the packet as cooking times will vary depending on the variety of pasta you are using.

Fresh pasta often takes a shorter time to cook than dried, so check the instructions well. The margarine prevents the pasta from sticking together.

10 mins Take out all the prepared ingredients for the Greek salad and combine them in a salad bowl. Add 6 tablespoons of olive oil and 2 tablespoons of wine vinegar. Season with freshly ground pepper, a pinch of salt and 1 teaspoon of mustard. Toss the salad well, garnish with chopped parsley and place on the table to serve.

Check the dressing to see if it suits your taste; you can always add more oil or vinegar, or even some lemon juice.

See Handy Tip 7, page xviii for frozen chopped parsley.

2 mins Pour the boiling water over the pasta and cook on a medium to high heat. If the pasta will take only a few minutes to cook, it is a good idea to cook it after you have eaten the starter.

0 mins Wash up and clear away.

Cook the pasta only if you are a few minutes away from serving it, or it will be overcooked.

Watch points

PROBLEMS AND HANDY TIPS

Once the meal has started, it is difficult to predict how long each course will take. The following instructions are given only as a guide.

The main course can be kept hot in the oven while you eat the starter; it will not spoil if the starter takes longer than expected.

Serve the starter, and don't forget to put the ciabatta bread and some butter on the table for your guests to help themselves. Put a serving dish and the main course plates in to warm if you have the facility.

The aubergines are cooked once the skins have started to shrink back a bit and the cheese on top is golden brown. If in doubt, use a sharp knife to pierce the side of the aubergines though the skin – it should pass through easily. The aubergine can sit happily in a warm oven while you eat the starter.

Cook the pasta if you have not already done so, then drain it and transfer to a warmed serving dish. Take the aubergines out of the oven and serve them.

Decorate the dessert with toasted flaked almonds before serving.

Do not allow the pasta to overcook – keep it al dente.

Summer picnic hamper

7

Moderately difficult to prepare and cook
Cost level: good value
Serves: 4

There is no break incorporated in this menu.

Starter	Home-made tuna fish dip[F*] **or** cottage cheese and cucumber dip with crudités, pitta bread or tortilla chips	*Preparation time = 20 minutes* *Cooking time = None*
Main course	Home-made savoury pizza[F*]	*Preparation time = 35 minutes* *Cooking time=25–30 minutes*
	Mixed pasta salad	*Preparation time=25 minutes* *Cooking time = None*
	Spicy chicken drumsticks[F*]	*Preparation time = 20 minutes* *Cooking time = 50 minutes*
	Smoked salmon and cream cheese **or** roast beef and mustard croissants	*Preparation time = 10 minutes* *Cooking time = None*
Dessert	Fresh fruit kebabs **or** vanilla custard tarts[F*]	*Preparation time = 15 minutes* *Cooking time = None* *Preparation time = 20 minutes* *Cooking time = 35–45 minutes*
Drink	Anything light – chilled rosé, sparkling wine, or even a light red wine, chilled	

This summer picnic menu can be adapted to suit any occasion. Choose a wide variety of dishes for the picnic as it is always lots of fun to see what comes out of the hamper. Make sure you cook a few things for vegetarians, especially if you are going in a big group and will be meeting people for the first time. Picnics are always shared, and it is nice to pass things around and have a taste of everyone's goodies.

Crudités are raw vegetables which have been cut into thin slices or sticks and are dunked into the dip; pitta bread and tortilla dips can also be used in the same way.

The pizza can be made with or without meat. Two versions are offered in the method to give you more choice. The filled croissants make an interesting change from the boring old sandwich. They can be made in advance and packed easily for transporting.

The custard tarts can be made well in advance and frozen; they are light to eat and easy to transport. The fruit kebabs are great fun. You can use any seasonal fruit, and they can also be dipped in crème fraîche or thick cream. They will need to be transported in a container with a lid as they are rather delicate.

MENU 7

Equipment needed – Menu 7

Starter

1 tin opener
1 mixing bowl or food processor
1 fork or savoury wooden spoon
1 tablespoon
1 potato peeler
1 sharp knife
1 savoury chopping board
1 pair kitchen scissors
1 serving bowl

Main course

cling film, aluminium foil and plastic containers
    with lids for transporting the food
1 picnic hamper, with cutlery, glasses or cups
Savoury pizza
  1 medium mixing bowl
  1 colander
  1 cheese grater
  1 savoury chopping board
  1 sharp knife
  2 plates or small bowls
  1 frying pan
  1 fish slice
  1 tablespoon
  1 rolling pin or clean wine bottle
  1 large rectangular baking tray or 1 10 inch/25
      cm pie dish
  1 tin opener
Mixed pasta salad
  1 large saucepan
  1 teaspoon
  1 tablespoon
  1 colander
  1 tin opener
  1 fine sieve
  1 sharp knife
  1 savoury chopping board
  1 large mixing bowl
  1 pair kitchen scissors
  1 large salad bowl
Spicy chicken drumsticks
  1 savoury chopping board
  1 sharp knife
  1 medium mixing bowl

Shopping list – Menu 7

Starter

Tuna fish dip
  1 tin (7oz/200g) tuna fish in oil or brine
  *salt and pepper
  *1 tablespoon lemon juice
  *2 tablespoons mayonnaise
Cottage cheese and cucumber dip
  4oz/100g cream cheese
  4oz/100g curd cheese
  ½ cucumber
  1 small bunch fresh chives
  *salt, cayenne pepper
Crudités
  fresh vegetables, such as carrots
  celery and cauliflower
  tortilla chips (optional) or 4 pieces of pitta
    bread

Main course

Savoury pizza
  1 packet pizza base mix or 1 large ready-
    made pizza base or turn to page 205 to
    make the dough yourself
Traditional topping
  8oz/225g button mushrooms
  6oz/175g Cheddar cheese
  *1 onion
  *1oz/25g (1 tablespoon) cooking margarine
  6oz/175g ham, bacon or pepperoni
  *2 tablespoons tomato purée
  1 small tin (7oz/200g) chopped tomatoes
  1 small bunch fresh oregano or 1 teaspoon
    dried
  *salt, pepper, nutmeg
  2oz/50g pitted olives, black or green
Vegetarian topping
  3–4 sun-dried tomatoes
  1 small tin (7oz/200g) sweetcorn
  1 small tin (7oz/200g) artichoke hearts
Mixed pasta salad
  1 packet (18oz/500g) mixed colour pasta
    shells
  *1 teaspoon margarine

1 garlic crusher (see Handy Tip 1, page xvii)
1 tablespoon
1 teaspoon
1 roasting tin
1 spatula

Filled croissants

1 savoury chopping board
1 sharp knife
1 round-ended knife
1 teaspoon
1 pair kitchen scissors

Dessert

Fresh fruit kebabs

1 colander
1 sweet chopping board
1 sharp knife
8 bamboo skewers
1 container to transport them

Vanilla custard tarts

1 tablespoon
1 rolling pin or clean wine bottle
1 pastry cutter, larger than the bun tin holes
12- or 18-holed bun tin (non-stick or greased)
1 measuring jug
1 small saucepan or microwave-safe container
1 mixing bowl
1 fork
1 fine sieve
1 cooling rack

*salt
8oz/225g button mushrooms
1 small tin (7oz/200g) red kidney beans
1 bunch fresh chives
*3 tablespoons mayonnaise
*2 tablespoons French dressing
½ teaspoon cayenne pepper

Spicy chicken drumsticks
*1 onion
*1 clove garlic
2 tablespoons tandoori paste
*1 tablespoon light soya sauce
*2 teaspoons lemon juice
*freshly ground black pepper
8 chicken drumsticks

Smoked salmon croissants
4 croissants
7oz/200g cream cheese
4–5oz/100–125g fresh smoked salmon
*2 teaspoons lemon juice
*freshly ground black pepper

Roast beef croissants
4 croissants
*2–3oz/50–75g butter or margarine
4 large slices roast beef
2 teaspoons coarse-grain mustard
*freshly ground black pepper
1 punnet fresh cress

Dessert

Fresh fruit kebabs
strawberries, peaches, nectarines,
raspberries, bananas, seedless grapes
(black or white)
4oz/100g crème fraîche, natural yoghurt or
thick cream to serve (optional)

Vanilla custard tarts
*1–2 tablespoons plain flour
1 small packet (8oz/225g) sweet shortcrust
pastry or 8 ready-made pastry cases or turn
to page 204 if you would like to make the
pastry yourself
*¼ pint/150ml full or half fat milk
*1 egg
*1oz/25g (1 tablespoon) caster sugar
*1 teaspoon vanilla essence
*pinch grated nutmeg

*Check store cupboard

MENU 7

Countdown – Menu 7

If you are going to prepare all the dishes for the picnic, you will need 145 minutes (2 hours 15 minutes). There is no break incorporated in this menu as so many things can be made in advance, and even frozen if you wish. If you are a slow cook, add 5–10 minutes to each course to ensure that you do not run out of time. Remember, the times given are only a guide as each cook will take different lengths of time to complete each task.

Choose one of the dips and serve either crudités or pitta bread with it. The pizza gives 4 generous servings; if it is accompanied by other savoury dishes, you might want to halve the quantities. On the other hand, any extra pizza can be frozen and used on another occasion. Make sure you have a wide variety of dishes to add flavour and fun to the picnic.

Starter
Tuna fish dip

PROBLEMS AND HANDY TIPS

> Preparation time: 8 minutes
> Cooking time: None

Assemble all the ingredients and equipment you need for the dip. It can be made in a food processor if you prefer; this saves time and also gives the dip a smoother finish. Set your timer for 8 minutes.

A food processor will make a very smooth dip, but the dip tastes just as good if slightly textured.

8 mins Open the tin of tuna fish and drain off the oil or brine. Place the tuna in a mixing bowl and mash with a fork or wooden spoon until it becomes flaky.

Make sure you drain all the oil from the tuna fish, or the dip will be greasy.

6 mins Season well with ground black pepper, then add 1 tablespoon of lemon juice and 2 tablespoons of mayonnaise. Mix well and check the seasoning.

1 min Place the tuna dip in a serving bowl and chill until required.

0 mins Wash up and clear away.

Cottage cheese and cucumber dip

Preparation time: 10 minutes
Cooking time: None

Assemble all the ingredients and equipment you need for the dip. It can be made in a food processor if you prefer; this saves time and also gives the dip a smoother finish. Set your timer for 10 minutes.

10 mins Place 4oz/100g of cream cheese and 4oz/100g of curd cheese in a mixing bowl or food processor. Mix well until the two cheeses combine.

6 mins Take the cucumber half and peel it with a potato peeler. Cut flesh in half and then quarters lengthways. Slice it into very small dice and mix with the cream cheese.

Do not put the cucumber through the food processor as it will become too liquid and make the dip runny.

2 mins Season with salt and a pinch of cayenne pepper and mix well. Take a small bunch of fresh chives, wash well and shake off any excess water. Using a pair of kitchen scissors, snip the chives into the bowl with the cream cheese and cucumber. Mix well and check the seasoning.

Season the dip well as both cucumber and cottage cheese can be rather bland.

1 min Place the dip in a serving bowl and chill until required.

0 mins Wash up and clear away.

Crudités

Preparation time: 10 minutes

If you are going to use vegetables for dipping rather than pitta bread or tortilla chips, prepare them after you have made the dip. Wash them well, then slice into thin strips 2 inch/5 cm long. Alternatively, put them through the thin chip slicing blade on a food processor. Arrange the vegetables on a serving plate, then cover and chill until required.

Remember to keep the crudités small and thin so that they are easy to dip.

For extra crispness, place the crudités in a small bowl or plastic bag and add a few cubes of ice. This will keep them fresh until required.

MENU 7

Main course
Savoury pizza

Preparation time: 35 minutes
Cooking time: 25–30 minutes

Assemble all the ingredients and equipment you need for the pizza. Remember, you can adapt the topping to suit your own and your guests' preferences. Set your timer for 35 minutes. If you are going to cook the pizza straight away, preheat the oven to 220°C/425°F/Gas mark 7.

35 mins Turn to page 205 if you are going to make the pizza base yourself, or make up the packet of pizza dough according to the instructions, then leave it to relax while you prepare the topping. If you have bought a ready-made pizza base, unwrap it and place it on a baking tray ready to add the toppings.

30 mins Take 8oz/225g of button mushrooms and wash them well. Discard the stalks and leave the tops to drain in a colander. Measure out 6oz/175g Cheddar cheese, grate it coarsely on to a plate and set aside.

25 mins Take the drained mushrooms and slice thinly, then place on a plate or in a bowl and set aside. Take the tinned artichoke hearts, quarter then set aside. Take 1 onion, peel and chop it finely, then place in a frying pan with 1oz/25g (1 tablespoon) of margarine over a medium heat. While the onion is cooking, chop 6oz/175g of bacon, or pepperoni. Add to the frying pan and cook for 12 minutes, then turn off the heat.

If the bacon has rind, trim it off with a pair of kitchen scissors before chopping the meat.

If you are making a vegetarian pizza, chop the sun-dried tomatoes instead of the bacon, and place them in the frying pan with the onion; cook briskly for 2 minutes, then turn off the heat.

If the sun-dried tomatoes have been soaking in olive oil, use a piece of kitchen paper to remove the excess oil.

17 mins Take the pizza dough out of the bowl and make a tight, firm ball. If you are going to make more than one pizza, cut the dough in half before rolling it out. Place the dough on a clean, well-floured work surface and using either a rolling pin or clean bottle, roll it out as thick or thin as you like. Remember to keep the shape of the baking tin in mind at all times so that the pizza base will fit on it.

12 mins To move the dough on to the baking tray, wrap it carefully around the rolling pin, then lift it up and place it on the baking tray or in the pizza pan. Make sure the dough is pressed well into the corners. Now take 2 tablespoons of tomato purée and spread it over the dough. Open the tin of chopped tomatoes and pour the contents over the purée.

9 mins Take a few leaves of fresh oregano (if using), wash them well and chop finely. Add the onion and bacon, ham or pepperoni (or sun-dried tomatoes) to the pizza base, cover with the sliced mushrooms (and artichoke hearts if using), freshly ground pepper, a good pinch of nutmeg and a little salt. (Use very little salt if your topping includes bacon or ham.)

5 mins Add the grated cheese and a few whole or halved olives; on the vegetarian pizza you can also add some sweetcorn. Place in the preheated oven for 25–30 minutes. (If you are making more than one pizza, check them after 15 minutes and swap their positions in the oven as the top one will probably be cooking faster than the bottom one.)

0 mins Wash up and clear away.

Mixed pasta salad

Preparation time: 25 minutes
Cooking time: None

Assemble all the ingredients and equipment you need for the pasta salad. Set your timer for 25 minutes.

25 mins Fill the kettle and put it on to boil. Take a large saucepan, empty the packet of mixed pasta into it and add 1 teaspoon of margarine and a pinch of salt.

You need to decide what size and thickness the pizzas will be before you start rolling out the dough.

If the tin is not non-stick, it is a good idea to grease it well to prevent the pizza from sticking.

The fresh oregano adds more flavour than dried.

Season the pizza well.

If the pizzas are very thin, they will probably take only 20–25 minutes to cook.

PROBLEMS AND HANDY TIPS

MENU 7

22 mins Pour the boiling water over the pasta and cook for 11–13 minutes. (Check the instructions on the packet as different brands will vary in their cooking times.) Stir the pasta well so that it becomes coated with the margarine.

20 mins While the pasta is cooking, take 8oz/225g of button mushrooms and wash them well. Discard the stalks and leave the tops to drain in a colander.

15 mins Open a tin of kidney beans and drain them in a fine sieve. Wash the beans under cold running water and leave to drain.

12 mins Check the pasta. If it is cooked, drain it in a colander, then rinse under warm running water, Return it to the saucepan and cover with warm water. Set aside.

10 mins Take the mushrooms and slice them thinly into a bowl. Add the kidney beans and mix well. Take the fresh chives, wash them under cold running water and pat dry on kitchen paper. Using a pair of kitchen scissors, snip the chives into the bowl with the mushrooms and beans. Set aside.

7 mins Place 3 tablespoons of mayonnaise in a small mixing bowl, add 2 tablespoons of well-mixed French dressing and season with ½ teaspoon cayenne pepper and a little salt. Mix well.

4 mins Drain the pasta through a colander, shake off any excess water, then place in the bowl with the beans, mushrooms and chives. Pour in the mayonnaise dressing, mix well and chill until required.

0 mins Wash up and clear away.

Spicy chicken drumsticks

Preparation time: 20 minutes
Cooking time: 50 minutes

Assemble all the ingredients and equipment you need for the main course. Set your timer for 20 minutes. Preheat the oven to 200°C/400°F/Gas mark 6.

20 mins Take 1 onion, peel and chop it finely, then place it in a medium-sized mixing bowl.

If you are using fresh pasta, it will take less time to cook, so check the instructions on the packet.

The margarine coats the pasta and prevents it from sticking together.

Keeping the pasta in warm water stops it from sticking together before being added to the salad.

Make sure you snip the chives as finely as possible.

Check the seasoning carefully as it is easier to adjust it now rather than later.

PROBLEMS AND HANDY TIPS

52

15 mins Peel and crush 1 clove of garlic and add it to the chopped onions. Add 2 tablespoons of tandoori paste, 1 tablespoon of light soya sauce, 2 teaspoons of lemon juice and some ground black pepper. Mix well.

10 mins Take 8 chicken drumsticks, with the skin on, and roll each one in the onion paste. Place the drumsticks in a roasting tin and pour the remaining sauce over them. Place in the preheated oven for 50 minutes. (Check the drumsticks after 20 minutes, and turn them over with a spatula so that they cook evenly and become crisp on all sides.)

0 mins Wash up and clear away.

Make sure all the ingredients are mixed together well before coating the chicken.

Don't worry about the onion falling off the drumsticks as the remaining sauce will be poured over them.

Smoked salmon and cream cheese croissants

PROBLEMS AND HANDY TIPS

Preparation time: 10 minutes
Cooking time: None

Assemble all the ingredients and equipment you need for the croissants. Set your timer for 10 minutes.

10 mins Take 4 croissants and slice them in half horizontally. Using a round-ended knife, spread a generous amount of cream cheese on each side, then insert one piece of fresh smoked salmon.

5 mins Add a drop of lemon juice to the salmon, grind some black pepper over the top and sandwich the halves together pressing lightly. Wrap up each croissant in cling film and place in the fridge to chill until required.

0 mins Wash up and clear away.

The filled croissants can be kept wrapped up in the fridge for approximately 4–6 hours without spoiling. Do not keep them longer than this or they will become soggy and lose their flavour.

The pepper and lemon juice can be left out if you prefer.

Roast beef and mustard croissants

PROBLEMS AND HANDY TIPS

Preparation time: 10 minutes
Cooking time: None

Assemble all the ingredients and equipment you need for the croissants. Set your timer for 10 minutes.

MENU 7

10 mins Take 4 croissants and slice them in half horizontally. Spread a thin layer of butter or table margarine over each half. Take a piece of roast beef and place it on one half of the croissant.

6 mins Spread a small amount of mustard over the roast beef and add some ground black pepper. Wash the cress well and shake off any excess water. Using a pair of kitchen scissors, snip some cress on to the beef and mustard. Sandwich the croissant halves together, pressing lightly.

1 min Wrap each croissant in cling film and place in the fridge to chill until required.

0 mins Wash up and clear away.

Dessert
Fresh fruit kebabs

> *Preparation time: 15 minutes*
> *Cooking time: None*

Assemble all the ingredients and equipment you need for the dessert. These kebabs should be made only 2–3 hours before being eaten, as they will not keep and will start to fall off their sticks. Set your timer for 15 minutes.

15 mins Take all your fresh fruit, place in a colander and wash well under cold running water.

10 mins Peel the peaches or nectarines, cut them in half and remove the stones and cut the flesh into bite-sized pieces. Take 8 bamboo skewers and carefully thread a small piece of each fruit on to each stick. Mix the fruits up so that you have some of the harder fruits next to the softer fruits, and keep them packed close together.

2 mins Place the kebabs on a plate or in a plastic container, cover and chill until required.

0 mins Wash up and clear away.

Vanilla custard tarts

> *Preparation time: 20 minutes*
> *Cooking time: 35–45 minutes*

Assemble all the ingredients and equipment you

The filled croissants can be kept wrapped in the fridge for approximately 4–6 hours without spoiling. Do not keep them longer than this or they will become soggy and lose their flavour.

The mustard can be left out or replaced with horseradish cream.

PROBLEMS AND HANDY TIPS

The peaches or nectarines can have their skin left on if it is shiny and unblemished.

The kebabs are very delicate and will need to be handled and transported with care to prevent the fruit from falling off the sticks.

need for the dessert. Set your timer for 20 minutes. Turn to page 204 if you are going to make the pastry yourself. If you have bought ready-made pastry cases, you will only need to prepare the filling. Preheat the oven to 200°C/400°F/Gas mark 6.

20 mins Lightly flour a clean work surface. Place the sweet shortcrust pastry on it and roll out as thinly as possible without tearing it. Using a circular cutter that is bigger than the bun tin holes, cut out circles of pastry and carefully place them in the individual holes. You should allow two pastry cases per person. Place in the fridge if there is space available.

Make sure there are no holes in the pastry cases or the custard will leak out.

12 mins To prepare the filling, place ¼ pint/150ml of milk in a small saucepan and heat almost to boiling point; remove from the heat as soon as bubbles start to appear. (This is known as scalding point.)

See Cookery Terms, page 223, for a definition of 'scald'.

8 mins Break 1 egg into a mixing bowl, whisk with a fork, then mix in 1oz/25g (1 tablespoon) of caster sugar and 1 teaspoon vanilla essence. Slowly add the scalded milk to the egg and sugar, whisking all the time. Strain the egg mixture through a fine sieve into a measuring jug and carefully fill the pastry cases with it.

The eggs are strained to remove any specks which indicate that the egg has been fertilized.

2 mins Add a small pinch of nutmeg to the top of each individual tart. Place in the preheated oven.

0 mins Wash up and clear away.

Check the tarts after 15 minutes and reduce the temperature to 160°C/325°F/Gas mark 3. Continue to bake for a further 20–30 minutes. The tarts are cooked when the custard has set and the pastry is golden brown and has shrunk away from the edges. Place them on a cooling rack until cold, then cover and chill them until required.

The cooking times will vary depending on the size and quantity of tarts you have made. Check them after 30 minutes' cooking.

Watch points

PROBLEMS AND HANDY TIPS

Since this is a picnic menu and all the dishes are served cold there are very few watch points.

Pack your picnic basket carefully, placing heavy

and solid items at the bottom. Place the plastic containers on top of these things, and then insert the delicate items such as the croissants.

Don't forget to pack plates, cutlery, glasses, cups and lots of napkins. Remember to take a corkscrew or bottle opener if you are having wine. You will also need a picnic blanket.

If it is a very hot and sunny day, it would be a good idea to pack perishables and drinks in a cool box with an ice-pack.

Vegan menu

Moderately difficult to prepare and cook
Cost level: good value
Serves: 4

8

A 30-minute break is incorporated in this menu.

Starter	Fresh asparagus with vinaigrette and French bread	*Preparation time = 10 minutes* *Cooking time = 10-15 minutes*
Main course	TVP and tomato meatloaf [F*] Baked potatoes French beans	*Preparation time = 40 minutes* *Cooking time = 45 minutes*
Dessert	Pears in red wine	*Preparation time = 20 minutes* *Cooking time = 30 minutes*
Drink	Why not drink more of the red wine you poached the pears in?	

This menu is suitable for those who do not eat any meat, poultry, fish, eggs or dairy products. If you prepare this menu, you must buy special vegan margarine or use vegetable, soya or olive oil.

The starter is best made on the day to keep it fresh, but it can be served hot or cold. The vinaigrette can be made in advance, but if time is short, buy a ready-made one.

The main course can be made in advance and frozen. It should be heated up on the night. The baked potatoes will cook in the oven with the main course to save time and energy.

The dessert must be made in advance to allow it time to absorb the juice and to be well chilled. Serve the pears decorated with toasted almonds.

MENU 8

Equipment needed – Menu 8

Starter

1 savoury chopping board
1 sharp knife
1 medium saucepan
1 colander or sieve

Main course

1 savoury chopping board
1 sharp knife
1 medium saucepan
1 garlic crusher (or see page xvii)
1 tablespoon
1 small wine glass
1 food processor or mixing bowl
1 loaf tin 8 × 4inch/20 × 10cm
1 tin opener

Dessert

1 measuring jug
1 medium saucepan with lid
1 sweet wooden spoon
1 sharp knife or potato peeler
1 sweet chopping board
1 serving bowl
1 tablespoon
1 small bowl

Shopping list – Menu 8

Starter

1lb/450g fresh asparagus
*salt
*¼ pint/150ml French dressing (see page 201)
1 long French loaf

Main course

4 large or 8 small baking potatoes
*1 onion
1oz/25g (1 tablespoon) vegan margarine
*1 clove garlic (optional)
4oz/100g button mushrooms
*salt, pepper, mustard powder
*nutmeg
4 fresh sage leaves or 1 tablespoon *dried sage
*3 tablespoons tomato purée
*1 small glass red wine
1 packet (12oz/350g) minced TVP (textured vegetable protein)
2oz/50g (2 tablespoons) fresh breadcrumbs
*1 small tin (7oz/200g) chopped tomatoes
2lb/900g French beans or green vegetable of your choice

Dessert

*¼ pint/150ml water
¼ pint/150ml red wine
*5oz/125g caster sugar
*1 cinnamon stick or pinch of cinnamon
*1 lemon
4 firm William or Conference pears
*1 tablespoon cornflour
*1oz/25g (1 tablespoon) toasted almonds for decoration

*Check store cupboard

Countdown – Menu 8

If you are going to prepare the whole menu, you will need 120 minutes (2 hours), which includes a 30-minute break. If you are a slow cook, add 5–10 minutes to each course to ensure that you do not run out of time. Remember, the times given are only a guide as each cook will take different lengths of time to complete the task. The starter is best made on the day so that it remains fresh, but it can be served hot or cold. The vinaigrette should be made in advance. The main course can be made and frozen in advance, then heated up on the day. The dessert should be prepared and cooked in advance to allow the flavours to develop.

Dessert

PROBLEMS AND HANDY TIPS

Preparation time: 20 minutes
Cooking time: 30 minutes

Assemble all the ingredients and equipment you need for the dessert. Set your timer for 20 minutes.
20 mins Place ¼ pint/150ml of water and ¼ pint/150ml of red wine in a saucepan. Add 5oz/125g of caster sugar to the saucepan and put over a low heat to dissolve, stirring constantly. Add the cinnamon stick or a good pinch of cinnamon.
15 mins Take one lemon and using a sharp knife or potato peeler, pare some of the rind into the wine mixture. Cut the lemon in half and squeeze one half of the juice into the saucepan. Stir well.
10 mins Take 4 pears, leave the stalks on, but carefully peel off the skin. (Firm pears are easier to keep intact.)
5 mins Place the pears upright in the saucepan of liquid and put over a low heat to cook. Spoon some of the liquid over each pear so that they take on the colour of the wine. Leave them to simmer on a very low heat for at least 30 minutes: the longer and slower the pears cook, the better.
0 mins Wash up and clear away.

If you don't have any scales to weigh out the sugar, measure out 5 tablespoons, which will be accurate enough.

Choose a saucepan that the pears will fit into snugly so that the liquid will cover as much of them as possible.

Roll the lemon on a work surface under the palm of your hand to loosen the flesh. This also increases the amount of juice you can get out of the lemon.
The stalk of the pear is left on as decoration and to keep the pear together while it is cooking.

Make sure that the syrup only simmers or the pears will cook too quickly and fall apart.
The liquid should be like a thin jelly – runny enough to pour but thick enough to coat.

MENU 8

Once the pears are soft, turn the heat off, remove them from the liquid and place them in a serving bowl. Return the pan to the heat and boil the liquid until you have approximately half the amount you started with. Place 1 tablespoon of cornflour in a small bowl, add 1 tablespoon of water and mix to a thin paste. Lower the heat under the reduced liquid, then pour in the cornflour. Return slowly to the boil, stirring constantly, until the liquid thickens. When the liquid becomes clear and gooey, pour it over the pears and place in the fridge to chill. Do not decorate until just before serving.

Main course

Preparation time: 40 minutes
Cooking time: 45 minutes

Assemble all the ingredients and equipment you need for the main course. If you have a food processor, it can be used to mince up the TVP, which makes the loaf bind better. Preheat the oven to 160°C/325°F/Gas mark 3. Set your timer for 40 minutes.

40 mins Take 4 large or 8 small baking potatoes, wash them well and pat dry. Using a sharp knife, make a shallow lengthways cut all the way around each potato. This helps them to cook more evenly. Place in the preheated oven to bake.

30 mins Peel and chop the onion, then place in a saucepan with 1oz/25g (1 tablespoon) of vegan margarine. Cook over a low heat.

25 mins While the onion is cooking, peel and crush 1 clove of garlic, if using. Once the onion is soft, add the garlic and cook for 2 minutes. Turn off the heat.

20 mins Take 4oz/100g button mushrooms, wash them, discard the stalks and cook roughly. Add the mushrooms to the onion and cook for a few minutes. Turn the heat down and season with

PROBLEMS AND HANDY TIPS

As the potatoes start to cook, they will open up, which makes it easier to fill them later on.

If you have a food processor, you can use it to chop the onion and mushrooms, and to mince the TVP.

See Handy Tip 1, page xvii for an easy way to crush garlic without a garlic crusher.

If the mushrooms are very wet, dry them on kitchen paper before chopping them.

salt, freshly ground black pepper, a pinch of mustard powder and a pinch of nutmeg. Roughly chop 4 fresh sage leaves, measure out 1 tablespoon of dried sage, and add to the mixture. Add 3 tablespoons of tomato purée and a small glass of red wine. Mix well.

15 mins Cook for a few minutes, stirring well, then turn off the heat. If you have a food processor, place the minced TVP and 2oz/50g (2 tablespoons) of fresh breadcrumbs in the bowl and process quickly. This helps the mixture to bind. If you don't have a processor, place the TVP in a mixing bowl, beat well, then mix in the fresh breadcrumbs.

10 mins Mix the TVP mixture with the mushroom sauce to bind all the ingredients together, then place in the loaf tin, pressing it well into the corners.

5 mins Open a small tin of chopped tomatoes (if using), pour them over the meatloaf and spread out evenly. Place in the preheated oven, either below, or on the same shelf as, the potatoes and cook for 45 minutes.

0 mins Wash up and clear away.

Relax

Have a 30-minute break. Take your timer with you. When you return you will only have to cook the asparagus and French beans, check the meatloaf and baked potatoes, and the dessert.

Welcome back

Feeling better after your break?

Starter

Preparation time: 10 minutes
Cooking time: 10–15 minutes

Assemble all the ingredients and equipment you need for the starter. Set your timer for 10 minutes.
10 mins Take the asparagus and wash it well under

TVP is rather bland, so season the loaf well.

See Handy Tip 3, page xvii for an easy way to make fresh breadcrumbs from frozen bread.

It is important that the meatloaf binds well so that it will hold its shape and not fall apart.

The tinned tomatoes are optional, but they will keep the meatloaf from drying out.

PROBLEMS AND HANDY TIPS

MENU 8

cold running water. Cut off any hard, woody-looking stalks. Place the asparagus in a saucepan and sprinkle with a little salt.

5 mins Fill the kettle and put it on to boil. If you have not made the vinaigrette, this would be a good time to make it (see page 201). It is best made in advance as it has time to mature. If you have bought a ready-made vinaigrette you will only need to shake it well before using it.

2 mins Pour the boiling water over the asparagus and cook for approximately 10-15 minutes (this will vary depending on the thickness and freshness of the asparagus). Make sure the asparagus doesn't overcook.

0 mins Wash up and clear away.

Be careful not to break the tips off the asparagus while you are washing it.

Always shake a vinaigrette dressing really well before using it as the oil floats to the top very quickly.

Do not overcook the asparagus – it tastes much better if it is still slightly firm.

Last-minute tasks

Set your timer for 20 minutes. This is how long you have before sitting down to eat the starter.

20 mins While the asparagus is cooking, prepare the French beans or your green vegetable. Top and tail the beans and place them in a saucepan with a pinch of salt. Fill the kettle again and put it on to boil. Place the bread to accompany the starter in the oven to warm through.

10 mins Check the asparagus to see whether it is cooked yet. When ready, drain off the water and, depending on whether you are going to serve it hot or cold, leave it in the saucepan to keep warm, or place on a serving dish to cool.

6 mins Check the meatloaf and the baked potatoes. If they are cooked, turn the heat right down to 110°C/225°F/Gas mark ¼. They can both sit quite happily in a warm oven without spoiling.

4 mins Pour the boiling water over the beans and cook them over a medium heat. If you are worried that the beans might overcook while you are eating the starter, cook them after you have eaten it.

0 mins Wash up and clear away.

If you do not have room in the oven to warm the bread, take out the meatloaf and put it back once the bread is hot. Alternatively, serve the bread cold.

It is much better to serve crisp vegetables than overcooked ones. Your guests can wait a few minutes for the beans if necessary.

Watch points

Once the meal has started, it is difficult to predict how long each course will take. The following instructions are given only as a guide.

Put the main course plates in to warm if you have the facility.

Place a few asparagus spears on each starter plate. Shake the vinaigrette well and pour a small amount over each serving of asparagus. Alternatively, place the vinaigrette on the table for your guests to help themselves.

If you have warmed the bread, take it out of the oven and serve with vegan margarine.

Put the beans back over a medium heat to cook. Take the meatloaf, baked potatoes and warmed plates out of the oven. Place the potatoes in a serving bowl or basket lined with a napkin. Place on the table with some vegan margarine. Drain the beans and place them in a serving dish on the table.

Serve the meatloaf. Any extra tomato sauce from the meatloaf can be put in a bowl and offered to your guests separately to accompany the baked potatoes.

The dessert should be served with some of the syrup and decorated with a few toasted almonds.

If you are going to turn out the meatloaf, make sure the serving plate is bigger than the loaf tin. If it starts to fall apart, don't worry: patch it up with the tomato sauce and serve it as best you can.

Chinese stir-fry menu

Moderately difficult to prepare and cook
Cost level: good value
Serves: 4

9

A 30-minute break is incorporated in this menu.

Starter	Hot and sour soup	*Preparation time = 25 minutes* *Cooking time = 10 minutes*
Main course	Lemon chicken with cashew nuts Egg-fried rice Quick-fried bean sprouts and bamboo shoots	*Preparation time = 55 minutes* *Cooking time = 55 minutes*
Dessert	Frozen mango crunch [F*]	*Preparation time = 20 minutes* *Cooking time = None* *Freezing time = 8–10 hours*
Drink	Try to find some Chinese beer or even some sake (rice wine) if you're feeling adventurous. Check out your local Chinese food shop.	

This menu provides a real taste of the Orient. The soup can be made in advance and heated up just before serving. The dessert must be made in advance so that it has time to freeze. If this is not possible, you could serve fresh or tinned mangoes instead. Stir-fries always involve a lot of preparation, as there are numerous ingredients involved. The actual cooking time, however, is very short and should be done at the last minute. A deep frying pan can be used instead of a wok, but make sure it is large enough to accommodate all the ingredients. If you don't have a lid for it, you can make one out of aluminium foil. Serve the main course in small Chinese bowls, and provide chopsticks rather than cutlery; this will make the meal really authentic and lots of fun.

MENU 9

Equipment needed – Menu 9

Starter

1 savoury chopping board
1 sharp knife
1 wok or medium saucepan
1 tablespoon
1 fine grater
1 tin opener
1 fine sieve
1 measuring jug
1 spatula or fish slice
1 ladle

Main course

Lemon chicken
1 savoury chopping board
1 sharp knife
1 medium-sized bowl
1 garlic crusher (or see page xvii)
1 fine grater
1 lemon squeezer
2 small bowls
1 tablespoon
1 wok or deep frying pan
1 spatula or fish slice
1 heatproof serving dish with lid
Egg-fried rice
1 medium saucepan with lid
1 teaspoon
1 small bowl
1 fork
1 fine colander or sieve
1 wok or deep frying pan
1 tablespoon
1 spatula or fish slice
1 heatproof serving dish with lid
Quick-fried vegetables
1 savoury chopping board
1 sharp knife
4 bowls
1 fine grater
1 small plate
1 tin opener
1 fine sieve
1 wok or deep frying pan
1 tablespoon

Shopping list – Menu 9

Starter

4 spring onions
*1 tablespoon sesame oil
1 inch/2.5 cm root ginger
1 tin (11oz/300g) whole button mushrooms
1 pint/300ml fresh chicken or vegetable stock
    or *1 chicken or vegetable stock cube
*1 tablespoon dark soya sauce
*1 tablespoon light soya sauce
*2 teaspoons white wine vinegar
*freshly ground black pepper

Main course

Lemon chicken
2 large chicken breasts or 4 chicken thighs,
    boned and skinned
*1 clove garlic
1 inch/2.5 cm piece fresh ginger
*1 lemon
4oz/100g cashew nuts
*2 tablespoons dark soya sauce
*1 tablespoon light soya sauce
*4–6 tablespoons water
*2 tablespoons dry sherry (optional)
*1 tablespoon cornflour
*1 tablespoon stir-fry oil
Egg-fried rice
8oz/225g long-grain, easy-cook rice
*1 teaspoon margarine
*2 eggs
*salt
*1 tablespoon stir-fry oil
*3 tablespoons light soya sauce
Quick-fried vegetables
1 small tin (8oz/225g) bamboo shoots
1 large tin (12oz/350g) baby corn
*2 carrots
1 inch/2.5 cm piece fresh root ginger
4oz/100g fresh bean sprouts
8oz/225g fresh mushrooms
*3 tablespoons stir-fry oil
*2 tablespoons light soya sauce
*2 tablespoons dark soya sauce
*1 teaspoon lemon juice

65

MENU 9

1 spatula or fish slice
1 teaspoon
1 heatproof serving dish with lid

Dessert

1 tin opener
1 small saucepan
1 fine sieve
1 sweet chopping board
1 sharp knife
1 freezer container with lid or clingfilm cover
1 tablespoon

Dessert

1 tin (15oz/425g) mango slices in syrup
*2oz/50g (2 tablespoons) granulated sugar
1 tablespoon sesame seeds

*Check store cupboard

Countdown – Menu 9

If you are going to prepare the whole menu, you will need 175 minutes (2 hours 55 minutes), which includes a 30-minute break . If you are a slow cook, add 5–10 minutes to each course to ensure that you do not run out of time. Remember, the times given are only a guide as each cook will take different lengths of time to complete each task. If you have a food processor with a thin slicing blade, all the vegetables for the starter and main course can be put through it. This will save time and energy. However, the menu can still be made quite easily by chopping everything with a knife. Don't forget that the starter should be made in advance and heated up just before serving. The dessert should also be made in advance to allow it time to freeze. For the main course, use a sesame, peanut or stir-fry oil for any of the recipes, and prepare as much as possible in advance so that you have only the cooking to do when your guests arrive.

Dessert

PROBLEMS AND HANDY TIPS

Preparation time: 20 minutes
Cooking time: None
Freezing time: 8–10 hours

Assemble all the equipment and ingredients you need for the dessert. Set your timer for 20 minutes.
20 mins Open a tin of mangoes and drain the liquid into a small saucepan through a fine sieve. Place the mango pieces on a sweet chopping board and chop roughly. Transfer the pieces to a freezer container, cover with a lid or cling film and place in the deep freeze.
15 mins Place the saucepan containing the mango juice over a low to medium heat and add 2oz/50g (2 tablespoons) of granulated sugar. Stir constantly until the sugar dissolves, then boil rapidly until the liquid reduces and becomes a thicker syrup. This will

Any excess liquid from the mangos once they have been chopped up can be put into the container alongside the mangos.

After boiling rapidly for 10 minutes, turn the syrup off, even if you are unsure whether it has reduced enough: 10 minutes' rapid boiling is sufficient.

MENU 9

take approximately 10 minutes, but you must watch the syrup in case it burns. Once it has reduced, turn the heat off and add 1 tablespoon of sesame seeds.
5 mins Take the mangoes out of the deep freeze and pour the syrup over them. Stir well, replace the lid or cling film, and put back into the deep freeze for 8–10 hours.
0 mins Wash up and clear away.

It is a good idea to stir the mangoes after 2 hours. The texture will vary depending on how frozen the mixture has become.

The frozen mango crunch can be kept in the deep freeze for up to 2 months and used when required.

To turn out the mango crunch, stand the freezer container in a small amount of warm water for a few seconds, then quickly invert the container on to a serving plate.

Starter

PROBLEMS AND HANDY TIPS

Preparation time: 25 minutes
Cooking time: 10 minutes

Assemble all the ingredients and equipment you need for the starter. You can make the soup in a wok or a saucepan: a wok will give a more authentic flavour. Set your timer for 25 minutes.
25 mins Take 4 spring onions, remove the outer layer of skin, then cut off the tops and roots. Slice the onions finely, using as much of the green parts as possible. Place the onion in your wok or saucepan, add 1 tablespoon of sesame oil and set aside.
20 mins Take approximately 1 inch/2.5 cm of fresh root ginger, peel it and remove any blemishes, then grate the ginger into the wok with the onions.
15 mins Open a tin of mushrooms and drain them through a fine sieve, discarding all the liquid. Set aside.
12 mins Measure out 1 pint/600 ml of fresh chicken or vegetable stock, or if using a stock cube, crumble it into a measuring jug and add 1 pint/600ml of boiling water. Leave to dissolve.
10 mins Place the wok containing the onion and ginger over a medium to high heat and cook for 2–3 minutes, then add the mushrooms and cook for a further 2 minutes.
5 mins Add the stock to the wok, mix well and bring to the boil. Add 1 tablespoon of dark soya sauce, 1

Do not use any dark green leaves that look tough; stop short of the top of the spring onion.

Use peanut or stir-fry oil if you prefer.

Discard any hairy or rough pieces of ginger.

Make sure all the stock cube is dissolved before using it.

68

tablespoon of light soya sauce and 2 tablespoons of vinegar, then season with black pepper. Bring to the boil and simmer for 5 minutes. If you are not going to serve the soup straight away, set aside. The soup will be reheated just before serving.

0 mins Wash up and clear away.

Check the seasoning and add any extra ingredients to suit your taste.

Main course
Lemon chicken with cashew nuts

PROBLEMS AND HANDY TIPS

Preparation time: 30 minutes
Cooking time: 20 minutes

Assemble all the ingredients and equipment you need for the main course. Set your timer for 30 minutes. If you are going to have a break, prepare all the ingredients in advance so that when you return you will only have to stir-fry everything.

30 mins Take the skinned and boned chicken, cut it into thin strips, place in a medium-sized bowl and set aside.

22 mins Take 1 clove of garlic and 1 inch/2.5 cm of fresh ginger. Peel both and crush the garlic, then either crush or grate the ginger, and add both to the chicken. Mix well.

15 mins Take 1 lemon and roll it around on a work surface to loosen the skin. Wash the lemon under cold running water, dry it and grate the rind into the bowl with the chicken pieces. Mix well. Cut the lemon in half, squeeze both halves through a lemon squeezer and set the juice aside.

10 mins Measure out 4oz/100g of cashew nuts, place in a small bowl and set aside. In another small bowl place 2 tablespoons of dark soya sauce, 1 tablespoon of light soya sauce, 4 tablespoons of water and 2 tablespoons of dry sherry. (If you are not using the sherry, add 2 extra tablespoons of water to the bowl.) Add 1 tablespoon of cornflour and mix well to form a thin paste. Set aside.

4 mins Now all the stir-fry ingredients are prepared and ready to cook. Cover the bowls with a tea

Don't forget you will need lots of little bowls for the stir-fry ingredients, as it is important to keep them separate.

If the chicken has bones and skin you will need to remove them before you can slice the meat into thin strips.

See Handy Tip 1, page xvii for an easy way to crush garlic if you don't have a garlic crusher.

Rolling the lemon under your hand releases the flesh, makes the fruit easier to squeeze and gives you more juice.

Adding all the liquid ingredients to the bowl now saves time and will ensure that you don't forget any of them.

MENU 9

towel or cling film and set aside until it is time to cook.

0 mins Wash up and clear away.

Egg-fried rice

Preparation time: 10 minutes
Cooking time: 10 minutes

Assemble all the ingredients and equipment you need for the rice. Set your timer for 10 minutes. The rice needs to be partially cooked in advance; it is then stir-fried for 5 minutes before it is served.

10 mins Fill your kettle and put it on to boil.

9 mins Measure out 8oz/225g of long-grain easy-cook rice and place it in a medium-sized saucepan. Add 1 teaspoon of margarine and pour enough boiling water over the rice to cover by 1 inch/2.5 cm. Place over a medium heat and boil for approximately 8 minutes. Remember that the rice should be only partially cooked at this stage, so boil it for 2 minutes less than the packet instructions suggest.

6 mins Break 2 eggs into a small bowl, add a pinch of salt and beat with a fork. Set aside.

2 mins Check the rice for readiness: it should be slightly firm. Drain the rice through a fine sieve, then run warm water through it to remove any excess starch and to stop it from cooking. Fork through the rice to break up any lumps and allow excess water to drain away. Set aside.

0 mins Wash up and clear away.

Quick-fried vegetables

Preparation time: 15 minutes
Cooking time: 10 minutes

Assemble all the ingredients and equipment you need for the vegetables. You must prepare all the

If you are going to take a long break, it is a good idea to cover the chicken and put it in the fridge to chill.

PROBLEMS AND HANDY TIPS

Check the cooking instructions on your packet of rice, as different brands vary in the length of time they take to cook.

Adding margarine to the water prevents the rice from sticking together during and after cooking.

Place the egg in the fridge if you are going to have a long break.

PROBLEMS AND HANDY TIPS

70

vegetables before your break so that when you return you have only the stir-frying to do. Set your timer for 15 minutes.

15 mins Top and tail 2 carrots, peel them and cut into pieces 2 inch/5 cm long. Then slice the pieces into very thin strips. Place the carrots in a bowl and set aside.

Make sure all the vegetables are cut to roughly the same size so that they will all cook in the same time.

9 mins Take a 1 inch/2.5 cm fresh piece of root ginger and peel using a potato peeler or sharp knife. Cut out any blemishes. Using a fine grater, carefully grate the ginger on to a small plate and set aside.

It is important to drain the rice well before it is stir-fried, as it gives a better result.

Discard the long, hairy parts of the ginger; use only the fine parts.

6 mins Measure out 4oz/100g beansprouts and place them in a bowl. If including the mushrooms, wash and chop them into thin slices. Place them in a separate bowl and set aside.

1 min Open the tins of bamboo shoots and baby corn, drain through a fine sieve, then place in a bowl and set aside.

If any of the pieces of the bamboo shoots are very large, it will be necessary to cut them up.

0 mins Wash up and clear away.

If you would like to have a break, now is a good time as once you start the stir-fry, you can't stop. Before your break, cover all the bowls of chopped ingredients with a clean tea towel. If you plan to take a very long break, cover the bowls with cling film and put in the fridge.

If preparing this menu in hot weather, it is a good idea to put the food in the fridge anyway to stop it from spoiling.

Relax

Have a 30-minute break, or more if you like. When you return you will only need to cook all the main course dishes and reheat the soup.

Welcome back

Feeling better after your break?

Last-minute tasks

PROBLEMS AND HANDY TIPS

Now it is time to stir-fry the various dishes and reheat the soup. Set your timer for 45 minutes. Preheat the oven to 120°C/250°F/Gas mark ½.

MENU 9

Remember, this should be fun. Once you have cooked the rice and vegetables and they are safely in the oven, you could ask your guests to sit down at the table and watch you perform your wonders on the stir-fry chicken.

45 mins Prepare the wok by washing it well and drying it with some kitchen paper. Place over a medium heat and add 1 tablespoon of stir-fry oil. Allow the oil to become very hot and smoky, then turn the heat down to low.

Make sure the wok is completely dry before adding the oil.

40 mins Add the rice and cook rapidly, stirring all the time with a spatula or fish slice. Add 3 table-spoons of light soya sauce and stir well. Carefully pour in the beaten egg and cook rapidly, stirring constantly, for 4–5 minutes. Place the rice in an ovenproof dish with a lid and put it in the oven to keep warm.

You must stir the rice all the time to stop it from sticking to the wok. If it sticks, add a little extra oil.

35 mins Take the grated ginger and place it in the wok with 2 tablespoons of stir-fry oil, put over a high heat and cook rapidly for 1 minute. Add the carrots and cook over a medium to high heat, stirring constantly, until slightly softened.

Do not overcook the vegetables – they should be crisp and crunchy, not soft and soggy.

30 mins Add the mushrooms and 1 extra table-spoon of stir-fry oil. Continue to cook, adding 2 tablespoons of light soya sauce. Next add the drained bamboo shoots, baby corn and the beansprouts. Stir-fry for 2–3 minutes, then add 2 tablespoons of dark soya sauce and 1 teaspoon lemon juice.

25 mins Place the cooked vegetables in an oven-proof serving dish with a lid, and put them in the oven with the rice to keep warm.

23 mins Put the soup into a saucepan and put it over a low to medium heat to warm through.

20 mins Meanwhile, put the wok over a medium to high heat, add 1 tablespoon of stir-fry oil and heat until hot. Add the chicken, garlic, ginger and lemon rind and cook rapidly for 5–10 minutes, turning occasionally. Cover the wok in between stirring so that it gets really hot.

Make sure you stir the chicken well and keep turning it over so that it cooks evenly.

10 mins Once the chicken starts to brown and you can no longer see any pink on the meat, stir the cornflour mixture, then pour it over the chicken. Stir and turn the chicken constantly.

5 mins When the chicken is almost cooked, add the lemon juice and cashew nuts and cook for 2 minutes. Stir well, allowing the mixture to thicken, and cook for a further 2 minutes. If the mixture looks dry at any time, add 1 tablespoon of water. The chicken should be cooked for a minimum of 10 minutes.

1 min Taste the sauce and add any extra seasoning if required. Transfer the chicken to a serving dish with a lid and put it in the oven to keep warm, or cover the wok and turn the heat off. Everything is ready to serve. Check the soup and turn up the heat if it is not piping hot.

0 mins Serve the soup.

Watch points

Once the meal has started, it is difficult to predict how long each course will take. The following instructions are given only as a guide.

Serve the soup piping hot.

Don't forget to use chopsticks with the main course if you have them: it is much more fun and makes the meal more authentic. If you have left the chicken in the wok while eating the soup, turn it up to a medium heat and heat through. When hot, transfer to a serving dish.

Take the rice and vegetables (and chicken) out of the oven and place on the table for your guests to help themselves.

Turn out the frozen mango crunch on to a plate and serve. There are no extras needed.

Check that you have not forgotten to add any of the bowls of chopped ingredients.

Make sure the chicken is well cooked. If you are uncertain, cook it a little longer to be on the safe side. Cut a large piece of chicken in half to see whether it is still pink.

If you are leaving the chicken in the wok, remember to reheat it well before serving. This can be done while you are clearing away the starter and laying up the main course.

Remember, you can always put the food back in the oven to keep warm.

Don't forget to turn the oven off once the main course is finished, and before serving the dessert.

Take the mango crunch out of the deep freeze a few minutes before serving to allow it to soften slightly. To turn it out, place the container in some warm water for a few seconds, then turn it on to a serving plate.

Summer or winter menu

10

Moderately difficult to prepare and cook
Cost level: good value
Serves: 4

*A 30-minute break is incorporated in this
menu.*

Starter	Artichoke hearts with croûtons and lemon vinaigrette	*Preparation time = 20 minutes* *Cooking time = None*
Main course	Pork chop casserole F* with apple and sage Oven-fried potatoes F* Red or white buttered cabbage	*Preparation time = 45 minutes* *Cooking time = 1¼–2 hours*
Dessert	Lemon or orange pancakes F*	*Preparation time = 15 minutes* *Cooking time = 20 minutes*
Drink	Normandy, or any good-quality dry cider, chilled	

This menu is ideal for a dinner party. It would suit hungry guests and can be adapted to suit both your taste and the time and money available. You can leave out the starter if time is short, and substitute cheese and fresh fruit for the dessert.

The starter is refreshing and light. The main course is based on pork, so do make sure your guests can eat it. The dessert is fun and can either be prepared in advance or made while your guests watch and wait. The filling for the pancakes can vary depending on your own taste.

Equipment needed – Menu 10

Starter

1 *tin opener*
1 *fine sieve*
1 *savoury chopping board*
1 *sharp knife*
1 *salad bowl*
1 *lemon squeezer*
1 *measuring jug*
1 *teaspoon*

Main course

1 *savoury chopping board*
1 *sharp knife*
1 *ovenproof casserole dish with lid*
1 *tablespoon*
1 *savoury wooden spoon*
1 *measuring jug*
1 *potato peeler*
2 *medium saucepans, 1 with lid*
1 *baking tray or roasting tin*
1 *colander*
1 *teaspoon*

Dessert

1 *fine sieve*
1 *medium mixing bowl*
1 *small bowl*
1 *fork*
1 *measuring jug*
1 *frying pan, preferably non-stick*
1 *fish slice, preferably non-stick*
1 *heatproof plate*
kitchen paper
1 *lemon squeezer*
cling-film for freezing

Shopping list – Menu 10

Starter

1 tin (14oz/400g) artichoke hearts, pre-cooked
8oz/225g white seedless grapes
1 bunch watercress
*1 lemon
*¼ pint/150ml French dressing (see page 201)
*1 teaspoon caster sugar (optional)
1 packet plain or garlic croûtons

Main course

1½–2lb/650–950g boneless pork shoulder
    steaks or boneless loin chops
*2oz/50g (2 tablespoons) margarine
1 cooking apple
*2oz/50g (2 tablespoons) plain flour
½ pint/300ml fresh meat stock or *1 beef stock
    cube
½ pint/300ml dry cider
1 parsnip
*salt, pepper, mustard powder
*Worcestershire sauce
1 small bunch fresh sage or 1 heaped teaspoon
    dried sage
Oven-fried potatoes
*6–8 medium-sized old potatoes
*2oz/50g (2 tablespoons) margarine or butter
*salt, pepper, nutmeg
Buttered cabbage
½ head white or red cabbage
*salt and freshly ground black pepper
*1oz/25g butter or margarine
*1 tablespoon vinegar

Dessert

*4oz/100g plain flour
*1 egg
* salt
*½ pint/300ml milk
*2oz/50g (2 tablespoons) margarine or butter
*4 teaspoons caster sugar
1 orange or lemon
½ pint/300ml fresh single cream or crème
    fraîche to serve (optional)

Check store cupboard

MENU 10

Countdown – Menu 10

If you want to prepare the whole menu, you will need 130 minutes (2 hours 10 minutes), which includes a 30-minute break. If you are a slow cook, add 5–10 minutes to each course to ensure that you do not run out of time. Remember, the times given are only a guide, as each cook will take a different length of time to complete each task. The starter should be made on the night, a few hours in advance if you like, but do not dress it. The main course is cooked in the oven and gives you time to have a break. The dessert can be made in advance and frozen, or cooked in front of your guests on the night.

Dessert

PROBLEMS AND HANDY TIPS

> Preparation time: 15 minutes
> Cooking time: 20 minutes

Assemble all the ingredients and equipment you need for the dessert. Set your timer for 15 minutes. Preheat the oven to 120°C/250°F/Gas mark ½, but do so only if you are going to cook and serve the pancakes at once.

15 mins Weigh out 4oz/100g plain flour and sift it into a mixing bowl. Break 1 egg into a small bowl, add a good pinch of salt and whisk with a fork. Take ½ pint/300ml of milk and add the beaten egg to it. Mix well.

You can use semi-skimmed milk if you prefer. It will not change the taste of the pancakes.

8 mins Make a well or hollow in the centre of the flour and carefully pour in a small amount of the milk mixture. Stir gently so that the flour and liquid combine. Continue adding the liquid gradually and stirring all the time. This should ensure that the batter does not go lumpy. If time allows, place the batter in the fridge and chill until required.

If the mixture becomes lumpy, don't worry; wait until the very end when you have incorporated all the liquid, then sieve the whole mixture into a new mixing bowl.

0 mins Wash up and clear away.

Cooking the pancakes

PROBLEMS AND HANDY TIPS

Set your timer for 20 minutes.

20 mins It is best to cook the pancakes in a non-stick pan if possible. If you do not have one, make sure you use plenty of butter or margarine to prevent the pancakes from sticking. Place the pan over a medium to high heat with a knob (½oz/12g) of the butter or margarine. Once the pan is very hot and the butter is foaming, pour in a small amount of batter (enough to cover the surface of the pan thinly) and leave to cook.

15 mins Keep the frying pan moving to prevent the pancake from sticking. Once the pancake starts to shrink and the sides start to curl up, turn it over. To do this you can either toss it or turn it using a fish slice. Cook the second side until golden brown and mottled. When cooked, place the pancakes on a heatproof plate with kitchen paper between each pancake, and place them in the oven to keep them warm. There should be enough mixture to make at least 6–8 pancakes: it depends how thin you can make them.

5 mins To serve the pancakes, sprinkle them with caster sugar and freshly squeezed orange or lemon juice. Roll them up and serve warm, as they are, or with some crème fraîche or single cream.

0 mins Wash up and clear away.

The pancakes will freeze very successfully unfilled. Place a piece of cling film between each of them, then wrap the pile of pancakes in cling film. Freeze them flat; don't bend them or they will crack.

This batter mixture can also be used for savoury pancakes. Fill them with such things as cheese and mushrooms, bacon and onion, or chicken and vegetables.

You will need approximately 2–3 tablespoons of butter to cover the base of a frying pan.
Make the pancakes as thin as possible, to keep them crisp rather than rubbery and to ensure there is plenty of mixture to make enough pancakes for everyone.

Remember the first pancake is usually not the best one as the pan hasn't had enough time to heat up properly.

Starter

PROBLEMS AND HANDY TIPS

Preparation time: 20 minutes
Cooking time: None

Assemble all the ingredients and equipment you need for the starter. Set your timer for 20 minutes.

MENU 10

20 mins Open a tin of pre-cooked artichoke hearts, drain them in a fine sieve, then wash under cold running water. If they are very large, cut them in halves or quarters. Leave to drain.

20 mins Take 8oz/225g white seedless grapes and wash them well. If they are very large, cut them in halves. Place the grapes and artichoke hearts together in a salad bowl and set aside.

12 mins Take 1 bunch of watercress and wash it under cold running water. Shake off any excess water and add the watercress to the salad bowl. Put in the fridge to chill.

8 mins Take 1 lemon, cut it in half and squeeze the juice of one half into a small bowl. Set aside. The other half of lemon can be sliced and served as a garnish alongside the salad.

5 mins Take ¼ pint/150ml of French dressing, home-made or shop-bought. Add the freshly squeezed lemon juice and mix well. Taste the dressing and if it is too tart, add 1 teaspoon of caster sugar. Set aside.

0 mins Wash up and clear away.

If the salad is not going to be served immediately, do not dress it yet or add the croûtons: both should be done just before serving.

Main course

PROBLEMS AND HANDY TIPS

Preparation time: 30 minutes
Cooking time: 1½–2 hours

Assemble all the ingredients and equipment you need for the pork casserole. Set your timer for 30 minutes. Preheat the oven to 160°C/325°F/Gas mark 3.

30 mins Take the pork and, depending on the type of meat you have bought, cut away any excess fat and connective tissue. (If you are using loin chops, you will only need to cut away the rind.) Cut the meat into small, even-sized cubes, approximately 1 inch/2.5 cm square.

Make all the cubes roughly the same size so that they will cook evenly.

23 mins Place the ovenproof casserole over a low to medium heat (do not use a glass or ceramic casserole as it may crack if used on direct heat), add 2oz/50g (2 tablespoons) of cooking margarine and allow to melt. Once the fat is foaming, place all the cubed pork in the casserole to brown. Meanwhile, peel, core and quarter the cooking apple, then cut the quarters into 3 or 4 slices. Stir the meat so that it browns evenly on all sides.

Make sure that the fat doesn't get too hot or it will burn. The meat must be browned all over to seal it.

18 mins Once the meat is brown all over, turn off the heat and add 2oz/50g (2 tablespoons) of plain flour. Mix well so that the meat is coated then put back over a low heat to cook for 2 minutes. Turn the heat off.

The margarine and flour mixture is called a roux (see Glossary of Cookery Terms, page 223).

15 mins If using a stock cube, crumble it into the flour and meat mixture and add ½ pint/300ml of water. Alternatively, use ½ pint/300ml of fresh stock. Stir well, then add ½ pint/300ml dry cider. Put the casserole over a medium heat and stir while it slowly thickens. Once the sauce has thickened, boil the mixture for 2 minutes. Add the sliced apple and leave on a very low heat to simmer.

When you add the cider to the casserole, don't worry if the mixture bubbles – it will die down quite quickly.

10 mins Meanwhile, peel the parsnip, discarding the root and top. Slice it into 1 inch/2.5 cm pieces, add to the meat mixture and stir well.

5 mins Season the casserole with a pinch of salt and mustard powder, some ground black pepper and a dash of Worcestershire sauce. Add 2 sprigs of fresh sage or a heaped teaspoon of dried sage. Place in a preheated oven for 1½–2 hours.

Check the seasoning before putting the casserole in the oven.

0 mins Wash up and clear away.

Oven-fried potatoes

PROBLEMS AND HANDY TIPS

Set your timer for 15 minutes.

15 mins Peel the potatoes, cut them in half and place in a saucepan with just enough cold water to cover them. Place over a medium to high heat, bring rapidly to the boil, then simmer for 5 minutes.

Par-boiling the potatoes first helps them to roast evenly and become crisp.

10 mins While the potatoes are simmering, take a baking tray or roasting tin and grease it with either butter or margarine.

MENU 10

8 mins Take the potatoes off the heat, drain them in a colander and run cold water over them. Place the potatoes on a chopping board, being careful not to burn your fingers, then slice them as thinly as possible. Make a layer of potatoes in the greased tin, then season with salt, ground black pepper and a good pinch of nutmeg. Dab small amounts of butter or margarine all over the potatoes. Depending on the size of your tin, make another layer of potatoes, adding seasoning and butter as before. Continue the layering until you have used all the potatoes. Place the tin on the top shelf of the oven above the casserole for approximately 1½ hours.

If cooking the potatoes separately from the casserole, place them on the top shelf of a hot oven preheated to 200°C/400°F/Gas mark 6 for 1 hour. If at the end of cooking, the potatoes are not very crisp, place them under a hot grill.

0 mins Wash up and clear away.

Make sure you season the potatoes well as they taste much better if they have absorbed the seasoning while cooking.

Relax

Have a 30-minute break. Take your timer with you. When you return you will only need to prepare and cook the cabbage, dress the starter and, if you have not done so already, cook the pancakes.

Welcome back

Feeling better after your break?

Last-minute tasks

PROBLEMS AND HANDY TIPS

Set your timer for 20 minutes.

20 mins Fill the kettle and put it on to boil.

18 mins Take your cabbage and shred it using a sharp knife. Place in a colander and wash well under cold running water. Transfer the cabbage to a medium-sized saucepan, add a pinch of salt and pour in just enough boiling water to cover the cabbage. Place over a medium to high heat and cook for 8–10 minutes.

10 mins Check the dishes in the oven. If the potatoes are very brown and the pork is well cooked, turn the heat down to 110°C/225°F/Gas mark ¼.

5 mins Take the bowl of artichokes, grapes and watercress out of the fridge. Shake or stir the French dressing really well and pour it all over the salad. Scatter the croûtons over the top and garnish with the lemon slices. Serve the salad in individual bowls or place the large bowl on the table for your guests to help themselves.

2 mins Check the cabbage and if it is cooked, drain it through a colander. Put it back into the saucepan and add 1oz/25g (1 tablespoon) of margarine or butter, salt and pepper and 1 tablespoon of vinegar. Stir well. Replace the lid and set aside. The cabbage will be reheated after you have eaten your starter.

0 mins Wash up and clear away.

Watch points

Once the meal has started, it is difficult to predict how long each course will take. The following instructions are given only as a guide.

Just before serving the starter, check the casserole and potatoes. If you are worried that they might overcook, turn the oven off. If there is room, put the main course plates in the oven to warm. Serve the starter.

Before getting everything out of the oven, put the cabbage back over a medium heat and stir well until hot. Place in a warmed serving dish. Take the pork casserole, potatoes and warm plates out of the oven. Serve the main course.

To serve the pancakes, sprinkle a little caster sugar and freshly squeezed orange or lemon juice over each one, then roll up carefully and serve warm. The pancakes can also be served with fresh cream or crème fraîche.

If you feel that the potatoes might need a little extra cooking, leave the temperature the same and move the casserole down to the bottom of the oven, or remove the casserole until the potatoes are almost ready.

Check the seasoning in the cabbage; do not make it too tart.

PROBLEMS AND HANDY TIPS

If you have not yet cooked the pancakes, see the method on page 77.

Barbecue menu

Moderately difficult to prepare
Cost level: good value
Serves: 4

11

There is no break incorporated in this menu.

Starter	Herb and garlic bread F*	*Preparation time = 20 minutes* *Cooking time = 25–30 minutes*
Main course	Lamb, fish or vegetarian kebabs F*	*Preparation time = 40 minutes* *Cooking time = 25–30 minutes*
	Marinated chicken legs or spare ribs F*	
	Baked potatoes or rice Mixed green salad and coleslaw	*Salads preparation = 35 minutes* *Baked potatoes cooking time = 60 minutes*
Dessert	Home-made chocolate cheesecake F*	*Preparation time = 40 minutes* *Cooking time = None*
Drink	Lager, chilled, or full-bodied spicy red wine	

This barbecue menu can be adapted to suit your guests. You can add some sausages to it if you like. Most of the preparation can be done on the day itself, except the chicken legs or spare ribs, which must be marinated overnight; this gives them time to soak up all the flavours in the marinade. The lamb, fish or vegetarian kebabs can be made in advance and chilled until required. If you plan to serve chicken or spare ribs, it is a nice idea to 'balance' the menu with fish or vegetarian kebabs rather than lamb.

The herb and garlic bread can be made in advance and frozen, or even bought ready-made to save time. The dessert should be made in advance to allow it time to set and chill; it can also be frozen. There is no break in this menu as most of the work can be done in advance, which will leave only the cooking and last-minute tasks to do on the day itself.

You will need a French dressing for the mixed salad. If you want to make it yourself, turn to page 201 for instructions. Remember, the dressing is best made in advance to allow it time to mature. Alternatively, you can buy a ready-made dressing of your choice.

If your barbecue is rained off, don't panic – everything can cook in the oven or under the grill just as well. Preheat the oven to 200°C/400°F/Gas mark 6, or the grill to a high setting. The chicken legs or spare ribs will need approximately 45 minutes in the oven. They can also be crispened under the grill after cooking them in the oven.

MENU 11

Equipment needed – Menu 11

Starter

1 mixing bowl
1 savoury chopping board
1 sharp knife
1 garlic crusher (or see page xvii)
1 savoury wooden spoon
1 bread knife
large sheet of tin foil
1 round-ended knife
1 baking tray
kitchen paper

Main course

Marinated chicken legs or spare ribs
1 savoury chopping board
1 sharp knife
1 small mixing bowl
1 tablespoon
1 teaspoon
1 small wineglass
1 fine grater
1 garlic crusher (or see page xvii)
1 roasting tin
Kebabs
1 savoury chopping board
1 sharp knife
1 medium-sized bowl
1 colander
4 large or 8 small skewers
2, 3 or 4 baking trays (depending on the meats
     you are cooking)
cling film or aluminium foil
1 plate
1 lemon squeezer
1 tablespoon
1 barbecue
Coleslaw and mixed green salad
1 savoury chopping board
1 potato peeler
1 sharp knife
1 cheese grater or food processor
1 mixing bowl
1 teaspoon
1 tablespoon
1 small bowl

Shopping list – Menu 11

Starter

*4oz/100g butter or margarine
*2 cloves garlic
1 large bunch fresh mixed herbs, e.g. coriander,
     parsley, chives, thyme and sage
1 long French loaf, brown or white

Main course

Marinated chicken legs or spare ribs
     *1 onion
     *4 tablespoons tomato purée
     *2 tablespoons wine or cider vinegar
     *1 teaspoon sugar
     *2 teaspoons lemon juice
     *1 tablespoon Worcestershire sauce
     *1 small glass red wine
     *½ inch/1 cm fresh root ginger
     *1 clove garlic (optional)
     8 chicken drumsticks or 8 spare ribs
Lamb kebabs
     4 lamb cutlets or chops, approx. 1½lb/675g
     *2 onions
     4 tomatoes
     2 green, red or yellow peppers
     8oz/225g button mushrooms
     3–4 sprigs fresh mint
     *2 tablespoons olive oil
     *salt, pepper, dried rosemary
     1 small jar mint sauce **and/or** redcurrant jelly
Fish kebabs
     8oz/225g fresh sole or haddock fillets,
         skinned
     4oz/100g king prawns, ready to use
     4oz/100g fresh scallops, ready to use
     8 cherry tomatoes
     2 courgettes
     2 green, red or yellow peppers
     *2 tablespoons olive oil
     *salt and freshly ground black pepper
     *lemon juice
Vegetarian kebabs
     selection of vegetables, but remember to
         include a wide variety of textures and
         colours, e.g. onions, tomatoes, courgettes,
         peppers, mushrooms, aubergines,

1 colander
1 fork
1 salad bowl
kitchen scissors
1 measuring jug
Side dishes
1 sharp knife
1 medium saucepan with lid
1 teaspoon
1 colander

Dessert

1 double saucepan or heatproof bowl that fits
  tightly inside a large saucepan
2 small saucepans
2 mixing bowls
1 strong plastic bag or bowl
1 rolling pin or clean wine bottle
1 sweet wooden spoon
1 8 inch/20 cm loose-bottomed tin or ceramic
  ovenproof dish
2 tablespoons
1 dessertspoon
1 balloon whisk or hand-held electric mixer
1 flexible spatula

gherkins, olives
*2 tablespoons olive oil
*salt, pepper, lemon juice
Coleslaw
*2 carrots
*1 small onion
2 eating apples
*2 teaspoons lemon juice
½ firm white cabbage (approx. 8oz/225g)
*2oz/50g (2 tablespoons) sultanas
*3 tablespoons mayonnaise
*2 tablespoons French dressing
*salt and freshly ground black pepper
bunch fresh parsley (see page xviii)
Mixed green salad
1 small iceberg lettuce
1 small cucumber
1 punnet fresh cress
*¼ pint/150ml French dressing
Side dishes
4 baking potatoes or *8oz/225g easy cook
  rice
*1 teaspoon cooking margarine
*salt
*4oz/100g butter or table margarine and/or
  8oz/225g sour cream to serve
selection of barbecue sauces of your choice

Dessert

*3oz/75g plain chocolate
*2oz/50g (2 tablespoons) of butter or table
  margarine
6oz/175g chocolate digestive biscuits
*1 level dessertspoon gelatine
*1 egg
4oz/100g cream cheese
2oz/50g (2 tablespoons) curd cheese
*1oz/25g caster sugar
*1 large chocolate Flake to decorate
¼ pint/150ml single cream to serve (optional)

*Check store cupboard

MENU 11

Countdown – Menu 11

If you want to prepare and cook the whole menu, you will need 150 minutes (2 hours 30 minutes). There is no break, as so many dishes are made in advance. If you are a slow cook, add 5–10 minutes to each course, to ensure that you do not run out of time. Remember, the times given are only a guide, as each cook will take different lengths of time to complete each task. The herb and garlic bread can be made in advance and frozen, as can the dessert. Before serving, the bread should be placed in a hot oven to make it crisp. The chicken or spare ribs should be marinated the night before to allow them to absorb all the flavours. The kebabs, salads and potatoes or rice can be prepared a few hours before cooking. It is a good idea to do as much as possible beforehand so that you too can enjoy the barbecue.

Main course
Marinated chicken legs or spare ribs

Preparation time: 15 minutes
Cooking time: 25–30 minutes

Assemble all the ingredients and equipment you need for the marinade. It is important that the meat marinates overnight, or for at least 10 hours, as this improves the flavour. Set your timer for 15 minutes.

15 mins Take 1 small onion, peel and chop it finely, then place in a small mixing bowl.

Mix all the ingredients really well to make a delicious, full-flavoured marinade.

10 mins Measure out 4 tablespoons of tomato purée, 2 tablespoons of wine or cider vinegar, 1 teaspoon of sugar, 2 teaspoons of lemon juice, 1 tablespoon of Worcestershire sauce and 1 small glass of red wine. Mix everything together in a bowl and set aside.

7 mins Take a ½ inch/1 cm piece of fresh root ginger, peel and grate it on a fine grater and place it in the bowl with the marinade. Peel and crush 1

The garlic and ginger can be left out if you prefer. Substitute a dash of Tabasco sauce to give the marinade a little kick.

clove of garlic and add it to the bowl. Mix well.
2 mins Place 8 chicken drumsticks or 8 spare ribs in a small roasting tin and pour over the marinade. Make sure that the meat is coated all over. Cover with cling film and chill overnight or for a minimum of 10 hours. The longer the meat marinates the more flavour it will have.
0 mins Wash up and clear away.

See Handy Tip 1, page xvii for an easy way to crush garlic if you don't have a garlic crusher.

Dessert

PROBLEMS AND HANDY TIPS

Preparation time: 40 minutes
Cooking time: None

Assemble all the ingredients and equipment you need for the dessert. Set your timer for 40 minutes.
40 mins Weigh out 3oz/75g of plain chocolate and break it up into the top of a double saucepan. Place a small amount of warm water in the bottom of the double saucepan. Alternatively, place the chocolate in a heatproof bowl and sit it over a pan of warm water that comes no higher than halfway up the bowl. Place over a medium heat and bring to the boil.

Use only a very small amount of water in the saucepan or it might splash into the bowl with the melting chocolate. If this happens, the chocolate will go hard. In this case, remove it from the heat immediately and allow to cool. When the egg yolks are added to the chocolate later on, the mixture should become smooth again.

36 mins Take 2oz/50g of butter or margarine and melt it in a bowl in a microwave oven or in a small saucepan over a low heat until it is liquid. Weigh out 6oz/175g (approximately 10) chocolate digestive biscuits. Place the biscuits in a plastic bag and break them up into fine crumbs using a rolling pin or clean wine bottle. Alternatively, place the biscuits in a mixing bowl and use a wooden spoon to break them up. Add the crushed biscuits to the melted butter and mix well.

Make sure the biscuits are crushed very finely as this makes a stronger base.

30 mins Pour the biscuit and butter mixture into a loose-bottomed or ceramic flan dish. Press down well with the back of a tablespoon, making the base as firm and as smooth as possible. Place the base in the fridge to harden while you make the filling.

It is important that the base is very well packed down.

26 mins Take a small saucepan and place 2 tablespoons of water in it. Sprinkle in 1 level dessertspoon of gelatine and leave to soak for 5 minutes.

22 mins Stir the chocolate and remove it from the heat if melted. Carefully separate 1 egg and place the yolk in the bowl with the melted chocolate. Put the egg white in a separate bowl. Take 4oz/100g of cream cheese, add it to the chocolate mixture and stir well. Add 2oz/50g (2 tablespoons) of curd cheese, beating hard to remove any lumps.

17 mins Place the gelatine over the lowest heat possible and allow it to dissolve slowly. Do not let it get too hot or it will lose its setting properties. When completely dissolved and there are no granules to be seen, pour the gelatine into the chocolate mixture and stir well.

12 mins Take the bowl with the egg white and use a balloon whisk or hand-held electric mixer to beat it until it becomes stiff and holds its shape. Once you have reached this stage, slowly add 1oz/25g (1 tablespoon) of caster sugar. Beat for a further 2 minutes until the egg white becomes thick and silky.

5 mins Fold the egg white into the chocolate mixture, or vice versa if the chocolate bowl is not big enough. Make sure you lift and fold the mixture carefully to keep it light and airy.

3 mins Take the cheesecake base out of the fridge and carefully pour the chocolate filling over it. Spread the filling out using a flexible spatula and make sure there are no gaps at the edges. Chill for a minimum of 2 hours to allow it to set. Decorate just before serving.

0 mins Wash up and clear away.

Starter

Preparation time: 20 minutes
Cooking time: 25–30 minutes

Assemble all the ingredients and equipment you need for the starter. Set your timer for 20 minutes. Preheat the oven to 200°C/400°F/Gas mark 6.

It is important that the gelatine has long enough to soak as it then becomes thick and spongy.

If you fear the gelatine is too hot, take it away from the heat. The saucepan should never be too hot to handle.

The egg white must be able to stand in peaks before being added to the mixture. This will ensure that the filling is the right consistency.

See the Glossary of Cookery Terms, page 223 for a definition of 'folding'.

Do not overfill the flan dish. If there is too much filling, place it in a separate bowl. It can be served on its own.

Once the cheesecake has set, it can be removed from the loose-bottomed tin and decorated before serving.

PROBLEMS AND HANDY TIPS

Heat the oven only if you are going to cook the herb and garlic bread immediately.

20 mins Weigh out 4oz/100g butter or margarine, place in a bowl and leave to soften at room temperature. Alternatively, soften it in a micro-wave for a few seconds. Peel and crush 2 cloves of garlic and place in the bowl with the softened butter.

16 mins Take a large bunch of fresh mixed herbs of your choice, wash them well and pat dry with some kitchen paper or a clean tea-towel. Place the herbs on a chopping board and chop finely using a very sharp knife. Add to the bowl with the butter and garlic and mix well with a wooden spoon.

12 mins Place the French bread on a chopping board and cut into it diagonally at 1 inch/2.5 cm intervals. Take care not to cut right through the base of the bread so the loaf will keep together.

10 mins Take a piece of aluminium foil large enough to be wrapped around the French loaf at least twice. Place the bread in the middle of the foil, but do not wrap it up yet.

8 mins Using a round-ended knife, spread the herb and garlic butter on each side of the diagonal slices. Continue all the way along the loaf. Do not butter too heavily at first as you will need enough for the whole loaf; you can always add more butter to each piece later.

2 mins Once all the bread has been buttered, wrap the loaf up in the foil and seal both ends well. Freeze or chill until required.

0 mins Wash up and clear away.

Main course
Lamb kebabs

If the butter or margarine hard and you don't have a microwave, beat it with a wooden spoon to soften it.

See Handy Tip 1, page xvii for an easy way to crush garlic if you do not have a garlic crusher.

If you are using freeze-dried ready-chopped herbs, mix them straight into the butter.

Try not to cut right through the bread or it will fall apart. Keeping the bread in one long piece makes it easier to handle.

The aluminium foil keeps the bread moist and stops it from drying out and burning while cooking.

Place the foil-wrapped bread in a plastic bag or cling film before freezing it.

Don't forget to defrost the herb and garlic bread at least 4–6 hours before you are going to use it.

PROBLEMS AND HANDY TIPS

Preparation time: 25 minutes
Cooking time: 12–15 minutes

The kebabs should be made in advance, then covered with aluminium foil or cling film and chilled until cooking. Assemble all the ingredients and equipment you need for the kebabs. Set your timer for 25 minutes.

MENU 11

25 mins Take 4 lamb cutlets or chops, remove any bone or gristle and cut the meat into even-sized pieces, cubes if possible. Place the lamb cubes in a bowl and set aside.

20 mins Take 2 onions and peel them, keeping the root at the base intact: this will prevent the onions from falling apart during cooking. Cut the onion into quarters, or eighths if they are very large. Set aside.

16 mins Wash and dry 4 tomatoes, cut them into quarters and set aside.

12 mins Take 2 mixed peppers of your choice. Cut them in half, remove the stalk and seeds, then wash them under cold running water. Pat dry on kitchen paper, then cut into pieces of a similar size to the onion and tomato. Set aside.

8 mins Take 8oz/225g button mushrooms, wash well under cold running water and leave to drain in a colander. Take a few sprigs of fresh mint, wash well and leave to drain.

6 mins Now all the ingredients for the kebabs are ready to be assembled. Take 4 large or 8 small skewers. Start with a piece of meat followed by a small sprig of mint, then alternate the vegetables, meat and mint along the skewer, remembering to keep the kebabs colourful. Finish with a piece of meat to secure the whole kebab together.

1 min Place the finished kebabs on a baking tray, cover with aluminium foil or cling film and chill until required.

0 mins Wash up and clear away.

Remove any fat from the lamb to minimize the greasiness.

Do not take out the eye of the tomato, as this will keep it together while cooking.

If the peppers are very long, you will need to cut them in half so that they won't take up too much room on the barbecue.

There will be more vegetables than meat, so it is important to place several pieces in between the meat.

Make sure the kebabs are well covered so that they do not dry out.

Fish kebabs

PROBLEMS AND HANDY TIPS

Preparation time: 25 minutes
Cooking time: 10–12 minutes

Assemble all the ingredients and equipment you need for the fish kebabs. Set your timer for 25 minutes.

25 mins Take 8oz/225g of skinned haddock or sole fillets. Cut them in half lengthways and roll them up into parcels. Set aside. Place the king prawns and scallops on a plate, ready to use.

20 mins Take 2 courgettes, wash well, then top and tail them. Cut into 1 inch/2.5 cm pieces. Place in a colander, sprinkle lightly with salt and leave them to degorge (see page 222).

16 mins Take 8 cherry tomatoes, wash and dry them and set aside.

14 mins Take 2 mixed peppers of your choice. Cut them in half, discard the stalk and seeds, then wash the peppers under cold running water. Pat dry on kitchen paper, then cut into pieces of similar size to the onion and tomato. Set aside.

9 mins Take 1 lemon and wash and dry it well. Cut it in half lengthways and cut one half into 4 lemon wedges to serve with the kebabs. Squeeze other half and set the juice aside to be used later.

7 mins Wash the courgettes under cold running water to remove the salt, then leave to drain.

5 mins Now all the ingredients for the kebabs are ready to be assembled. Take 4 large or 8 small skewers. Start with a cherry tomato followed by a piece of rolled fish fillet, then add prawns, scallops and vegetables. Alternate the ingredients, remembereing to keep the kebabs colourful, and to end with a piece of courgette or pepper to secure the whole kebab.

1 min Place the finished kebabs on a baking tray, cover with aluminium foil or cling film and chill until required.

0 mins Wash up and clear away.

Vegetarian kebabs

Preparation time: 20 minutes
Cooking time: 8–10 minutes

Prepare the vegetables as set out in the lamb and fish kebab countdowns. Remember to wash the vegetables very well. When you put the kebabs together, make sure each skewer has a variety of

If the fish fillets have not been skinned, you will need to skin them before rolling them up.

The courgettes are degorged to remove the bitter flavour they sometimes have.

If the peppers are very long, you will need to cut them in half or they will take up too much room on the barbecue.

It is important to wash all the salt off the courgettes or the final flavour will be spoiled.

Make sure you pierce the centre of each piece of fish to prevent it falling off during cooking.

PROBLEMS AND HANDY TIPS

Make sure you use a wide variety of colours and textures in the kebabs.

vegetables and keep them colourful. Start and end with a piece of courgette or pepper to secure the whole kebab.

Coleslaw

Preparation time: 20 minutes
Cooking time: None

Assemble all the ingredients and equipment you need for the salad. Set your timer for 20 minutes. If you have a food processor with a thin slicing blade, you can put the onion, cabbage, carrots and apple through it. This will save time and give an even finish to the ingredients.

Try to make all the vegetables and fruit roughly the same size and thickness, as this gives it a better appearance.

20 mins Peel 2 carrots and 1 onion. Cut the onion in half and chop it as finely as possible. Top and tail the carrots, then slice very thinly or grate coarsely. Place the onion and carrot in a mixing bowl.

15 mins Take 2 blemish-free eating apples, wash them and cut into quarters. Remove the cores and slice very thinly or grate coarsely. Place the apple in the bowl with the onion and carrot. Add 2 teaspoons of lemon juice and mix well. This will prevent the apple from going brown.

If the apple skin is rough and bruised, peel it off before slicing the flesh.

10 mins Take half a firm white cabbage and remove the tough base with a sharp knife. Cut the cabbage into thin slices about 2 inch/5 cm long, place in a colander, wash and drain well. Add to the other ingredients. Measure out 2oz/50g sultanas and add them to the bowl. Mix well.

The cabbage is best shredded or grated as finely as possible.

2 mins Place 3 tablespoons of fresh mayonnaise in a small bowl and add 2 large tablespoons of well-mixed French dressing. Mix well and season with a little extra salt and black pepper. Pour the dressing over the coleslaw and mix well, making sure all the ingredients are well coated. Cover and place in the fridge to chill.

Mix the French dressing well before adding it to the mayonnaise.

0 mins Wash up and clear away.

Mixed green salad

Preparation time: 15 minutes
Cooking time: None

Assemble all the ingredients and equipment you need for the salad. Set your timer for 15 minutes.
15 mins Take a small iceberg lettuce and chop it into bite-size pieces. Wash it well and leave to drain in a colander.
10 mins Take a small cucumber and wash it well under cold running water. Peel it, or if you would like a decorative effect, run a fork down the whole length of the cucumber through the skin: when you slice it, each piece will have a frilly skin, which contains all the vitamins. Slice the cucumber thinly and place in a salad bowl.
5 mins Take the cress and wash it well. Using a sharp pair of kitchen scissors, snip the cress into the salad bowl. Add the drained iceberg lettuce. Mix all the ingredients together and set aside. You will need a French dressing for the salad; use either a ready-made dressing, or make one yourself from the recipe on page 201.
0 mins Wash up and clear away.

If the cucumber skin is rough and bruised, you will have to peel it before slicing the flesh.

Last-minute tasks

Set your timer for 15 minutes. Preheat the oven to 200°C/400°F/Gas mark 6.
15 mins Take 4 baking potatoes and wash and dry them. Using a sharp knife, make a shallow cut all the way around the potato lengthways: this helps them to cook more evenly. If you are using rice instead of potatoes, weigh out 8oz/225g, place it in a saucepan and add 1 teaspoon of margarine and a pinch of salt. Fill the kettle and put it on to boil.
10 mins Put the potatoes straight on to the top shelf of the oven and bake for approximately 1 hour, maybe a little more if they are very large.
8 mins Take the sour cream and/or butter out of

As the potatoes start to cook, they open up, which makes them easier to fill.

The margarine coats the grains of rice, preventing them from sticking together.

the fridge. Collect up all the sauces to serve with the main course. Take the wrapped garlic bread, put it on a baking tray and place in the oven on the shelf below the potatoes. Heat for 25–30 minutes.

5 mins Pour the boiling water into the saucepan with the rice, stir well, place over a low heat and cook slowly. Take the green salad and coleslaw out of the fridge so that they are ready to be dressed and served.

0 mins Wash up and clear away.

Light the barbecue and leave it to get red hot. Take all the foods to be barbecued out of the fridge. Remove the herb and garlic bread from the oven before you start barbecuing: that way, your guests can be eating the starter and watching the cooking at the same time. The barbecue is ready once the charcoal has become white.

Place the chicken legs on the barbecue first as they will take approximately 30 minutes. The spare ribs will take approximately 15–20 minutes.

Brush the lamb kebabs with olive oil and season with a little salt, pepper and diced rosemary; barbecue for 12–15 minutes. Serve with mint sauce or redcurrant jelly.

Brush the fish kebabs with olive oil and season with salt, pepper and freshly squeezed lemon juice. Barbecue for 10–12 minutes.

Brush the vegetarian kebabs with olive oil and season with salt and pepper. Barbecue for 8–10 minutes.

Remember, if there is not enough space on the barbecue for all the food at one time, you can cook it in batches and keep it warm in the oven.

Watch points

Once you have started the barbecue, it is difficult to predict how long each course will take. The following instructions are given only as a guide.

PROBLEMS AND HANDY TIPS

The potatoes should be perfectly cooked during the time it takes to heat and eat the herb and garlic bread, and to barbecue the meat.

If the barbecue has lots of flames, sprinkle a very small amount of beer or water over the coals to dampen them down. This also prevents the food from burning.

Check the herb and garlic bread in the oven; if it is crisp and golden, take it out and place in a bread basket or in the foil on a plate. Check the baked potatoes and turn them over. If cooking rice, check it is ready (you will need to check cooking instructions on the packet of rice, as these may vary), drain the water away through a colander, then place the rice in a serving dish and keep warm.

Serve the herb and garlic bread with some napkins while the meat is cooking.

Just before all the meat is ready, dress the green salad with the French dressing (don't forget to shake it well). Mix the coleslaw and place it in a serving dish. Take the baked potatoes out of the oven and serve with sour cream or butter. Serve the rice as it is. Place everything at the table and serve the meat.

If you have used a loose-bottomed tin for the cheesecake, push the bottom up, allowing the ring to slide down your hand, on to your arm. Place the cheesecake with the metal base on a serving plate. Decorate with crumbled chocolate Flake sprinkled over the top. Serve with extra single cream if desired.

If the herb and garlic bread is not crisp enough, unwrap the foil to expose the bread, and cook for a further 5 minutes.

The bread can be very greasy, so make sure you hand it round with paper napkins.

Indian curry menu

Moderately difficult to prepare and cook
Cost level: good value
Serves: 4

12

A 30-minute break is incorporated in this menu.

Starter	Dahl soup ^{F*} with nan bread	*Preparation time = 40 minutes* *Cooking time = 40 minutes*

Starter _____ Dahl soup ^{F*}
with nan bread

Preparation time = 40 minutes
Cooking time = 40 minutes

Main course _____ Lamb rogan josh ^{F*}
with cucumber raita
Almond sag
Saffron or pilau rice with
poppadoms

Preparation time = 75 minutes
Cooking time = 2 hours

Dessert _____ Lemon and lime sorbet ^{F*}

Preparation time = 20 minutes
Cooking time = None
Freezing time = 10–12 hours

Drink _____ Lager, chilled – look for
an Indian brand in your
local supermarket

This curry menu is moderately difficult to prepare and cook. If time is short you can always buy some ready-made samosas, onion bhajis or chicken tikka from a good supermarket or Indian shop. Don't forget some nan bread, poppadoms and chutneys to go with the curry.

The soup and curry can be mild, medium or hot, depending on your taste. It is a good idea not to make the curry very hot in case your guests prefer less spicy food. Extra spice can be added with a lime pickle or sauce at the table. Lager is traditionally served with a curry menu as it complements the flavours, as well as helping to relieve the heat.

The sorbet must be made in advance and frozen. It is deliciously refreshing and takes some of the sting out of the curry. If you do not have enough time to make the sorbet, you could serve fresh mangoes or even a ready-made dessert from an Indian shop.

Equipment needed – Menu 12

Starter

1 fine sieve
1 medium saucepan with lid
1 savoury chopping board
1 sharp knife
1 savoury wooden spoon
food processor **or** liquidizer **or** fine sieve and
  mixing bowl
1 large saucepan with lid
1 tablespoon
1 measuring jug

Main course

1 savoury chopping board
1 sharp knife
1 large bowl
1 ovenproof casserole dish with lid
1 tablespoon
1 savoury wooden spoon
1 garlic crusher (or see Handy Tip 1, page xvii)
1 fine grater
1 teaspoon
1 measuring jug
Cucumber raita
  1 potato peeler
  1 sharp knife
  1 savoury chopping board
  1 mixing bowl
  1 measuring jug
  1 serving bowl
Almond sag
  1 large saucepan
  1 measuring jug
  1 colander or sieve
  1 tablespoon
  1 wooden spoon or saucer
  1 teaspoon
Saffron or pilau rice
  1 medium saucepan with lid
  1 teaspoon
  1 fine sieve or colander

Shopping list – Menu 12

Starter

8oz/225g green or yellow lentils
*2 onions
1 small green chilli
2 cardamom pods
*1 tablespoon curry powder
*1 bay leaf
*2 tablespoons cooking oil
2 teaspoons mustard seeds
2 crushed dried chillies
2oz/50g (2 tablespoons) creamed coconut
*½ pint/300ml water
*2 teaspoons lemon juice
*salt
2 nan bread (optional)

Main course

2lb/900g lean cubed lamb **or** 1 boneless leg
  joint
*1 onion
*1oz/25g (1 tablespoon) butter
*1oz/25g (1 tablespoon) cooking oil
1 small green chilli
*2 cloves garlic
*1 inch/2.5 cm piece fresh root ginger
*1 teaspoon medium or hot curry powder
*2 tablespoons tomato purée
*2oz/50g (2 tablespoons) plain flour
½ pint/300ml fresh beef or lamb stock **or**
  *1 beef stock cube
½ teaspoon turmeric
2 cardamom pods
1 teaspoon mustard seeds
*1 teaspoon brown sugar
4 poppadoms
1 jar lime pickle
1 jar mango **or** peach chutney
Cucumber raita
  ½ cucumber
  2 spring onions
  1 pint/600ml plain yoghurt
Garnish
  1 small green chilli
  *paprika

MENU 12

Dessert

1 measuring jug
1 small saucepan
1 sharp knife
1 potato peeler
1 lemon squeezer
1 fine sieve
2 small bowls
1 large mixing bowl
1 balloon whisk or hand-held electric mixer
1 freezer container (1 pint/600ml)
1 fork

Almond sag
   14oz/400g fresh spinach
   *salt
   *1oz/25g (1 tablespoon) margarine or butter
   1 teaspoon Bombay curry powder
   2oz/50g ground almonds
Saffron or pilau rice
   8oz/225g saffron or pilau rice
   *1 teaspoon cooking margarine
   *salt

Dessert

*½ pint/300ml water
*4oz/100g granulated sugar
1 lime
*1 lemon
*2 egg whites
¼ pint/150ml chilled, concentrated apple juice
1 packet dessert biscuits of your choice

*Check store cupboard

Countdown – Menu 12

If you want to prepare the whole menu, you will need 185 minutes (3 hours 5 minutes), which includes a 30-minute break. If you are a slow cook, add 5-10 minutes to each course to ensure that you do not run out of time. Remember, the times given are only a guide as each cook will take different lengths of time to complete each task. You have the choice of leaving out a course if you think it is too much, or if time is limited. The soup is best made one or two days before needed to allow all the flavours to combine. The sorbet must also be made in advance to allow it plenty of time to freeze properly. The main course can be made in advance or on the night, but the almond sag and rice should be made just before serving.

Lemon and lime sorbet

PROBLEMS AND HANDY TIPS

> *Preparation time: 20 minutes*
> *Cooking time: None*
> *Freezing time: 10–12 hours*

Assemble all the ingredients and equipment you need for the dessert. Set your timer for 20 minutes.
20 mins Place ½ pint/300ml of water and 4oz/100g granulated sugar in a saucepan. Take 1 lime and 1 lemon and using either a sharp knife or a potato peeler, remove a few strips of rind from each fruit and place in a saucepan with the sugar and water. Put the saucepan over a medium to high heat and allow the sugar to dissolve, then boil rapidly for 15 minutes.
15 mins While the syrup is boiling, cut the lemon and lime in half and squeeze them both. Strain the juice through a fine sieve into a bowl and set aside. Take 2 eggs and separate them, putting the whites into a large mixing bowl and the yolks into a separate small bowl. Either using a balloon whisk or a hand-held electric mixer, beat the whites until they are stiff and hold their shape.

Roll the lime and lemon under the palm of your hand on a work surface to release the flesh. This makes squeezing the fruit easier and more efficient.

Make sure the sugar has dissolved before turning up the heat and boiling the syrup rapidly.

See Handy Tip 2, page xvii, for an easy way to separate eggs without breaking the yolk.

The egg yolks can be kept, covered in the fridge for 1–2

MENU 12

10 mins Remove the sugar syrup from the heat, strain it through a fine sieve, to remove the rind, and pour it into the bowl with the lemon and lime juice. Add ¼ pint/150ml of chilled apple juice and stir well.

5 mins Using a balloon whisk, carefully mix the fruit into the egg whites. Whisk well, place in a freezer container with a tight-fitting lid and put into the freezer.

0 mins Wash up and clear away.

You will need to stir the mixture after 3–4 hours to prevent it from separating: use a fork to break up any ice particles and freeze for a further 4–6 hours before serving.

Starter

Preparation time: 40 minutes
Cooking time: 40 minutes

Assemble all the ingredients and equipment you need for the starter. Set your timer for 40 minutes. (**Note:** This soup is best made one or two days before serving so that the flavours have time to combine.)

40 mins Take 8oz/225g of green or yellow lentils, place them in a fine sieve and wash them thoroughly under warm running water. Place in a medium saucepan with enough cold water to cover by 1½ inch/3 cm.

35 mins Take 1 onion, peel and chop it finely, then place in the saucepan with the lentils. Take 1 small green chilli, cut it in half, discard all the seeds and chop it finely. Add it to the lentils with 2 cardamom pods, ½ tablespoon of curry powder and 1 bay leaf. Stir well, put over a medium heat and bring to the boil. Allow them to boil rapidly for 10 minutes, then reduce the heat and simmer gently, with a lid on, for a further 15–20 minutes. Check regularly that there is enough liquid so that they do not burn dry.

days, and used in rich shortcrust pastry or hollandaise sauce (see Additional Recipes, pages 204 and 200).

If the mixture seems to be separating after whisking, don't worry; put it into the freezer for 2–3 hours, then mix it well with a fork to recombine the sorbet. Repeat if necessary after a few more hours.

PROBLEMS AND HANDY TIPS

Don't use too much water in the lentils or all the flavour is lost during cooking.

Be sure to wash your hands well after chopping the chilli, and do not rub your eyes as they will sting very badly.

Make sure there is always enough water in the lentils or they will dry out.

20 mins When the lentils are cooked, drain it all but 2–3 tablespoons of the water, and discard the bay leaf. Place the lentils in a food processor or liquidizer, and blend to a fine but still slightly textured purée. Alternatively, rub them through a fine sieve with the back of a spoon. Place the purée in a bowl and set aside.

The cooked lentils should be moist, like thick porridge. This consistency makes it easier to purée them.

10 mins Take 1 onion, peel and chop it finely and place in a large saucepan with 2 tablespoons of cooking oil. Fry the onion until it is golden brown. Add 1 teaspoon of mustard seeds, 1 teaspoon of curry powder and 1 crushed dried chilli. Cook for a few more minutes. Now add all the puréed lentils, mix well and cook for 10 minutes, stirring occasionally.

Add the curry powder cautiously if you prefer a mild soup. You can add extra later if it is not hot enough, but you cannot take it away.

5 mins Add 2oz/50g (1 tablespoon) of creamed coconut and ½ pint/300ml of water, and mix well. Add 2 teaspoons of lemon juice and season with a little salt. Taste the soup and adjust to your taste. Remove from the heat and allow to cool. Place in the fridge for 1–2 days so that the flavours develop.

As the soup will gain flavour with time, it is a good idea to taste it and adjust the seasoning just before serving it.

0 mins Wash up and clear away.

Main course

PROBLEMS AND HANDY TIPS

Preparation time: 40 minutes
Cooking time: 2 hours

Assemble all the ingredients and equipment you need for the main course. Set your timer for 40 minutes.

40 mins Take the lamb and if it is not cubed, cut it into 1 inch/2.5 cm cubes, removing any connective tissue or skin. Place the cubes in a bowl and set aside.

It is important to remove all the connective tissue, or the meat will be tough and stringy.

35 mins Peel and chop 1 onion and place half of it in a medium-sized ovenproof casserole dish. Add 1oz/25g (1 tablespoon) of butter and 1 tablespoon of cooking oil, place over a medium heat and cook the onion.

A mixture of oil and butter is used because it can reach a higher temperature without burning.

30 mins Meanwhile, take 1 small green chilli, cut it in half, discard the seeds and chop it finely. Peel and crush 2 cloves of garlic, then add to the casserole with the chilli. Cook for 2 minutes, then

Be very careful not to get chilli in your eyes or in any cuts as it will be very painful.

turn off the heat. Take a 1 inch/2.5 cm piece of root ginger, then peel it and crush it through a garlic crusher or grate it. Add to the casserole, put the heat back on and cook the mixture for 2 minutes. Add 1 teaspoon of medium or hot curry powder and 2 tablespoons of tomato purée and cook for a further 2 minutes.

20 mins Turn the heat off and add 2oz/50g (2 tablespoons) plain flour to the mixture in the casserole dish. Put the mixture back over a low heat and cook for a further 2–3 minutes to remove the floury taste. Preheat the oven to 150°C/300°F/Gas mark 2.

15 mins Take the casserole off the heat and carefully pour in ½ pint/300ml of fresh stock. If using a stock cube, crumble it into the mixture and add ½ pint/300ml of cold water. Stir well and add ½ teaspoon of turmeric, 2 cardamom pods, 1 teaspoon of mustard seeds and 1 teaspoon of brown sugar. Put back over a medium heat and bring to the boil, stirring constantly as the sauce thickens. Simmer for 2 minutes.

2 mins Add the lamb to the sauce, stir well and place in a preheated oven for approximately 2 hours. Stir occasionally during the cooking time.

0 mins Wash up and clear away.

Cucumber raita

This must be made at least 1 hour before serving. Set your timer for 10 minutes.

10 mins Take half a cucumber, peel it and cut it lengthways in half and then into quarters. Slice the cucumber into small dice, place in a bowl and set aside.

5 mins Take 2 spring onions, discard one layer of skin, the root and the top, then chop finely into the bowl with the cucumber.

2 mins Add 1 pint/600ml of plain yoghurt, then pour the mixture into a serving bowl and chill for at least 1 hour. Garnish just before serving.

0 mins Wash up and clear away.

Almond sag

Reset your timer for 25 minutes.

See Handy Tip 1, page xvii, for an easy way to crush garlic, if you don't have a garlic crusher.

If you like hot curries, you may like to add an extra 1–2 teaspoons of curry powder.

It is important that the curry cooks slowly so that all the spices can penetrate the meat.

Do not use the dark green top parts of the spring onions: use the paler bits lower down.

25 mins Fill the kettle and put it on to boil. Take the spinach and wash it well under cold running water to remove any sand or grit. Discard any long stalks and place the spinach in a large saucepan.

20 mins Pour in a very small amount of boiling water, no more than ¼ pint/150ml, add a pinch of salt and cook on a medium to high heat for 4–5 minutes.

15 mins Remove from the heat and drain through a colander. Wash out the saucepan and put it back over a low heat with 1oz/25g (1 tablespoon) of margarine or butter. While the fat is melting, squeeze any excess water out of the spinach in the colander by pressing it with the back of a wooden spoon or a saucer. Set aside.

10 mins Add 1 teaspoon of Bombay curry powder to the melted fat and cook for a few moments. Add 2oz/50g (2 tablespoons) of ground almonds, stir well and add the spinach. Mix well and set aside if you are going to have a break. The almond sag can be reheated just before serving.

0 mins Wash up and clear away.

Relax

Have a 30-minute break. Take your timer with you. When you return you will only have to heat up the soup and cook the rice before serving.

Welcome back

Feeling better after your break?

Last-minute tasks

Set your timer for 20 minutes. This is how long you have before serving the starter.

20 mins Fill the kettle and put it on to boil for the rice.

18 mins Place the soup in a saucepan over a low heat to warm through slowly.

15 mins Check the lamb in the oven. If you think that it is almost cooked, turn the heat right down

Make sure the spinach is washed well as it often has lots of sand and grit in it. Some supermarkets now sell ready-washed spinach. Add only a very small amount of water or all the goodness from the spinach is lost in the water.

Do not cook the spinach longer than stated. It is better undercooked than overcooked at this point as it will be cooked further with the other ingredients.

Do not make the sag (spinach) too spicy; extra spice can be added later when you have tasted it.

PROBLEMS AND HANDY TIPS

and leave it until you are ready to serve. Put all the serving dishes, soup bowls and main course plates in the oven to warm.

11 mins Place the rice in a saucepan and add 1 teaspoon of cooking margarine and a pinch of salt. Pour in enough boiling water to cover the rice, then place over a medium to high heat and cook for 10 minutes.

6 mins Place the saucepan of almond sag over a low heat and warm it up slowly.

4 mins Check the soup and stir it well. If you are going to serve nan bread with it, put it in the oven to warm through. If you are serving poppadoms, check the instructions on the packet to see whether they need to be warmed through. Check the rice and stir well. If you are worried that it will overcook while you are eating the soup, turn it off and finish cooking it once the starter is finished.

2 mins Turn off the almond sag and either leave it covered in the saucepan or put it into a serving dish and keep warm in the oven.

0 mins Wash up and clear away.

Adding a teaspoon of margarine to the rice prevents it from sticking together during and after cooking.

Check the cooking instructions on the rice packet, as different brands will take different lengths of time to cook.

If you prefer, the rice may be cooked, placed in a serving dish with a lid and kept warm in the oven until needed.

Watch points

PROBLEMS AND HANDY TIPS

Once the meal has started, it is difficult to predict how long each course will take. The following instructions are given only as a guide.

Check the soup, stir it well and bring to the boil for the last time. Take the nan bread or poppadoms out of the oven and serve with the soup.

Check the rice and if it is cooked, drain it through a colander or sieve. Transfer to a warmed serving dish. Check that the almond sag is hot, then put it into a serving dish. Garnish the cucumber raita with 1 finely chopped chilli and a pinch of paprika. Place it on the table with the other chutneys. Lastly, take the lamb rogan josh and the warmed plates out of the oven and serve.

The dessert is served as it is, or with some dessert biscuits of your choice.

The soup must be boiling hot before it is served.
Make sure all the dishes are piping hot. Leave the oven on a low-temperature so that you can keep any leftovers warm for second helpings.

Take the sorbet out of the deep freeze 10 minutes before serving so that it will have time to soften slightly.

Winter or spring dinner party menu

Moderately difficult to prepare and cook
Cost level: good value
Serves: 4

A 30-minute break is incorporated in this menu.

Starter	Tomato and orange soup ^{F*} with croûtons or French bread	*Preparation time = 30 minutes* *Cooking time = 20 minutes*

Starter — Tomato and orange soup F* with croûtons or French bread

Preparation time = 30 minutes
Cooking time = 20 minutes

Main course — Chicken casserole with peanut and ginger sauce F*
Spiced mixed vegetables with yoghurt
Plain or saffron rice

Preparation time = 65 minutes
Marinating time = 4 hours minimum
Cooking time = 60 minutes

Dessert — Mousse au chocolat

Preparation time = 20 minutes
Cooking time = None
Chilling time = 3–4 hours

Drink — Spicy, dry white wine, chilled

This menu would make an excellent winter or early spring dinner party. The soup is rich and best served very hot. It has a strong, fresh taste of tomato and orange and is served with croûtons or French bread. The chicken needs to be marinated at least 4 hours before cooking, so it could be made the night before, which gives it even longer to absorb all the flavours in the marinade. The saffron rice is colourful and easy to prepare, while the spicy vegetables cook in the oven with the chicken to save time and energy. The dessert is very rich and should be made in advance to allow it to set and chill. Serve it with some wafer biscuits and single cream, if desired.

MENU 13

Equipment needed – Menu 13

Starter

1 savoury chopping board
1 sharp knife
1 medium saucepan with a lid
1 tablespoon
1 savoury wooden spoon
1 lemon squeezer
1 potato peeler
1 tin opener
1 measuring jug

Main course

Chicken casserole
1 medium mixing bowl
1 tablespoon
1 savoury wooden spoon
1 lemon squeezer
1 savoury chopping board
1 sharp knife
1 potato peeler
1 fine grater
1 heatproof bowl
1 ovenproof casserole dish with lid
1 colander or fine sieve
1 measuring jug
Vegetables
1 savoury chopping board
1 sharp knife
1 colander
1 ovenproof dish or roasting tin
1 tin opener
1 mixing bowl
1 teaspoon
Rice
1 medium saucepan
1 colander or fine sieve

Dessert

1 double saucepan or heatproof bowl that fits
   tightly inside a large saucepan
1 large mixing bowl
1 small mixing bowl

Shopping list – Menu 13

Starter

*1 large onion
*2oz/50g (2 tablespoons) cooking margarine
*1 large carrot
2 oranges
*1 tin (16oz/450g) plum tomatoes
*2oz/50g (2 tablespoons) plain flour
*2 tablespoons tomato purée
1½ pints/900ml fresh chicken or vegetable
   stock **or** 1 chicken or vegetable stock cube
*salt, pepper, mustard powder
*1 tablespoon demerara sugar
*2 teaspoons oregano
1 long French loaf **or** 1 packet croûtons
1 bunch fresh coriander to garnish
*4oz/100g butter or table margarine
¼ pint/150ml single cream (optional)

Main course

1 jar (approx. 7oz/200g) satay sauce
*3 tablespoons white wine vinegar
*3 tablespoons dark soya sauce
*2 tablespoons brown or white sugar
1 lime
1 inch/2.5 cm piece fresh root ginger
8 chicken thighs **or** 6 chicken breasts, skinned
   and boned
12 small pickling onions
*1oz/25g (1 tablespoon) cooking margarine
*1oz/25g (1 tablespoon) plain flour
½ pint/300ml fresh chicken stock **or** *1 stock
   cube
Vegetables
1½lb/675g fresh broccoli
*1oz/25g (1 tablespoon) butter **or** margarine
*salt and freshly ground black pepper
1 red pepper
1 small tin (approx. 7oz/200g) butter beans
*1 small tin (approx. 11oz/300g) sweetcorn
12oz/350g plain yoghurt
*3 teaspoons chilli powder
*2 teaspoons garlic purée
Rice
*8oz/225g plain or saffron rice
*salt

1 teaspoon
1 balloon whisk or hand-held electric mixer
1 sweet wooden spoon
1 flexible spatula
4 individual ramekins or 1 small serving bowl

Dessert

*4oz/100g plain chocolate
*4 eggs
*1 teaspoon vanilla essence
1 packet wafer biscuits of your choice
½ pint/150ml single cream (optional)

*Check store cupboard

MENU 13

Countdown – Menu 13

If you want to prepare the whole menu you will need 160 minutes (2 hours 40 minutes), which includes a 30-minute break. If you are a slow cook, add 5–10 minutes to each course to ensure that you do not run out of time. Remember, the times given are only a guide, as each cook will take different lengths of time to complete each task. The soup can be made in advance and frozen, but remember it must be defrosted at least 12 hours before serving. The main course is best made on the day to keep it fresh and aromatic. The spicy vegetables are cooked in the oven alongside the chicken casserole, which saves time and energy. The rice is cooked and served straight away. The dessert should be made the night before needed to give it time to set and chill.

Dessert

PROBLEMS AND HANDY TIPS

Preparation time: 20 minutes
Cooking time: None
Chilling time: 3–4 hours

Assemble all the ingredients and equipment you need for the dessert. Set your timer for 20 minutes.

20 mins Place 6oz/175g plain chocolate in the top of a double saucepan or in a heatproof bowl over a saucepan of boiling water. Leave the chocolate to melt over a low to medium heat.

Do not overfill the pan with water or it might splash into the bowl of melting chocolate. If this happens the chocolate will go hard.

15 mins Separate 4 eggs: place the whites in the large mixing bowl and the yolks in the small bowl. Add 1 teaspoon of vanilla essence to the yolks.

See Handy Tip 1, page xvii for an easy way to separate eggs without breaking the yolk.

10 mins If the chocolate has almost melted, turn off the heat. Take a balloon whisk or hand-held electric mixer and beat the whites until they are stiff and hold their shape.

5 mins Add the egg yolks to the melted chocolate and mix well, then add this mixture to the egg

If the chocolate has become rather hard, don't worry: it will soften up once the egg yolks have been added.

whites. Be careful to fold this mixture as carefully as possible to keep it light. When there is no more egg white to be seen, pour the mixture into the individual ramekins or a small glass serving bowl and chill for 3–4 hours before serving.

0 mins Wash up and clear away.

Main course

Preparation time: 15 minutes
Marinating time: 4 hours minimum
Cooking time: None

Assemble all the ingredients and equipment you need for the main course. The chicken needs a long time in the marinade so that it has time to absorb all the flavours before being cooked. Set your timer for 15 minutes.

15 mins Empty the jar of satay sauce into a medium-sized bowl. Add 3 tablespoons of white wine vinegar, 3 tablespoons of soya sauce and 2 tablespoons of brown or white sugar. Mix well.

10 mins Take 1 lime, wash it well and cut it in half. Squeeze one half, adding the juice to the marinade. The other half of the lime should be sliced thinly and set aside to garnish the dish later.

6 mins Take a 1 inch/2.5 cm piece of fresh root ginger, peel it with a knife or potato peeler and remove any blemishes. Using a fine grater, grate the ginger into the marinade. Discard any rough or hairy bits and make sure you scrape the rest off the back of the grater.

6 mins Take the chicken pieces, cut the meat into 1 inch/2.5 cm strips and place them in the marinade. Mix well to ensure all the chicken is coated, then cover the bowl and place in the fridge for a minimum of 4 hours, but preferably overnight.

0 mins Wash up and clear away.

PROBLEMS AND HANDY TIPS

Make sure all the ingredients are well mixed to make a flavoursome marinade.

Do not use any hairy or rough parts of the ginger as these are unpleasant to eat.

Try to make all the chicken pieces roughly the same size so that they will cook evenly.

The longer the chicken sits in the marinade, the stronger the flavours will be.

MENU 13

Starter

Preparation time: 30 minutes
Cooking time: 20 minutes

The soup can be made in advance and frozen. Don't forget to defrost it at least 12 hours before it is to be served. The soup can be put through a food processor or blender to give a smooth consistency. Serve it piping hot with French bread or warm toast.

Assemble all the ingredients and equipment you need for the starter. Set your timer for 30 minutes.

30 mins Take 1 onion, chop it finely and place it in a medium saucepan with 2oz/50g (2 tablespoons) of cooking margarine. Cook over a medium heat.

> The onion doesn't have to be cut up very finely as it will cook down.

25 mins Meanwhile, peel 1 large carrot and slice it into thin circles or strips. Add to the onion, stir well and cook until soft – about 5 minutes.

> The carrots should be roughly the same size so that they cook evenly.

20 mins While the onion and carrot are cooking, take 2 oranges, cut them in half and squeeze them. Set the juice aside as it will be used later. Stir the onion and carrot, and turn down the heat if they are cooking too fast. Open a tin of plum tomatoes.

> Roll the oranges under the palm of your hand before squeezing them. This releases the flesh and increases the amount of juice you get out of the oranges.

15 mins Remove the saucepan containing the onion and carrot from the heat and stir in 2oz/50g (2 tablespoons) of plain flour. Crumble in 1 stock cube (if using), place the pan over a low heat and cook the roux for 2 minutes to remove the starchy flavour.

> The margarine and flour mixture is called a roux. A roux is the basis for all soups, sauces and casseroles.

12 mins Turn off the roux and allow it to cool. Stir in 2 tablespoons of concentrated purée, add the tin of tomatoes and mix well. Slowly add 1 pint/600ml of cold water to the mixture. If using fresh stock, add 1 pint/600ml of it now. Make sure the mixture remains smooth and has no lumps.

> If you don't like the seeds and stalk ends found in the tinned tomatoes, you can sieve the soup before serving it.

8 mins Add another ½ pint/300ml of water or stock, put the saucepan over a low heat and bring the soup to the boil. Remember to stir it often to prevent lumps forming. Once it has thickened, boil the soup for a few minutes.

> Don't worry if you can still see lumps of stock cube – these will dissolve as the soup cooks.

> Make sure you stir the liquid into the roux well so that no lumps appear. If the soup is lumpy, beat it with a wooden spoon, or sieve it at the end just before serving it.

5 mins Reduce the heat and add a pinch of salt, mustard powder, nutmeg and freshly ground black pepper, 2 teaspoons of dried oregano, 2 table-spoons of demerara sugar and the freshly squeezed orange juice. Stir well and simmer on the lowest heat possible until you are ready to go for your break.

0 mins Wash up and clear away.

Before going for your break, turn off the soup and put the lid on the saucepan. When you return the soup can be sieved or put through a food processor or blender to give it a smooth consistency. Reheat it just before serving.

Check the seasoning of the soup again1 as the taste will change when the tomatoes and orange juice are added. You can always add extra orange juice if you like.

Make sure you put the soup on the lowest heat possible to stop it from boiling and burning on the bottom of the saucepan.

The soup seasoning should be checked again before the final cooking and again before serving.

Relax

Have a 30-minute break. Take your timer with you. When you return you will only have to cook the main course, vegetables and rice.

Welcome back

Feeling better after your break? It is now time to prepare and cook the main course.

Main course

PROBLEMS AND HANDY TIPS

Preparation time: 30 minutes
Cooking time: 60 minutes

Assemble all the remaining ingredients and equipment you need for the main course. Set your timer for 30 minutes.

30 mins Fill the kettle and put it on to boil.

29 mins Place 12 pickling onions in a heatproof bowl. Pour the boiling water over them and leave to stand for 5–10 minutes.

Soaking the onions in the boiling water loosens the outside skin of the onions and makes them easier to peel.

25 mins Take an ovenproof casserole dish and add 1oz/25g (1 tablespoon) of cooking margarine. Place the casserole over a medium heat until the margarine has melted, then turn off the heat.

MENU 13

22 mins Drain the hot water from the onions, being careful not to burn yourself. Run the onions under cold water to cool them off. Take a sharp knife and carefully remove the outside skin of the onions (it should come away easily). Try to keep the root end intact as this keeps the onion together during cooking.

If the onions are still too hot to handle you can run them under cold water again to cool them off.

15 mins Place the peeled onions in the casserole with the melted margarine and cook over a medium heat until slightly brown. Turn off the heat. Preheat the oven to 180°C/350°F/Gas mark 4.

Take care not to burn the margarine when browning the onions.

12 mins Add 1oz/25g (1 tablespoon) of plain flour and stir to make a thick roux. Return the casserole to a low heat and cook for 2 minutes to remove the starchy flavour.

The mixture of margarine and flour is called a roux. This paste forms the basis of most soups, sauces and casseroles.

7 mins Turn off the heat. If using fresh stock, measure out ½ pint/300ml and slowly add it to the roux. If using a stock cube, crumble it into the roux mixture, then stir in ½ pint/300ml of cold water. Put the casserole over a low heat and bring to the boil, stirring constantly until thick. Cook for 2 minutes to remove the starchy flavour.

Don't worry if you can still see some of the stock cube – it will dissolve as the sauce cooks.

3 mins Take the marinated chicken out of the fridge and stir both the meat and marinade into the casserole. Bring back to the boil, stirring all the time. Place the chicken casserole in the preheated oven for approximately 1 hour.

Make sure the chicken is well mixed with the sauce and heated through before putting it in the oven to cook.

0 mins Wash up and clear away.

Spiced mixed vegetables

PROBLEMS AND HANDY TIPS

Preparation time: 20 minutes
Cooking time: 40–45 minutes

Assemble all the ingredients and equipment you need for the vegetables. Set your timer for 20 minutes.

20 mins Take all the fresh broccoli, discard the thick stalks and cut the remainder into small, even-sized sprigs. Wash well under cold running water, shake dry and place in an ovenproof dish or

Make the broccoli sprigs small and all roughly the same size so that they cook evenly.

roasting tin. Dot small amounts of margarine or butter over the sprigs, and season with a pinch of salt and some ground black pepper.

15 mins Take 1 red pepper, cut it in half and discard all the seeds and stalks. Wash the peppers under cold running water, cut into thin slices and add to the broccoli in the ovenproof dish.

Washing the peppers removes any hidden seeds that you might have missed.

10 mins Open a small tin of butter beans, place them in a colander or sieve and wash under cold water. Pour the beans over the broccoli and peppers. Open a small tin of sweetcorn and discard the liquid. Scatter the corn over the broccoli, peppers and beans.

It is important to wash the butter beans really well before adding them to the dish.

5 mins Place 12oz/350g of plain yoghurt in a mixing bowl and add 3 teaspoons of chilli powder, 2 teaspoons of garlic purée and a pinch of salt and pepper. Mix well and pour the mixture over the vegetables.

You can use more or less chilli depending on your own taste for spicy dishes.

1 min Place the vegetables in the oven above the chicken to cook for approximately 40–50 minutes, or until golden brown. They should have softened but still retain a little bite.

The oven should be already preheated to 180°C/350°F/Gas mark 4.

0 mins Wash up and clear away.

The vegetables might need to cook a little longer if the broccoli sprigs are rather large.

Last-minute tasks

PROBLEMS AND HANDY TIPS

Set your timer for 15 minutes. This is how long you have before sitting down to eat the starter.

15 mins Fill the kettle and put it on to boil.

14 mins If you have not already sieved or blended the soup and wish to do so, do it now. Return the soup to the saucepan and add the remaining stock or water if you think it is too thick. Place over a low heat to warm gently. Stir the chicken casserole and make sure the vegetables are not browning too much. The casserole and vegetables will continue to cook in the oven while you eat your soup.

Check the soup for seasoning as it might need a little lift after sitting for some time.

The soup doesn't have to be sieved or blended. You can serve it as it is with a slight texture.

12 mins Place 8oz/225g of plain or saffron rice in a medium saucepan. Check the instructions on the packet as different brands vary in the length of time they take to cook. Add a pinch of salt.

Adding a teaspoon of margarine to the rice while it is cooking will prevent it from sticking together.

MENU 13

10 mins Stir the soup and turn up the heat if it is not yet boiling. It will need to simmer for 10 minutes before serving.

8 mins Check the chicken casserole in the oven and give it a good stir. If it is cooking well, move it down to the bottom shelf, keeping the vegetables nearer the top.

5 mins If you are using bread rather than croûtons, put the loaf in the oven to warm through. Place the butter on the table to serve with the bread. If you are going to use fresh coriander, wash it well, shake off any excess water and chop finely to serve with the soup.

2 mins Pour the boiling water over the rice and put it over a medium heat to cook slowly. If the rice needs 20 minutes or more, leave it to cook on a low heat while you eat the soup. Otherwise you can cook it while you are putting the main course together.

0 mins Wash up and clear away.

If you prefer you could leave the cooked rice in just-boiled water while you finish everything else off. It will continue to cook very slowly while you are completing the last-minute tasks.

Watch points

PROBLEMS AND HANDY TIPS

Once the meal has started, it is difficult to predict how long each course will take. The following instructions are given only as a guide.

Check the rice before you sit down to eat the soup. If you are worried that it might overcook, turn it right down or even turn it off; it can continue to cook while you are getting everything ready for the main course. The chicken casserole and vegetables should continue to cook in the oven for 20–25 minutes, or until you are ready to serve the main course.

If you have the facility to warm the plates and dishes for the main course, put them in now.

Serve the soup piping hot with some freshly chopped coriander sprinkled over the top. If you are using single cream and croûtons, add a small teaspoon of each to each soup bowl and serve. Take the warmed bread out of the oven and place it in a basket or bowl to serve.

Make sure all the main course dishes and food are keeping warm in the oven before you sit down to eat the soup.

114

Check the rice to see whether it is cooked. Drain it and place in a serving dish. Take the vegetables and casserole out of the oven and transfer to warmed serving dishes if you like. Serve the main dish.

When you drain the rice, it is a good idea to run some hot water through it to remove any excess starch and to stop it from sticking together.

Serve the mousse au chocolat, allowing your guests to help themselves to wafer biscuits and single cream.

The mousse can go straight from the fridge to the table.

All-season menu

Difficult to prepare and cook
Cost level: good value
Serves: 4

14

A 40-minute break is incorporated in this menu.

<u>Starter</u>	Mixed cheese and croûton salad	*Preparation time = 20 minutes* *Cooking time = None*
<u>Main course</u>	Boeuf bourguignonne [F*] Potato and spinach layer Vichy carrots	*Preparation time = 70 minutes* *Cooking time = 2–3 hours*
<u>Dessert</u>	Crème brûlée	*Preparation time = 20 minutes* *Cooking time = 35 minutes*
<u>Drink</u>	Full-bodied red wine – Burgundy would be ideal	

This menu can can be used all year round. The mixed cheese and croûton salad makes a delicious change from the usual salads. It can also be served with fresh bread or rolls. The beef can be made in advance and frozen, but do give it plenty of time to defrost. It can be cooked in the oven, along with the potato layer, which saves time and energy. The crème brûlée should be made in advance to allow it time to chill. The caramel for the topping is added just before serving.

Equipment needed – Menu 14

Starter

1 savoury wooden spoon
1 savoury chopping board
1 tablespoon
1 teaspoon
1 sharp knife or food processor
1 potato peeler
1 measuring jug
1 small mixing bowl or jam jar

Main course

Boeuf bourgignonne
1 heatproof bowl
1 savoury chopping board
1 sharp knife
1 medium bowl
1 tablespoon
1 colander
1 ovenproof casserole with lid
1 savoury wooden spoon
1 garlic crusher (or see page xvii)
1 pair kitchen scissors
Potato and spinach layer
1 colander
1 potato peeler
1 savoury chopping board
1 sharp knife
1 mixing bowl
1 cheese grater or food processor
1 plate
1 measuring jug
1 savoury wooden spoon
1 medium roasting tin, approx. 2½ inch/6 cm
 deep

Dessert

1 double saucepan or 1 heatproof bowl that fits
 tightly inside a large saucepan
1 small saucepan
1 measuring jug
1 small bowl
1 tablespoon
1 balloon whisk or hand-held electric mixer
1 teaspoon
4 ramekins or 1 large heatproof dish
1 roasting tin which the ramekins will fit into

*Check store cupboard

Shopping list – Menu 14

Starter

2 red or green dessert apples
2 sticks celery
½ small white or red cabbage
*2 tablespoons lemon juice
salt and freshly ground black pepper
2oz/50g blue cheese
*2oz/50g Cheddar cheese
2oz/50g feta cheese
*2oz/50g (2 tablespoons) sultanas
3 tablespoons natural yoghurt or sour cream
*2 tablespoons olive oil
1 teaspoon French mustard
1 packet plain or garlic croûtons

Main course

Boeuf bourgignonne
12 small pickling onions
2lb/900g braising or stewing steak
*2oz/50g (2 tablespoons) plain flour
*salt and freshly ground black pepper
*1oz/25g (1 tablespoon) cooking margarine
*1 clove garlic (optional)
*4oz/100g bacon, preferably rindless
½ pint/300ml fresh beef stock or *1 stock cube
½ pint/300ml red wine
*1 tablespoon tomato purée
*1 bouquet garni (see page 222)
*mustard powder, nutmeg
8oz/225g button mushrooms
Potato and spinach layer
8oz/225g fresh spinach
*4 medium-sized potatoes
*6oz/175g Cheddar cheese
*½ chicken or vegetable stock cube
*1oz/25g (1 tablespoon) margarine or oil
*salt, pepper, nutmeg, mustard powder
Vichy carrots
4 large carrots
*1oz/25g margarine or butter
*1 teaspoon sugar
*chopped parsley to garnish (see page xviii)

Dessert

½ pint/300ml double cream
*4 egg yolks
*2oz/50g (2 tablespoons) caster sugar
*1 teaspoon vanilla essence

MENU 14

Countdown – Menu 14

If you want to prepare the whole menu you will need 170 minutes (2 hours 50 minutes), which includes a 40-minute break. If you are a slow cook, add 5–10 minutes to each course to ensure that you do not run out of time. Remember, the times given are only a guide as each cook will take different lengths of time to complete each task. The starter should be made on the day and dressed at the last minute before serving. The main course can be made in advance and frozen. Remember to defrost the meal at least 12 hours before you are going to use it. The dessert must be made in advance to allow it to set and chill. The caramel topping is added just before serving.

Dessert

Preparation time: 20 minutes
Cooking time: 35 minutes

Assemble all the ingredients and equipment you will need for the dessert. Set your timer for 20 minutes. Preheat the oven to 160°C/325°F/Gas mark 3.

20 mins Take a large saucepan or the bottom half of a double boiler, half fill it with water and place it over a medium heat to boil.

18 mins Take a small saucepan and pour in ½ pint/300ml of double cream. Place over a very low heat and warm gently: do not allow it to bubble or boil. Take 4 eggs and carefully separate them, making sure not to break the yolks. Place the yolks in a heatproof bowl or the top part of a double saucepan, but do not put them over the heat yet.

12 mins Add 1oz/25g (1 tablespoon) of the caster sugar to the egg yolks and beat using either a balloon whisk or hand-held electric mixer until thick and light in colour. Place the mixture over the pan of boiling water and continue to beat. If the cream is very hot, turn it off.

See Handy Tip 2, page xvii for an easy way to separate eggs.

Make sure the heatproof bowl is large enough to hold all the cream as well as the whisked egg yolk.

It is important that the cream doesn't boil. Turn it off as soon as you see bubbles appearing.

118

7 mins Once the mixture is thick and light, slowly add the scalded cream, whisking all the time until light and fluffy. Remove from the heat, add 1 teaspoon of vanilla essence and mix well. Spoon the mixture into 4 ramekin dishes or one large heatproof dish.

3 mins Place the ramekins in a roasting tin and pour cold water around them. Place the tin in the preheated oven and cook for 35 minutes.

0 mins Wash up and clear away.

Once the crème brûlée is set, allow it to cool before placing it in the fridge to chill for a minimum of 4–6 hours. The caramel topping is added just before serving.

If at any time the egg mixture looks as though it is cooking or curdling, take it off the heat immediately. If the egg and cream have really started to separate, add an ice cube to the mixture and beat well. This sometimes brings the mixture back together again.

The water bath in which the crème brûlée cooks is called a bain-marie. See Cookery Terms, page 222.

Crème brûlée is very rich, so it is not necessary to serve any extra cream with it.

Main course

PROBLEMS AND HANDY TIPS

Preparation time: 40 minutes
Cooking time: 2–3 hours

Assemble all the ingredients and equipment you need for the boeuf bourgignonne. Set your timer for 40 minutes.

40 mins Fill the kettle and put it on to boil. Place 12 pickling onions in a heatproof bowl, pour the boiling water over them and leave to stand for 5–10 minutes.

The boiling water loosens the outer skin of the onions and makes them easier to peel.

35 mins Take the beef and chop it into 1 inch/2.5 cm cubes. Place the meat in a bowl and sprinkle 1 heaped tablespoon of plain flour over it. Add a good pinch of salt and some ground pepper, then mix well. Set aside.

A mixture of plain flour, salt and pepper is called seasoned flour, and is often used to coat meat and fish.

30 mins Drain the onions in a colander and run lots of cold water over them to cool. Cut a small amount off the top and bottom of each onion, then cut a slit in the skin; it should peel off easily.

Leave as much root as possible on the onions as this prevents them falling apart during cooking.

22 mins Place the peeled onions in the ovenproof casserole. Add 1oz/25g (1 tablespoon) of cooking margarine, place over a low to medium heat and stir well. Peel and crush the garlic, if using, and add to the onions. Leave on a low heat, stirring occasionally, while you chop up 4oz/100g of bacon (if the bacon has rind, it will need to be removed). **14 mins** Add the bacon to the onions, put over a medium heat and cook rapidly, stirring all the time: this will ensure that the mixture does not burn. Preheat the oven to 160°C/325°F/Gas mark 3.

12 mins Once the bacon has started to cook, turn up the heat and add the floured meat. Stir well and cook for a few minutes so that the meat starts browning; do not allow it to stick to the bottom. If using a stock cube, crumble it into the meat, mix well and turn off the heat. Add ½ pint/300ml of water and stir again. If using fresh stock, add ½ pint/300ml of it now. Stir in ½ pint/300ml of red wine and 1 tablespoon of tomato purée.

6 mins Check the desserts in the oven: if they are set, take them out and leave to cool.

4 mins Put the casserole over a low heat and allow it to thicken very slowly. Leave the beef to cook for at least 2 minutes, then add 1 bouquet garni, some freshly ground pepper and a pinch of salt, mustard powder and nutmeg. Cover with a tight-fitting lid and place in the preheated oven for 2–3 hours.

0 mins Wash up and clear away.

The mushrooms should be added to the beef 15 minutes before serving, or they will overcook.

Potato and spinach layer

PROBLEMS AND HANDY TIPS

Preparation time: 30 minutes
Cooking time: 1½–2 hours

Assemble all the ingredients and equipment you need for the potatoes. Set your timer for 30 minutes.

30 mins Wash 8oz/225g of fresh spinach under cold running water. Discard any woody stems or damaged leaves. Tear very large leaves in half. Leave the spinach to drain in a colander.

See Handy Tip 1, page xvii for an easy way to crush garlic if you don't have a garlic crusher.

The rind must be removed from the bacon before cooking it, as it becomes tough when stewed.

It is important to seal the meat well so that all the juices are kept in: these will add flavour to the finished dish.

If you would rather not use the red wine, add an extra ½ pint/ 300ml of water instead.

Bouquet garni is explained in Cookery Terms, page 222.

Season the casserole well before putting it into the oven and checking it again before serving.

The mushrooms can be washed and sliced now so that they are ready to put into the casserole 15 minutes before serving.

The spinach should be thoroughly washed as it often contains lots of sand and grit.

25 mins Peel 4 medium-sized potatoes and slice them as thinly as possible. Place them in a mixing bowl and cover with warm water.

If you have a food processor, you can use it to slice the potatoes and grate the cheese.

18 mins Fill the kettle and put it on to boil. Take 6oz/175g of cheese, grate it on to a plate and set aside.

You might find that the spinach is very bulky, but it will reduce dramatically during cooking.

13 mins Take ½ a chicken or vegetable stock cube and crumble it into a measuring jug. Pour in ¼ pint/150ml of boiling water and stir well until the cube has dissolved. Set aside. Preheat the oven to 160°C/325°F/Gas mark 3 if it's not already on.

10 mins Grease an ovenproof dish or roasting tin with oil or margarine. Drain the potatoes, then arrange a layer of them in the bottom of the dish. Season with salt, pepper, nutmeg and a pinch of mustard powder. Add a layer of drained spinach followed by a layer of grated cheese. Continue to layer in the same way, ending with a layer of potato. Sprinkle the remaining cheese on top.

It is very important to season the layers well now as it is impossible to do so later.

Remember to leave enough grated cheese for the top. If in doubt, set half the cheese aside until the end.

2 mins Stir the stock, then pour it over the potato and spinach layers. Place the dish in the preheated oven above the beef and cook for 1½–2 hours.

0 mins Wash up and clear away.

If there is too much stock for your dish or tin, leave some out and add it later when the potatoes have absorbed some of the liquid. It is important to use all the stock as it prevents the potatoes and spinach from drying out.

Relax

Have a 40-minute break. Take your timer with you and when you return you will only have to finish off the salad and cook the vegetables.

Welcome back

Feeling better after your break? Before preparing the starter, check the dishes in the oven. The beef should be stirred, and if the potatoes are browning too quickly, move them to a shelf below the beef.

Starter

PROBLEMS AND HANDY TIPS

> *Preparation time: 20 minutes*
> *Cooking time: None*

Assemble all the ingredients and equipment you need for the starter. If you have a food processor, you can use it to cut up some of the vegetables, which will save you time and energy. Set your timer for 20 minutes.

20 mins Take the apples, celery and cabbage and wash them well under cold running water. If you have a food processor with a thin slicing blade, cut up the cabbage, then process it through the machine. Alternatively, chop the cabbage thinly with a sharp knife and place in a mixing bowl.

15 mins Cut the apples into quarters and remove the cores. Leave the skin on as it adds colour and flavour. Chop or process the apples and celery into small, thin pieces. Add them to the cabbage and mix well. Mix in 2–3 teaspoons of lemon juice and season with a pinch of salt and ground black pepper.

10 mins Take your selection of cheeses, cut them into bite-sized pieces and add to the mixing bowl. Add 2oz/50g of sultanas and mix well. Cover and set aside until needed; the dressing and croûtons will be added just before serving.

5 mins Take a small mixing bowl and add 3 tablespoons of natural yoghurt or sour cream, 2 tablespoons of olive oil, 1 tablespoon of lemon juice and 1 teaspoon of French mustard. Mix well and taste before seasoning with a little salt and pepper. Set aside.

0 mins Wash up and clear away.

Last-minute tasks

Set your timer for 20 minutes. This is how long you have before you serve the starter.

20 mins Prepare 8oz/225g of button mushrooms now if you have not already done so. Wash them well under cold running water, discard the stalks, cut into quarters and set aside.

15 mins Take the crème brûlée out of the fridge. Sprinkle a teaspoon of caster sugar over the top of each dessert and place under a hot grill until the sugar caramelizes. Watch carefully as

Make sure all the vegetables are finely chopped otherwise it may be difficult for your guests to eat.

The lemon juice will prevent the apples from discolouring.

You can mix all the ingredients for the dressing in a small jam jar with a tight-fitting lid; this can be shaken hard to mix the dressing before using.

PROBLEMS AND HANDY TIPS

The stalks can either be completely removed, or cut off in line with the mushroom.

the sugar can burn very easily. Once the brûlées are golden brown, remove from the grill and set aside.

10 mins Take 4 large carrots, peel and discard the top and tail. Cut them into thin even-sized slices and place in a saucepan with approximately 4–6 tablespoons of water. Add 1oz/25g (1 tablespoon) of margarine or butter and a teaspoon of sugar. Set aside.

5 mins Stir the prepared mushrooms into the boeuf bourguignonne. Taste the sauce, add a good pinch of nutmeg and more herbs and spices according to your taste. Put back in the oven until you are ready to serve it.

2 mins Mix the dressing for the starter again and pour over the salad, making sure all the ingredients are well covered. Sprinkle with the croûtons and place on the table ready to serve.

0 mins Wash up and clear away.

Before sitting down to eat the starter, put the carrots over a medium heat to cook. Once the water in the saucepan is boiling rapidly, lower the heat and simmer very gently. If you are worried that they might overcook while you are eating the starter, turn off the heat and finish cooking them just before serving the main course. They will need approximately 10 minutes.

When the sugar caramelizes, it bubbles and turns brown. When it cools, it forms a thin hard layer over the top of the crème brûlée.

The butter and sugar bring out the flavour of the carrots and add a little extra sweetness. There should be just enough water to cover the bottom of the saucepan, no more.

It is important to season the beef really well now so that all the flavours can be absorbed by the beef.

You will need to keep an eye on the carrots to make sure that the pan doesn't boil dry.

Watch points

Once the meal has started, it is difficult to predict how long each course will take. The following instructions are given only as a guide.

Put your serving dishes and plates for the main course in to warm if you have the facility.

Toss the salad again and serve with the croûtons sprinkled on top. Check the carrots to see if they are cooked. If they are not quite done, turn up the heat and continue to cook them while you take out

Turn the oven down if you are concerned about the serving dishes and plates getting too hot.

all the dishes for the main course. Place the carrots and any cooking juices in a warmed serving dish. Garnish with freshly chopped parsley if you have some. The boeuf bourguignonne and potato and spinach layer can be served straight from the dishes they have been cooked in. Take the warmed plates out of the oven and serve the main course.

The dessert is served as it is: there is no need for any extra cream as it is already very rich.

Keep the carrots slightly firm rather than overcooked and soggy. Your guests can always wait a few minutes while they finish cooking. Once cooked, there should be virtually no liquid left in the saucepan.

Summer lunch or dinner menu

15

Difficult to prepare and cook
Cost level: good value
Serves: 4

A 30-minute break is incorporated in this menu.

Starter	Chilled ratatouille^{F*} with French bread	*Preparation time = 40 minutes* *Cooking time = 10–15 minutes* *Chilling time = 4–6 hours*
Main course	Fillet of sole véronique^{F*} New potatoes Avocado and fresh spinach salad	*Preparation time = 30 minutes* *Cooking time = 20 minutes*
Dessert	Summer pudding with crème fraîche	*Preparation time = 30 minutes* *Cooking time = None* *Chilling time = 12 hours*
Drink	Crisp, dry white wine, chilled	

This menu would suit guests who prefer not to eat meat, but who enjoy eating fish. The starter can be made in advance and frozen. Remember to defrost it the night before or at least 8 hours before serving.

The fish is cooked in the style of véronique, which means in a white wine sauce garnished with white grapes. It is accompanied by a refreshing avocado and spinach salad. If you want to make the French dressing for it yourself, turn to page 201 for instructions.

The dessert should be made the day before needed so that the juice from the fruits has time to soak into the bread. It is then turned out on to a plate and served with fresh cream or crème fraîche.

It is a good idea to make this menu during the summer months when fillet of sole and summer fruits are readily available: if you try to buy these ingredients during the winter months, it can prove difficult and expensive. As this menu is quite light, it would make a very good summery lunch.

MENU 15

Equipment needed – Menu 15

Starter

1 savoury chopping board
1 sharp knife
1 colander
1 bowl
1 large saucepan with lid
1 tablespoon
1 savoury wooden spoon
1 garlic crusher (or see page xvii)
1 frying pan
1 tin opener
1 teaspoon
4 individual bowls or plates

Main course

1 savoury chopping board
1 sharp knife
1 ovenproof dish
1 lemon squeezer
1 small saucepan
1 tablespoon
1 savoury wooden spoon
1 measuring jug
1 teaspoon
1 salad bowl
1 medium saucepan
1 serving dish

Dessert

1 colander
1 sweet chopping board
1 sharp knife
1 bread board
1 pudding basin (2 pint/1.2l capacity)
1 medium saucepan
1 sweet wooden spoon
1 tablespoon
1 saucer, plate or bowl to fit inside the pudding
  basin and weights to keep it under pressure.
1 serving plate
1 round-ended knife

*Check store cupboard

Shopping list – Menu 15

Starter

4 courgettes
1 medium-sized aubergine
*salt, pepper, nutmeg, mustard powder
*1 onion
*1oz/25g (1 tablespoon) cooking margarine
*1 clove garlic (optional)
2 mixed peppers, either red, yellow or green
*1 tablespoon olive oil
*2 tablespoons tomato purée
*1 tin (14oz/400g) chopped tomatoes
*1 teaspoon of oregano
1 long French loaf or fresh rolls
parsley to garnish (see page xviii)
*4oz/100g butter or table margarine

Main course

8 fillets Dover or lemon sole, preferably
  skinned
*salt, pepper, mustard powder
2 lemons
16 small new potatoes
4 spring onions
*1oz/25g (1 tablespoon) butter or margarine
*1oz/25g (1 tablespoon) plain flour
½ pint/300ml fresh fish stock or *1fish or
  vegetable stock cube
*2 tablespoons white wine (optional)
6oz/175g white grapes (preferably seedless)
1–2 sprigs fresh mint

Salad

2lb/900g fresh young salad spinach
1 ripe avocado
1 small bunch red radishes
*¼ pint/150ml French dressing (see page 201)

Dessert

1lb 12oz/800g soft summer fruits, such as
  strawberries, raspberries, blackcurrants,
  redcurrants, blackberries
8–9 slices brown or white bread, depending on
  size of basin
*4oz/100g caster sugar
½ pint/300ml single cream or 8oz/225g crème
  fraîche

Countdown – Menu 15

If you want to prepare the whole menu, you will need 160 minutes (2 hours 40 minutes), which includes a 30-minute break. If you are a slow cook, add 5–10 minutes to each course to ensure that you do not run out of time. Remember, the times given are only a guide as each cook will take different lengths of time to complete each task. The starter should be made 4– 6 hours in advance or the day before to allow it time to chill. The dessert must also be made in advance to allow all the fruit juice to soak through the bread. The fish, potatoes and salad should be made on the night itself.

Dessert

PROBLEMS AND HANDY TIPS

> Preparation time: 30 minutes
> Cooking time: None
> Chilling time: 12 hours

Assemble all the ingredients and equipment you need for the dessert. Set your timer for 30 minutes.

30 mins Take all the summer fruits, place them in a colander and wash carefully under cold running water. Cut any large fruits into halves or quarters. Leave to drain.

If you are using frozen summer fruits, it is not necessary to wash them.

22 mins Take 6–7 slices of white or brown bread and cut off the crusts. Place 1 piece of bread in the bottom of your pudding basin, then add the remaining pieces of bread around the sides. You might need to cut the bread to fit.

The amount of bread needed will depend on the size of your pudding bowl. Make sure there are no gaps in the lining as the bread keeps the pudding together when it is turned out.

18 mins Put all the fruit in a medium-sized saucepan and add 4oz/100g of caster sugar. Put over a medium heat to dissolve the sugar, simmering gently for 4–5 minutes.

Do not overcook the fruits. Simmer for only 5 minutes, so that they remain firm and whole.

14 mins Turn off the heat and add 2–3 tablespoons of the fruit and juice to a lined pudding basin. Place 1 piece of bread on top of the fruit, press down lightly with a tablespoon, then continue to add the remaining fruit and juice to the

The piece of bread placed in the middle of the pudding basin absorbs some of the fruit and juices and helps to keep the dessert together once it is turned out.

basin. Stop when the fruit almost reaches the top of the bread lining.

11 mins Place another slice of bread on top of the fruit, filling in any gaps with the remaining slice of bread.

4 mins Loosely cover the top of the basin with cling film, then sit a flat saucer, plate or bowl on top, inside the basin. Place a weight on top of the plate so that it pushes down the pudding and forces the juices to soak into the bread. Leave the pudding in the fridge overnight.

If you do not have a weight, use something heavy like a jar of jam to sit on top of the plate.

0 mins Wash up and clear away.

Starter

PROBLEMS AND HANDY TIPS

Preparation time: 40 minutes
Cooking time: 10–15 minutes
Chilling time: 4–6 hours

Assemble all the ingredients and equipment you need for the starter. Set your timer for 40 minutes.

40 mins Wash the courgettes and aubergine under cold running water. Slice the courgettes thinly, place in a colander, sprinkle liberally with salt and leave to degorge. Take the aubergine and cut off the stalk and a small piece of the base. Slice the remainder into thin pieces roughly the same size as the courgettes. Place the aubergine in a second colander or bowl and sprinkle liberally with salt. Leave to degorge.

The ratatouille can be served hot, and in which case, reheat it before serving. However, it is a refreshing cold starter for a summer meal.

Try to make all the slices of courgettes and aubergine the same size so that they cook evenly.

30 mins Meanwhile, peel and chop 1 onion and place it in a large saucepan with 1oz/25g (1 table-spoon) of cooking margarine. Put over a low to medium heat and cook until soft.

To degorge means to draw out the bitter flavours found in these vegetables.

25 mins Peel and crush 1 clove of garlic, if using, and place in the saucepan with the onion. Cook for 2 minutes on a low heat.

See Handy Tip 1, page xvii, for an easy way to crush garlic if you do not have a garlic crusher.

20 mins Take your mixed peppers, cut them in half and remove the seeds and stalk. Wash them under cold running water, then slice into thin, even-sized strips.

128

15 mins Add the peppers to the onion and garlic and cook until the peppers have softened, approximately 5 minutes.

12 mins Rinse the courgettes and aubergine thoroughly and pat dry with kitchen paper. Add the courgettes to the onion mixture and continue to cook. Place the aubergine in a separate frying pan, add 1oz/25g (1 tablespoon) of olive oil and fry quickly over a high heat. Once the aubergine begins to shrink and brown slightly, add it to the onion mixture and continue to cook.

6 mins Mix in 2 tablespoons of tomato purée. Open the tin of chopped tomatoes and empty them into the vegetables. Season with a pinch of salt, nutmeg, mustard powder, some ground black pepper and 1 teaspoon of oregano. Mix well and cook on a very low heat for approximately 10–15 minutes, or until the courgettes and aubergine are soft but not falling apart. This will vary, depending on the size of your vegetables. Allow the ratatouille to cool before placing it in the fridge to chill.

0 mins Wash up and clear away.

Make sure you wash off all the salt, as any excess will spoil the taste of the ratatouille.

The olive oil adds an authentic Mediterranean flavour to the aubergines. Add a little extra if they start to look dry or burn.

Season the mixture well with your favourite herbs and spices.

Do not overcook the ratatouille: it tastes much better if the vegetables are slightly firm.

Main course

PROBLEMS AND HANDY TIPS

Preparation time: 30 minutes
Cooking time: 20 minutes

Assemble all the ingredients and equipment you need for the main course. It is a good idea to prepare everything so that after your break you will only have to cook the fish. Set your timer for 30 minutes.

30 mins Take 8 fish fillets and skin them, if necessary, with a sharp knife. Starting at the tail end, insert the knife under the skin and use a sawing action as you work slowly towards the head. Discard the skin.

25 mins Roll up the fillets, skinned side inside,

Place a piece of cling film or greaseproof paper over the chopping board to prevent the smell of fish penetrating the board.

If the fish is very fresh, the skin may come away easily just by pulling it gently. If it starts to tear, use the sharp knife again.

place them in an ovenproof dish and season with salt and freshly ground black pepper. Take 1 lemon and roll it under the palm of your hand on a work surface to loosen the flesh. Cut the lemon in half and squeeze both halves. Pour a small amount of juice over each rolled fish fillet, keeping the extra for the sauce. Set the fish aside.

20 mins Take the new potatoes and, if they are very dirty, soak them in warm water.

18 mins Take 4 spring onions, remove the outer skin, root and top, then slice the remainder thinly. Place in a small saucepan, add 1oz/25g (1 tablespoon) of butter or margarine and cook over a medium to high heat. This will take only a couple of minutes as the onions are so small.

12 mins Once the onions are cooked, remove from the heat and stir in 1oz/25g (1 tablespoon) of plain flour. Put back over a low heat and cook the mixture for 2–3 minutes, stirring all the time. Turn off the heat and leave to cool. Preheat the oven to 180°C/350°F/Gas mark 4 if you are going to cook the fish now.

9 mins Take ½ pint/300ml of fresh fish stock or dissolve 1 fish or vegetable stock cube in just under ½ pint/300ml of boiling water. Add 2 tablespoons of white wine to give the sauce a richer flavour.

6 mins Pour the stock into the roux very slowly, stirring all the time. Put back over a low heat and bring slowly to the boil, stirring constantly until the sauce thickens. Cook for 2–3 minutes. Season with salt, white pepper, a pinch of mustard powder and 1 teaspoon of freshly squeezed lemon juice. Check the seasoning before pouring the sauce over the fish. Either cook it straight away or, if you are going to have a break, cover and set aside. You will cook the fish when you return from your break.

2 mins Wash the white grapes and leave them to drain. Cut them open to remove the seeds, if necessary, before adding them to the fish.

0 mins Wash up and clear away.

Rolling the lemon under the palm of your hand increases the amount of juice extracted from the lemon when it is squeezed.

Use only the crisp-looking parts of the onion.

The mixture of margarine and flour is called a 'roux'. It forms the basis of most sauces.

The wine is optional. Don't add any more liquid instead of it.

If the sauce becomes lumpy, beat it well with a wooden spoon or whisk. If the lumps remain, wait until the sauce has thickened and cooked for a few minutes, then sieve it over the fish before cooking it in the oven. Discard the lumps.

It is important that the grapes are small and sweet or they can make the dish rather bitter.

Relax

Have a 30-minute break, or more if you like. Take your timer with you. When you return you will only have to put the fish in the oven, cook the new potatoes and prepare the salad.

Welcome back

Feeling better after your break?

Last-minute tasks

PROBLEMS AND HANDY TIPS

Set your timer for 30 minutes. This is how long you have before sitting down to eat the starter. If you have not already done so, preheat the oven to 180°C/350°F/Gas mark 4.

30 mins Take the ingredients you will need for the salad. Wash the spinach well, if necessary. If the leaves are very large, tear them into smaller pieces, discarding any woody stems, and place in a salad bowl.

Many supermarkets now stock pre-washed spinach which is ready to use. Discard any rough or damaged dark green leaves. Make sure you discard any old, tough spinach leaves. They should be young and bright green in colour.

25 mins Take the second lemon and wash it well under cold running water. Using a sharp knife, cut the lemon into 4 large or 8 small wedges and set aside to serve with the fish.

20 mins Take the fish and place it in the middle of the preheated oven for 20 minutes.

Remove any pips in the lemon wedges as they are unpleasant to bite into and spoil the appearance of the fish.

18 mins Rinse the new potatoes, place them in a medium saucepan of cold water and put over a medium to high heat with a pinch of salt and a few sprigs of fresh mint. Cook for 15–20 minutes. This will vary, depending on the size of the potatoes.

16 mins Cut the avocado in half, remove the stone, then peel off the skin. If this is not possible, carefully scoop the flesh out of the skin using a teaspoon. Chop it into small pieces, then add 2 teaspoons of lemon juice to prevent the flesh from discolouring. Wash the radishes and slice them

To peel the avocado, cut it in half lengthways. Pull the halves apart by twisting them in opposite directions. Remove the stone. Place the halves cut side down on a chopping board. Score the skin three times from top to bottom thinly. Set aside until you are ready to put the salad together.

10 mins Place the French bread or rolls in the oven to warm through.

8 mins Take the ratatouille out of the fridge, divide it between individual plates or bowls and garnish with some fresh chopped parsley. Put each serving on the table.

5 mins Take the prepared white grapes, sprinkle them over the fish, then put back in the oven to keep warm.

2 mins Check the new potatoes to see if they are cooked. If they are, turn off the heat, drain then return them to the saucepan or a warm serving dish.

0 mins Check the fish in the oven: if it is cooked, turn the heat right down to 110°C/225°F/ Gas mark ¼. Everything is now ready to serve.

with a sharp knife, then carefully peel off each section of skin.

The fish is cooked when it has shrunk and is very white in colour.

The fish will not spoil when keeping warm in the oven as it is covered by the sauce which prevents it from drying out.

Watch points

PROBLEMS AND HANDY TIPS

Once the meal has started, it is difficult to predict how long each course will take. The following instructions are given only as a guide.

Serve the starter. Don't forget to take the bread out of the oven and to put some butter on the table.

Toss the salad in the French dressing and put it on the table for your guests to help themselves. Take the fish out of the oven and turn off the heat. Serve with the lemon wedges and new potatoes.

Before serving the dessert, turn it out by placing a plate over the top of the basin and quickly turning it over. The pudding should fall out easily on to the plate. If not, run a round-ended knife around the inside edge of the bowl and try again. Serve with single cream or crème fraîche.

Don't turn the oven off if you are going to keep the fish and potatoes warm for guests who might like a second helping.

Smart winter dinner party

Difficult to prepare and cook
Cost level: good value
Serves: 4

16

A 30-minute break is incorporated in this menu.

Starter	Seafood vol-au-vents F*	Preparation time = 35 minutes Cooking time = 15 minutes
Main course	Noisettes of lamb cooked with orange and rosemary F* Brussels sprouts, buttered carrots and duchesse potatoes	Preparation time = 60 minutes Cooking time = 60 minutes
Dessert	Hazelnut meringue gâteau	Preparation time = 40 minutes Cooking time = 3 hours
Drink	Fruity, full-bodied white, chilled, or a light red wine	

This menu can be made all year round and is nice and filling. You can leave out the starter or dessert and serve cheese and biscuits or fresh fruit at the end of the meal, depending on how much time and energy you have. The starter is delicious and the seafood filling can be varied depending on your own taste. To save time you can buy frozen or pre-cooked vol-au-vent cases.

Most good supermarkets stock prepared noisettes; if not, ask your local butcher to prepare them for you. You could make them yourself, but this will add extra time and effort. The orange and rosemary really bring out the flavour of the lamb and the vegetables complement it perfectly. However, you can choose any seasonal vegetables to suit your taste. The meringues must be made in advance as they cook slowly and must then cool. They should be filled shortly before serving to prevent them becoming soft and soggy. The filling can be adapted to your own taste and can be made with crème fraîche instead of double cream.

MENU 16

Equipment needed – Menu 16

Starter

1 non-stick or greased baking tray
1 small mixing bowl
1 fork
1 pastry brush
1 tablespoon
1 small saucepan
1 measuring jug
1 savoury wooden spoon
1 savoury chopping board
1 sharp knife
1 teaspoon

Main course

1 savoury chopping board
1 sharp knife
1 ovenproof casserole with lid
fine string
1 tablespoon
1 savoury wooden spoon
1 measuring jug
1 lemon squeezer
1 frying pan
1 spatula
Vegetables
   1 savoury chopping board
   1 sharp knife
   2 medium saucepans with lids
   1 small saucepan
   1 teaspoon
   1 colander
   1 potato masher
   1 baking tray
   1 wooden spoon
   1 piping bag with wide fluted nozzle, or 2 teaspoons

Dessert

1 large mixing bowl
2 small bowls
1 baking tray
1 balloon whisk or hand-held electric mixer
2 sheets of parchment or silicone paper
1 tablespoon
1 piping bag with fluted nozzle (optional)
1 spatula
1 cooling rack

Shopping list – Menu 16

Starter

8 small vol-au-vent cases (frozen and ready to cook, or pre-cooked and ready to serve)
*1 egg
*salt, pepper
*1oz/25g (1 tablespoon) cooking margarine
*1oz/25g (1 tablespoon) plain flour
¼ pint/150ml fresh stock or *1 fish stock cube
4oz/100g fresh seafood cocktail
1 tablespoon lemon juice
*1 lemon
1 bunch watercress or fresh parsley

Main course

*1 onion
*1oz/25g (1 tablespoon) cooking margarine
8 noisettes of lamb, or 2lb/900g best end or loin of lamb
*1oz/25g (1 tablespoon) plain flour
½ pint/300ml lamb or beef stock or *1 stock cube
*salt and pepper
2 sprigs fresh or 2 teaspoons dried rosemary
1 orange
*2 tablespoons dry sherry (optional)
Vegetables
   2lb/900g old potatoes
   2 large parsnips
   *salt, pepper, nutmeg
   2lb/900g Brussels sprouts
   *8 large carrots
   *1oz/25g (1 tablespoon) cooking margarine
   *1 heaped teaspoon sugar
   *2oz/50g (1 tablespoon) butter or table margarine
   *1 egg
   *1 tablespoon dried breadcrumbs

Dessert

*3 eggs
3oz/75g chopped hazelnuts
*6oz/175g caster sugar
*2 drops vinegar
¼ pint/150ml double cream
8oz/225g fresh or frozen summer fruits

*Check store cupboard

Countdown – Menu 16

If you want to prepare the whole menu, you will need 190 minutes (3 hours 10 minutes). This includes a 30-minute break. If you are a slow cook, add 5–10 minutes to each course to ensure that you do not run out of time. Remember, the times given are only a guide as each cook will take different lengths of time to complete each task. The dessert must be made in advance to allow the meringues time to cool before being filled. The vol-au-vents and lamb can also be made in advance and frozen, then heated up on the night. The vegetables and duchesse potatoes are best made on the night.

Dessert

PROBLEMS AND HANDY TIPS

> *Preparation time: 40 minutes*
> *Cooking time: 3 hours*

Assemble all the ingredients and equipment you need for the dessert. Set your timer for 40 minutes. Preheat the oven to 200°C/400°F/Gas mark 6.

40 mins Take 3 eggs and separate them. Place the whites in a large mixing bowl, and the yolks in a small bowl. Make sure none of the yolk falls into the whites or the whites will not froth up.

See Handy Tip 2, page xvii, for an easy way to separate eggs.

35 mins Place 3oz/75g chopped hazelnuts on a baking tray and put them into the oven to toast for 10 minutes, or until they are golden brown.

Take care with the hazelnuts as they contain a lot of oil and can burn very easily.

32 mins Take a hand-held electric mixer or a balloon whisk and beat the egg whites until they are stiff and hold their shape.

24 mins Take the hazelnuts out of the oven and place in a bowl to cool. Turn the oven down to 110°C/225°F/Gas mark ¼. Place a large sheet of parchment paper on each of the two baking trays, securing the corners with dabs of egg white or egg yolk.

Secure the paper to the baking tray or it might stick to the side of the meringues.

20 mins Measure out 6oz/175g of caster sugar and add it to the egg whites, 1 tablespoon at a time, whisking constantly. The last few spoonfuls should

Make sure the egg whites are really stiff and holding their shape before adding the sugar.

be carefully folded in using a spatula or tablespoon. Add 2 drops of vinegar and all the toasted hazelnuts.

15 mins Using either a piping bag or a spoon, divide the mixture evenly between the two lined baking trays. Shape the 2 meringues into circles approximately ¾ inch/2 cm thick, using a spatula. If using a piping bag, start piping from the centre of the baking sheet, slowly working outwards until you have a large spiral circle. Place in the preheated oven for about 2 hours.

2 mins Keep your timer with you as the meringues should be turned over after 2 hours and the paper peeled off. Return them to the oven and cook for a further 1 hour. Set aside to cool.

0 mins Wash up and clear away.

If you do not have a piping bag, use a flexible spatula to make the circles.

The nozzle must not be too large or the mixture will pour out too quickly.

The meringues might take longer to cook, depending on their thickness and the accuracy of your oven.

Starter

PROBLEMS AND HANDY TIPS

Preparation time: 35 minutes
Cooking time: 15 minutes

Preheat the oven to 220°C/425°F/Gas mark 7. If you are going to make the filling the night before needed, you will not need to set the oven until you are going to cook the vol-au-vent cases. They should be filled shortly before serving, or they will become soft and soggy. Assemble all the ingredients and equipment you need for the starter. Set your timer for 35 minutes.

35 mins If using frozen vol-au-vent cases, place them on a non-stick baking tray. Break one egg into a small bowl, add a pinch of salt and beat with a fork. Using a pastry brush or your clean fingers, brush the top of each vol-au-vent with beaten egg. Place in the preheated oven for approximately 10 minutes.

30 mins While the vol-au-vents are cooking, make the seafood filling. Melt 1oz/25g (1 tablespoon) cooking margarine in a small saucepan over a low heat. Remove from the heat and stir in 1oz/25g (1 tablespoon) of plain flour. Put back over a low heat and cook for 2 minutes. Remove from the heat and add ¼ pint/150ml of fresh fish stock or 1

The vol-au-vents can be frozen when filled, though they are better frozen unfilled to keep them crisp.

The beaten egg brushed over the vol-au-vents will give them a shiny golden brown finish, which always looks appetizing.

stock cube dissolved in ¼ pint/150ml of water. Mix well, making sure there are no lumps, then put back over a medium to low heat and continue cooking until the sauce thickens. Boil the sauce for 2 minutes.

22 mins Check the vol-au-vents in the oven. If they are baking unevenly, turn the tray around. Put the vol-au-vents back in the oven and cook for another 3–4 minutes.

20 mins Turn off the sauce. Take the seafood cocktail and, if necessary, chop it into bite-sized pieces. Add the sauce and cook for 2 minutes.

15 mins Take the vol-au-vents out of the oven and carefully remove the central discs with a sharp knife. Put them on the baking sheet beside the vol-au-vent cases and put them back in the oven for 1 minute to dry out the pastry in the centre.

13 mins Season the sauce with ground black pepper, a pinch of salt and 1 tablespoon of lemon juice. If you are not going to serve the vol-au-vents straight away, do not fill them now or they will become soggy.

10 mins Take the vol-au-vent cases out of the oven and use a teaspoon to fill each case with some seafood sauce. Once all the cases have been filled, place the pastry lids on top and return to the oven to heat through for 10 minutes before serving.

0 mins Wash up and clear away.

If you have made the vol-au-vents in advance, allow them to cool and then place in the fridge until required. The vol-au-vents can also be frozen when cool, but they must be defrosted for a minimum of 6–8 hours at room temperature.

Main course
Vegetables

Preparation time: 30 minutes
Cooking time: 20–25 minutes

Take out all the ingredients and equipment you need for the vegetables. Set your timer for 30 minutes.

Make sure the sauce is smooth before adding the seafood. If it is lumpy, you will need to sieve it after it has cooked and before adding the seafood.

If the pastry cases lean to one side, this means that your oven is uneven. You can counteract this by turning the baking tray around halfway through the cooking time so that they lean the opposite way.

It might be necessary to cut around the tops if they have been baked on with the egg.

It is important to dry the cases out as it makes them crisper.

Put 1 teaspoonful of filling into each vol-au-vent case before doing any topping up. This will ensure the filling is equally distributed.

PROBLEMS AND HANDY TIPS

MENU 16

30 mins Peel the potatoes and 2 parsnips. Cut them into quarters and place in a saucepan half full of cold water. Add a pinch of salt, place the pan over a high heat and bring to the boil. Once boiling, turn down the heat and simmer for 20–25 minutes.

Make sure all the pieces of potatoes and parsnips are roughly the same size so that they will cook evenly.

25 mins Take 2lb/900g Brussels sprouts, trim the stems and discard any old or discoloured outer leaves. Cut a small cross on the base of each sprout, but do not cut too deeply or they will fall apart during cooking. Place the sprouts in a saucepan with a pinch of salt, cover with cold water and set aside. Peel 8 large carrots and trim the tops and bottoms. Cut into thin, even-sized circles and place them in a saucepan with 1oz/25g (1 tablespoon) of margarine, a pinch of salt and 1 heaped teaspoon of sugar.

Make sure you do not cut right through the Brussels sprouts or they will fall apart.

13 mins Check the potato and parsnip with a sharp knife: if the blade passes through them easily, turn off the heat and drain them. Put the potato and parsnip back in the saucepan and mash thoroughly using a potato masher. When the mixture is as smooth as possible, add 2oz/50g (2 tablespoons) of butter or margarine and 1 whole egg. Season with a pinch of salt, ground white pepper and nutmeg. Take out your baking tray and grease it, if necessary, with a thin layer of margarine.

The potatoes and parsnips must be soft, but not falling apart. If they are hard, they will not mash well.

It is important to grease the baking tray, especially if it is not non-stick, so that the potatoes can be easily removed.

8 mins Using a wooden spoon, beat the potato mixture well, then spoon it into a piping bag fitted with a fluted nozzle. Tie the bag up at the top, then carefully squeeze it so that the potato comes out in perfect, little round castles on to your baking tray. If you do not have a piping bag, use 2 teaspoons and make small, even-sized mounds instead.

Potatoes shaped with two teaspoons will obviously not look as even as piped ones, but will taste just as good.

2 mins Sprinkle the top of each duchesse potato with a small amount of dried breadcrumbs and place under a hot grill to brown all over before serving and then set aside until needed. They can be reheated in the oven with the lamb before serving.

Make sure the potatoes are golden brown before removing them from the grill.

0 mins Wash up and clear away.

If using frozen fruits in the filling for the gâteau, put them out to defrost before you take your break. Read the defrosting instructions on the packet.

Relax

Have a 30-minute break, or longer if you like. When you return you will prepare and cook the main course, fill the vol-au-vents, if they have not already been filled, and cook the vegetables. You will also fill and decorate the dessert, if it hasn't already been done.

Welcome back

Feeling better after your break?

Noisettes of lamb

PROBLEMS AND HANDY TIPS

Preparation time: 30 minutes
Cooking time: 25–30 minutes

Assemble all the ingredients and equipment you need for the main course. Set your timer for 30 minutes.

30 mins Peel and chop 1 onion and place it in an ovenproof casserole dish. Add 1oz/25g (1 table-spooon) of cooking margarine, place over a low heat and allow the onion to soften.

The onion doesn't have to be very small as it will cook down.

25 mins Meanwhile, if you are preparing the noisettes yourself from a joint of lamb, slice the meat into approximately 1 inch/2.5 cm slices, removing the bone if necessary. Roll up each slice of lamb and tie neatly using fine string. This keeps the meat together while it is cooking. The string is removed before serving. You will need to make a minimum of 8 noisettes. If you have bought prepared noisettes, set them aside.

Try to make the noisettes roughly the same size so that they will cook evenly.

18 mins Take the onion off the heat and stir in 1oz/25g (1 tablespoon) of plain flour. Put back over

The mixture of flour and melted margarine is called a roux.

a medium heat and cook for a few minutes. Off the heat, add ½ pint/300ml of lamb or beef stock, or 1 stock cube dissolved in ½ pint/150ml of boiling water. Stir the liquid into the roux, and when the mixture is smooth, put it back over a low to medium heat and bring to the boil. Season with a pinch of salt, ground black pepper and 2 sprigs of fresh rosemary. Leave to simmer.

13 mins Preheat the oven to 200°C/400°F/Gas mark 6. Take one large orange, cut in half and squeeze both halves. Add all the juice to the sauce, stir well and adjust the seasoning if necessary. Cook for a few minutes before turning off the heat.

9 mins Place a small amount of cooking margarine in a frying pan and place over a medium heat to melt. When it foams, add the noisettes of lamb. Cook briskly over a medium to high heat to brown them all over, turning when necessary. Add 2 tablespoons of dry sherry to the pan and cook for a further 1 minute. Turn off the heat and add the noisettes, juices and sherry to the sauce in the casserole. Stir well and cover with the lid.

2 mins Place in the preheated oven to cook for approximately 25–30 minutes.

0 mins Wash up and clear away.

If you are going to freeze the lamb, cook it for only 20 minutes at this stage. After it has been defrosted, it will be heated up and cooked for a further 10 minutes before serving.

Last-minute tasks

Set your timer for 25 minutes.

25 mins Fill the vol-au-vents with the seafood sauce if they have not already been filled, place the tops on them and put in the oven to heat through.

17 mins Fill and decorate the hazelnut meringue if you have not already done so. Take 7fl oz/210ml of double cream and beat it with an electric mixer or balloon whisk until it is stiff and holds its shape. Take the soft fruits and carefully fold them into the cream. (Don't worry if the fruit breaks up.)

Make sure the stock cube is completely dissolved before adding it to the roux.

Roll the orange under the palm of your hand before squeezing it. This loosens the flesh and increases the amount of juice you get out of the orange.

The sherry is optional, but it does add extra flavour to the lamb.

The meat is browned all over to seal the juices into the meat before cooking it in the casserole. Do not overcook the lamb: it is better left pink rather than tough and dried out.

PROBLEMS AND HANDY TIPS

If the vol-au-vents are already filled, place them in the oven to heat through.

Frozen summer fruits must be defrosted before being added to the cream. If the frozen fruit has a lot of juice, you will need to discard some of it or the cream will become liquid.

Spread the cream and fruit mixture on to one of the meringue circles, and place the second circle on top to form a gâteau. If there is too much filling, you can use the excess on top. Decorate with extra nuts, if you like.

7 mins Check the meat in the oven. If you think it might overcook, take it out but leave the lid on. Put the duchesse potatoes into the oven to warm through. The lamb can be returned to the oven just before sitting down to eat the vol-au-vents.

4 mins Take 1 lemon, wash it under cold running water and cut it into quarters or eighths, depending on its size. Place the wedges on a plate to serve with the vol-au-vents.

1 min Put the carrot and Brussels sprouts on to a medium heat to start cooking.

0 mins Wash up and clear away.

Watch points

Once the meal has started, it is difficult to predict how long each course will take. The following instructions are only given as a guide.

Take the vol-au-vents out of the oven – they should be piping hot by now. Before serving them, put the lamb back into the oven to keep warm and put the duchesse potatoes on a lower shelf if you think they are browning too much. If you think the vegetables might overcook while you are eating the starter, turn them off; you can continue cooking them after you have eaten the starter and while you are preparing everything for the main course.

Put your serving dishes and plates for the main course in to warm if you have the facility.

Serve the starter, garnished with watercress or parsley, and don't forget the lemon wedges.

Put the vegetables back on to cook if they were turned off while you were eating the starter. Take the lamb and potatoes out of the oven. Once the vegetables are cooked, drain them and put them into a warm serving dish. Serve the main course.

The dessert is served as it is – extra cream is not necessary.

Use the best circle for the top of the gâteau. If you break a circle, it won't be noticeable if used as the bottom of the gâteau.

Check the seasoning of the meat now as you might forget later when things get more hectic.

If you prefer, put the vegetables on to cook just before sitting down to eat the starter. Make sure they do not overcook.

PROBLEMS AND HANDY TIPS

The vol-au-vents must be really hot before serving them, especially if they were previously frozen.

If the serving dishes and plates are going to warm in the oven with the meat and potatoes, turn the heat down so that they do not get too hot or crack.

The dessert can be a bit tricky to serve as it sometimes cracks while being cut. Don't worry, it will still taste delicious.

Cocktail or drinks party menu

Difficult and time-consuming to prepare
and cook
Cost level: expensive
Serves: 24

17

*There is no break incorporated in this
menu.*

<u>Dips</u>	Guacamole dip or	*Preparation time = 15 minutes*
	Smoked mackerel dip ^{F*}	*Preparation time = 15 minutes*
	served with crudités and	*Preparation time = 15 minutes*
	tortilla chips	*Cooking time = None*
<u>Cold canapes</u>	Parma ham and	*Preparation time = 20 minutes*
	asparagus rolls	*Cooking time = None*
	Smoked salmon turn-ups	*Preparation time = 20 minutes*
	with fresh lime	*Cooking time = None*
	Grape and melon cheese	*Preparation time = 20 minutes*
	sticks	*Cooking time = None*
<u>Hot canapes</u>	Mushroom and coriander	*Preparation time = 30 minutes*
	meatballs^{F*} with mustard	*Cooking time = 45–50 minutes*
	sauce	
	Choux buns^{F*} stuffed	*Preparation time = 40 minutes*
	with Gruyère cheese	*Cooking time = 10–12 minutes*
	Scampi^{F*} with tartare	*Preparation time = 10 minutes*
	sauce	*Cooking time = 20–25 minutes*
	Pizza bits^{F*}	
<u>Drink</u>	Sparkling white wine,	
	chilled, freshly squeezed	
	orange juice – or mix	
	them together to make	
	buck's fizz	

This menu provides lots of ideas for a cocktail party, but it is not necessary to
make everything suggested. Choose 1 dip, 2 or 3 cold canapés and 2 or 3 hot

canapés. Keep in mind how much time and money are available and how many guests you have invited. The salmon and Gruyère cheese are expensive, and don't forget you will have to buy the drinks as well. The recipes serve 24 people, but you can easily double or halve the quantities depending on how many people you expect.

Nearly all the canapés can be made the day before needed. Check the countdown instructions to see which canapés suit the time available. Remember, you can always serve some shop-bought canapés with your home-made ones to fill out the menu. Ready-made canapés, such as scampi, mini pizzas, savoury tartlets and vol-au-vents, are widely available, and useful if you anticipate a lot of hungry guests. Buy some extra pâté and biscuits, or some French bread, plus crisps and nuts as fillers. If you are going to make the choux buns yourself, turn to the recipes on page 207. If time is short, buy ready-made buns, which will allow you more time to make the Gruyère filling.

Finger food can be messy to eat, so don't forget to buy cocktail sticks and lots of napkins.

MENU 17

Equipment needed – Menu 17

Dips and accompaniments

1 savoury chopping board
1 sharp knife
1 mixing bowl or food processor
1 fork or savoury wooden spoon
1 tablespoon
1 teaspoon
2 serving bowls
1 large bowl
1 small bowl
1 serving platter

Cold canapés

Parma ham and asparagus rolls
 1 tin opener
 1 fine sieve
 6 sheets greaseproof paper
 1 sharp knife
 1 roasting tin
 1 savoury chopping board
 kitchen paper
 1 round-ended knife
 1 baking tray or roasting tin
Smoked salmon turn-ups with fresh lime
 1 savoury chopping board
 1 round-ended knife
 1 sharp knife
 1 baking tray
 1 sheet greaseproof paper
 1 potato peeler
 1 lemon squeezer
 1 pastry brush
Grape and melon cheese sticks
 1 savoury chopping board
 1 sharp knife
 1 packet cocktail sticks
 1 colander
 1 plate

Hot canapés

Mushroom and coriander meatballs with mustard sauce
1 large mixing bowl
1 food processor or sharp knife
1 savoury chopping board

Shopping list – Menu 17

Dips and accompaniments

Smoked mackerel dip
 8oz/225g smoked mackerel fillets
 8oz/225g cream cheese
 8oz/225g cottage cheese
 3 tablespoons sour cream
 *salt and freshly ground black pepper
 *3 teaspoons of lemon or lime juice
 fresh or frozen parsley to decorate
Guacamole dip
 *1 small onion
 1 large or 2 small ripe avocados
 *2 teaspoons lemon juice
 8oz/225g curd cheese
 1 medium tomato
 *2 teaspoons Tabasco sauce
 *salt
 *1 teaspoon cayenne pepper
 ½ teaspoon ground coriander
Accompaniments
 selection of fresh vegetables, such as mixed
  peppers (red, green, or yellow), celery,
  carrots, cauliflower, cucumber or
  tortilla chips, plain or spicy

Cold canapés

Parma ham and asparagus rolls
 1 tin (12oz/350g) asparagus tips
 16 slices brown bread
 6oz/175g butter or margarine
 16 slices parma ham (approx. the same size
  as a slice of bread)
Smoked salmon turn-ups with fresh lime
 8–10oz/225–275g sliced smoked salmon
 12 slices brown bread
 *4oz/100g butter or margarine
 1 lime
 *freshly ground black pepper
 small bunch fresh parsley (optional)
Grape and melon cheese sticks
 8–10oz/225–275g mature Cheddar cheese
 1 ripe honeydew melon
 12 black seedless grapes
 12 white seedless grapes

1 savoury wooden spoon
1 teaspoon
2 small mixing bowls
1 baking tray or roasting tin
1 tablespoon
1 large serving platter
1 small serving bowl
Choux bun filling
  1 savoury wooden spoon
  1 sharp knife
  1 medium saucepan
  1 tablespoon
  1 flexible spatula
  1 cheese grater
  1 plate
  1 measuring jug
  1 teaspoon
  1 piping bag with small–medium nozzle
  (optional)
Scampi and pizza bits
  2 baking trays
  1 fish slice
  1 sharp knife
  1 serving platter

  Cocktail sticks
  Napkins

Hot canapés

**Mushroom and coriander meatballs with
  mustard sauce**
  2lb/900g lean minced beef
  *1 onion
  *2 pieces of bread to make fresh
    breadcrumbs
  8oz/225g button mushrooms
  *1 egg
  *salt, pepper, mustard powder, nutmeg
  1 bunch fresh coriander leaves or 1 teaspoon
    dried coriander
  *1oz/25g (1 tablespoon) plain flour
  *1oz/25g (1 tablespoon) dried breadcrumbs
  2 tablespoons natural yoghurt
  2 teaspoons whole grain mustard
Choux buns stuffed with Gruyère cheese
  *1 small onion
  *2oz/50g (2 tablespoons) cooking margarine
  8oz/225g Gruyère cheese
  *2oz/50g (2 tablespoons) plain flour
  *12 fl oz/375ml milk
  *white pepper, cayenne pepper
  *1 teaspoon fresh mustard
Scampi with tartare sauce
  2lb/900g fresh **or** frozen scampi in
    breadcrumbs
  1 small jar tartare sauce
Pizza bits
  fresh **or** frozen pizza bits
Optional extras
  assorted crisps and nuts
  biscuits
  French bread
  pâté
Garnishes
  1 bunch watercress
  fresh parsley
  fresh coriander
  cherry tomatoes

*Check store cupboard

MENU 17

Countdown – Menu 17

Canapés can be very time-consuming to prepare and cook, so make your selection keeping in mind your budget and how much time is available. If you are a slow cook, add 5–10 minutes for each canapé to ensure that you do not run out of time. Remember, the times given are only a guide as each cook takes different lengths of time to complete each task. Make as much as possible the day before to give yourself enough time on the night to complete all the last-minute tasks. If you are going to make the choux buns yourself, turn to the recipe on page 207. The buns can be made the day before, but should be filled only a few hours before the party.

Mushroom and coriander meatballs with mustard sauce

PROBLEMS AND HANDY TIPS

> *Preparation time: 30 minutes*
> *Cooking time: 45–50 minutes*

Assemble all the ingredients and equipment you need for this recipe. A food processor can be used to mix all the ingredients together, if you have one. Set your timer for 30 minutes. Preheat the oven to 200°C/400°F/Gas mark 6.

30 mins Take 2lb/900g of lean minced beef and place in a large mixing bowl. Peel and finely chop 1 onion and add to the meat. If you are making your own breadcrumbs, place two slices of bread on a chopping board and use a sharp knife to chop the bread as finely as possible. Add to the bowl along with 1 tablespoon tomato purée and mix well.

If you are using a food processor, make the breadcrumbs first, then set them aside. Next, process the onion followed by the meat, mushrooms, egg and coriander. Season well and then add the breadcrumbs.

See Handy Tip 3, page xvii for an easy way to make breadcrumbs from frozen bread.

22 mins Wash the mushrooms well, discarding the stalks. Chop roughly and add to the bowl with the meat. Break 1 egg into the mixture and mix well using either a wooden spoon or your clean hands. Season with salt, pepper, a pinch of mustard powder and nutmeg, and some chopped fresh

Make sure the seasoning is mixed in thoroughly before making the meatballs.

146

coriander leaves or a heaped teaspoon of dried coriander.

14 mins Place 1oz/25g (1 tablespoon) each of plain flour and dried breadcrumbs in a small bowl, season with a pinch of salt and freshly ground black pepper, mix well and set aside.

12 mins Using your hands, form the meat mixture into at least 24 bite-size balls. (The quantity given will make as many as 36, depending on the size of the balls.)

6 mins Roll each meatball in the seasoned flour and breadcrumb mixture so that they are completely coated. Place on a baking tray or in a roasting tin and put into the preheated oven for 40 minutes.

2 mins To make the mustard sauce, place 2 tablespoons of natural yoghurt in a small bowl, add 2 teaspoons of whole grain mustard and mix well. Cover and chill until required.

0 mins Wash up and clear away.

Smoked mackerel dip

Preparation time: 15 minutes
Cooking time: None

Assemble all the ingredients and equipment you need for this dip. It will be smoother and quicker to make if you use a food processor. Set your timer for 15 minutes.

15 mins Take 8oz/225g of mackerel fillets and remove the skin, either by pulling it away with your fingers or using a sharp knife. It should come away easily. Remove any visible bones.

10 mins Place the fillets in a bowl and mash with a fork or wooden spoon. Add 8oz/225g of cream cheese and mix well. Now add 8oz/225g of cottage cheese and 3 tablespoons of sour cream and beat thoroughly to form a slightly textured mixture.

3 mins Season with fresh ground black pepper and 3 teaspoons of lemon or lime juice. Taste the dip before adding salt as mackerel can be very salty.

See Cookery Terms, page 224 for a definition of seasoned flour.

Keep the meatballs small so that your guests can eat them easily.

PROBLEMS AND HANDY TIPS

If you have a food processor, place the fish in the bowl and blend well.

Add the cream cheese, cottage cheese and sour cream to the processor and blend again.

For a smooth, fine dip, keep the machine running for a minute or two longer.

MENU 17

Place in a serving dish and chill until required.
0 mins Wash up and clear away.

Guacamole dip

Preparation time: 15 minutes
Cooking time: None

Assemble all the ingredients and equipment you
need for the guacamole dip. Using a food processor
will save you time and energy. Set your timer for 15
minutes.

If you have a food processor,
prepare the onion, then add the
avocado. Add the other
ingredients as directed, blending
in each one. Don't overblend; the
dip is best if slightly textured.

15 mins Peel and finely chop 1 onion and place it
in a mixing bowl.
16 mins Cut 1 large or 2 small ripe avocados in
half lengthways and remove the stone. Spoon the
flesh out of the skins into the mixing bowl. Add 2
teaspoons of lemon juice and mash with a fork to
form a paste.
12 mins Add 8oz/225g curd cheese to the bowl
and mix well.
8 mins Take 1 tomato, wash it well and cut it in
half. Remove the stalk and 'eye', then chop finely.
Add to the avocado and mix well.
4 mins Season with 2 teaspoons of Tabasco sauce,
a generous pinch of salt, 1 teaspoon of cayenne
pepper and ½ teaspoon of ground coriander. Taste
to see if it is to your liking. The seasoning can be
adjusted again before serving.

Take care adding the Tabasco;
some people prefer not to have
things too spicy.

1 min Place the guacamole in a serving bowl and
chill until required.
0 mins Wash up and clear away.

Crudités

Preparation time: 15 minutes
Cooking time: None

Crudités are raw vegetables designed to serve
with dips. Assemble all the ingredients and
equipment you need. Set your timer for 15
minutes.

15 mins Peel the carrots and cut into sticks approximately 2 inches/5 cm long.
10 mins Wash the celery and peppers under cold running water. Slice the peppers in half, discard the seeds and stalks and slice the flesh into similar sized strips to the carrots. Remove any large strings from the celery and slice to match the carrots and peppers.

Wash the halved peppers under cold water to remove any stray seeds.

5 mins Wash the cucumber and peel it if the skin looks blemished and tough. Cut it into quarters and then make sticks roughly the same size as the other vegetables. Place the cucumber in a small bowl, cover and set aside. Wash the cauliflower and cut it into small sprigs.

If it is a very hot day, add some ice-cubes to the cold water for the vegetables; this will keep them really cool and crisp.

The cucumber strips would become soggy if placed in cold water.

1 min Place all the vegetables (except the cucumber) in a large bowl. Fill the bowl with ice-cold water, cover with cling film or a tea towel and set aside until required.
0 mins Wash up and clear away.

Do not dry the vegetables before serving them. Leave them damp as this makes them look particularly fresh.

Parma ham and asparagus rolls

PROBLEMS AND HANDY TIPS

Preparation time: 20 minutes
Cooking time: None

The rolls are best made the day before. Place them in a tin tightly packed together and chill for a minimum of 8 hours. Each roll should be sliced into 3 before serving (allow 2 rolls per person).

Be careful if using an old roasting tin as rust can discolour the rolls. Wash and dry the tin well, then line it with a large piece of cling film.

Assemble all the ingredients and equipment you need for the rolls. Set your timer for 20 minutes.
20 mins Open the tin of asparagus, discard the liquid and leave the asparagus to drain in a fine sieve.
18 mins Take a sheet of greaseproof paper 56 inches/142 cm long and fold it like a concertina into 7 inch/18 cm strips. Using a sharp knife, cut along the creases. Cut the resulting strips in half again to double the quantity. Make a total of 16 pieces.

If you prefer, you can simply cut individual strips of paper that will be large enough for each roll.

15 mins Place all the paper in a roasting tin, pour some warm water over it and allow it to soak.

MENU 17

14 mins Arrange 16 slices of bread on a chopping board. Spread each slice evenly with butter or margarine. Stack the buttered bread on a chopping board and cut off all the crusts.

10 mins Take 1 strip of wet greaseproof paper and pat dry with kitchen paper so that it is only damp. Place a slice of bread on the greaseproof paper. Place 1 slice of parma ham on to the bread and put 1 asparagus tip along one end of it. Holding the asparagus in place, roll it up in the bread, then roll the paper around the bread as tightly as possible. Prepare all the rolls in this way.

3 mins Place the finished rolls in a roasting tin or on a baking tray. Pack them tightly together so that they hold their shape. Chill for a minimum of 8 hours, or until required.

0 mins Wash up and clear away.

Smoked salmon turn-ups with fresh lime

Preparation time: 20 minutes
Cooking time: None

Assemble all the ingredients and equipment you need for the turn-ups. Set your timer for 20 minutes.

20 mins Unwrap the salmon and set it aside to breathe before using it. Arrange 12 slices of brown bread on a chopping board. Spread each slice evenly and generously with butter or margarine. Arrange the bread in a stack, then cut off all the crusts.

15 mins Prepare a baking tray by spreading a sheet of damp greaseproof paper on it.

13 mins Cut the buttered bread into quarters so that you have 48 individual squares.

10 mins Place a small piece of salmon on each square. Carefully pull all four corners into the centre and squeeze together hard to form a neat parcel with the salmon forced out of the middle. Repeat with all the squares, then place the finished parcels on the prepared baking tray.

If the butter is very hard, soften it in a microwave oven or by beating it in a bowl with a wooden spoon.

Practice will enable you to roll up the bread more quickly and neatly.

Make sure the greaseproof paper doesn't get rolled inside the bread. It must be rolled only around the outside to keep it together.

PROBLEMS AND HANDY TIPS

Allowing the salmon to breathe before using it helps the flavour and aroma to develop.

If the butter is very hard, soften it in a microwave oven or place it in a mixing bowl and beat hard with a wooden spoon.

The butter on the bread should keep the parcel stuck together.

4 mins Take 1 fresh lime and use a potato peeler or sharp knife to remove some of the zest (green skin). Cut the lime in half and squeeze 1 half. Using a pastry brush, brush each parcel with a little lime juice, then grind some black pepper on top.
2 mins Finely chop the lime zest and sprinkle over each parcel; if time is short, sprinkle with freshly chopped parsley instead. Cover the baking tray with another sheet of damp greaseproof paper to keep the turn-ups moist, then cover with cling film. Chill for a minimum of 1 hour before serving.
0 mins Wash up and clear away.

The lime zest makes a colourful garnish on each parcel. The remaining lime half should be cut into slices or thin wedges and used to garnish the platter of salmon turn-ups.

Grape and melon cheese sticks

PROBLEMS AND HANDY TIPS

Preparation time: 20 minutes
Cooking time: None

Assemble all the ingredients and equipment you need for the cheese sticks. Set your timer for 20 minutes.
20 mins Take 8–10oz/225–275g of mature Cheddar cheese and cut into 48 cubes about ¾ inch/2 cm square (24 for the grapes and 24 for the melon).
15 mins Cut the melon in half around the middle. Using a spoon, scoop out all the pips and discard them. Cut the melon into quarters, then slide a sharp knife under the flesh to remove the skin. Chop the flesh into 24 pieces that are roughly the same size as the cubes of cheese.
10 mins Place a cube of melon on a cube of cheese, then push a cocktail stick through both. Arrange the finished sticks on a plate. If you have any melon left over, cube it and place it in a bowl with cocktail sticks beside it for people to help themselves.
5 mins Wash and dry the grapes, then push each one on to a cocktail stick with a cube of cheese. Arrange on the plate with the melon sticks, cover with greaseproof paper and cling film, and chill until required.
0 mins Wash up and clear away.

Try to slide the knife as close to the melon skin as possible so as not to lose too much of the flesh.

Insert the sticks carefully so that the melon and cheese don't split and fall off.

The grapes should be seedless. If you have bought grapes with seeds, you will have to cut them in half and remove them. Put half a grape with each piece of cheese, alternating between white and black grapes to give lots of colour.

MENU 17

Choux buns stuffed with Gruyère cheese

Preparation time: 40 minutes
Cooking time: 10–12 minutes

Assemble all the ingredients and equipment you need for the filling. Set your timer for 20 minutes.

20 mins Peel and chop 1 small onion as finely as possible and place in a medium saucepan. Add 2oz/ 50g (2 tablespoons) of cooking margarine, then put over a medium heat to soften.

Make sure the onion is very finely chopped as it will have to pass through the nozzle of a piping bag when filling the buns.

15 mins Meanwhile, grate 8oz/225g of Gruyère cheese on to a plate. Stir the onion and turn down the heat if it is colouring too quickly.

12 mins Once the onion has softened, remove from the heat and add 2oz/50g (2 tablespoons) of plain flour. Mix well to form a roux. Put it back over a low heat and cook for 2–3 minutes. Remove from the heat and allow to cool.

8 mins Measure out 12 fl oz/375ml of milk and pour it into the roux. Stir well, making sure that no lumps appear. When the mixture is smooth, put the saucepan back over a low heat and allow the sauce to thicken, stirring constantly. Cook for 2–3 minutes, then remove from the heat and leave to cool slightly.

If the sauce becomes lumpy at any time, stop adding the milk and beat well or process. Once all the lumps are gone, continue adding the milk gradually.

3 mins Stir in the grated cheese and season with ground white pepper, a pinch of cayenne pepper and 1 teaspoon of fresh mustard. Set the sauce aside.

Do not cook the cheese or it will become stringy

0 mins Wash up and clear away.

Assemble all the ingredients and equipment you need to fill the choux buns. Reset your timer for 20 minutes. Preheat the oven to 200°C/400°F/Gas mark 6.

20 mins Take a piping bag, if you have one, and insert a small nozzle. Fill the bag with the cheese sauce, then push the nozzle into the hole already made in a choux bun. Squeeze the bag gently and fill the bun, being careful not to overfill it. (Once it starts to puff up and you can see the filling, stop.)

If the filling is very stringy and difficult to handle, use a knife to cut the mixture off at the nozzle. Fill all the buns in this way.

If you don't have a piping bag, cut the buns in half and use a teaspoon and a knife to insert some filling in both halves. When they are all filled, slide them back together again. You will find that this works very well as the filling is very sticky.

2 mins Place the filled buns on a baking tray and put in the preheated oven for 10–12 minutes to warm them through.

0 mins Wash up and clear away.

Twist the top of the piping bag firmly once it is full of sauce and hold it closed. Squeeze the top of the bag when filling the buns – the sauce should flow out easily. If the mixture stops flowing, push a sharp knife into the nozzle to release the blockage: it is likely to be a small piece of onion.

Only heat the buns now if you are going to serve them immediately.

Serving the cold canapés

PROBLEMS AND HANDY TIPS

Take the parma ham and asparagus rolls out of the fridge and carefully remove the greaseproof paper. Using a very sharp knife, slice the rolls into 3 pieces (4 if they are very large). Place on a serving platter.

Take the smoked salmon turn-ups out of the fridge, remove the cling film and paper, then arrange them on the same platter as the rolls. Garnish with sprigs of watercress, fresh parsley and a few wedges or slices of lime. Cover with cling film to keep moist if you are not going to serve them immediately.

The cheese sticks should be served on a separate platter garnished with a few cherry tomatoes to add colour.

Remember to put out some extra nibbles such as crisps and nuts. These will help to fill out the menu.

Serving the hot canapés

PROBLEMS AND HANDY TIPS

The meatballs should be placed on a baking tray or in a roasting tin and heated in the oven for 15–20 minutes. The choux buns will need only 10–12 minutes.

If you are serving ready-made pizzas and scampi, cook them according to the instructions on the packets.

Once they have warmed through, arrange the hot canapés on large platters. Don't forget to place

If there are too many hot canapés to be heated up at one time, put a mixed selection on 2 baking trays. Once these are hot serve them, while the next batch can be heated through.

MENU 17

the bowl of mustard sauce in the centre of the
meatballs and a bowl of tartare sauce in the centre
of the scampi. Garnish the platters with sprigs of
watercress, parsley or coriander and cherry tomatoes to add colour. Make sure you provide napkins
and an egg-cup containing cocktail sticks to be
passed around with the canapés.

Don't forget to remind your
guest that the canapés are very
hot. Hand round some paper
napkins at the same time as the
canapés so your guests can help
themselves.

Summer lunch or dinner buffet menu

18

Difficult to prepare and cook
Cost level: expensive
Serves: 12

A flexible break is incorporated in this menu.

Starter	Spinach and Gruyère roulade F*	Preparation time = 60 minutes Cooking time = 12–15 minutes
Main course	Cold roast beef with horseradish cream	Preparation time = 10 minutes Cooking time = 60 minutes
	Cold chicken in a tomato and basil sauce F*	Preparation time = 35 minutes Cooking time = 10–15 minutes
	Cold new potatoes with fresh chives	Preparation time = 15 minutes Cooking time = 15–20 minutes
	Mixed bean salad with walnut dressing	Preparation time = 25 minutes Cooking time = None
	Watercress and pepper salad	Preparation time = 10 minutes Cooking time = None
Dessert	Fresh fruit salad with cream	Preparation time = 35 minutes Cooking time = None
	Mixed cheese platter with biscuits	
Drink	Why not give your guests a choice – chilled crisp, dry white or fruity red wine	

This is a good summer lunch or dinner buffet menu. It caters for 12 people, but you can halve or double the quantities to suit. Everything can be eaten with a fork, which means that people don't have to sit down formally. Most of the menu can be prepared and cooked in advance, leaving only the salads to be made a few

MENU 18

hours before the party. There is a lot of preparation, but once everything is cooked, the whole menu is served cold, so there are very few last-minute tasks, which gives you time to relax and prepare yourself for the party. If you have invited some vegetarian guests, it would be a good idea to replace the chicken or beef with a vegetarian main course from another menu. The starter, salads and dessert will suit all dietary preferences.

The starter can be made the day before and chilled until the party. The roast beef should be cooked the day before to allow it to cool. A few hours before the party, it can be sliced as thinly as possible, placed on a large plate and garnished. For the chicken in basil and tomato sauce you will need a pre-cooked chicken. Turn to the additional recipes on page 210 for instructions on how to poach a chicken yourself. If time is very short, you can always buy a ready-cooked chicken. The meat must be sliced off the carcass before adding it to the sauce and chilling. The salads are made a few hours before serving, but not dressed until the last minute. Don't forget you will need a French dressing: turn to page 201 if you want to make your own, or buy a ready-made one.

The fruit salad can be made the day before, but it is best to add the soft fruits just before serving so that they don't go soggy. Serve the fruit salad with fresh cream and dessert biscuits. Offer a cheese platter as well as the dessert for those guests who prefer savoury to sweet, or who like both.

Equipment needed – Menu 18

Starter

2 standard high-sided roasting tins
1 pastry brush
4 large sheets of greaseproof paper
1 colander
1 large saucepan
1 measuring jug
1 savoury chopping board
1 sharp knife
1 medium saucepan
1 savoury wooden spoon
1 medium mixing bowl
1 large mixing bowl
1 tablespoon
1 small saucepan or bowl
1 balloon whisk or hand-held electric mixer
1 cheese grater
1 teaspoon

Main course

Cold roast beef
1 medium roasting tin
1 tablespoon
3 small bowls
1 large plate
1 carving knife
1 large serving platter
1 pair kitchen scissors
Cold chicken
1 savoury chopping board
1 sharp knife
1 medium saucepan with lid
1 tablespoon
1 savoury spatula
1 wine glass
1 teaspoon
1 mixing bowl
1 savoury wooden spoon
1 serving bowl
Cold new potatoes
1 large saucepan
1 sharp knife
1 colander
1 serving dish
1 pair of kitchen scissors

Shopping list – Menu 18

Starter

1½lb/675g fresh spinach
*1 tablespoon vegetable oil
*salt, pepper, nutmeg, mustard powder
12oz/350g button mushrooms
*6 eggs
*1oz/25g of butter or margarine
*2oz/50g (2 tablespoons) cooking margarine
6oz/175g Gruyère cheese
*1 teaspoon lemon juice
*1oz/25g (1 tablespoon) plain flour
8oz/225g sour cream
2–3 long French loaves

Main course

Cold roast beef
*1 tablespoon dripping fat
3lb/1.3kg beef off the bone (topside, top rump, silverside), 4–6oz/100–175g per person
*salt and freshly ground black pepper
1 punnet fresh mustard and cress
1 small jar horseradish cream
Cold chicken
*1 onion
*1 tablespoon cooking margarine
*1 tablespoon tomato purée
*½ glass red wine
1 small jar Italian spicy tomato sauce
*1 teaspoon brown sugar
*salt and freshly ground black pepper
1 large bunch fresh basil
2 medium chickens, raw or pre-cooked
*4 tablespoons mayonnaise
Cold new potatoes
4lb/1.75kg baby new potatoes (approx. 3 per person)
3–4 sprigs fresh mint
*salt
1 big bunch fresh chives
Mixed bean salad with walnut dressing
1lb/450g French beans
*salt, pepper
3 heads red chicory
1 small bunch spring onions
8oz/225g beansprouts

MENU 18

Mixed bean salad
  1 *savoury chopping board*
  1 *sharp knife*
  1 *colander*
  1 *medium saucepan*
  1 *large bowl*
  1 *tin opener*
  1 *fine sieve*
  1 *tablespoon*
  1 *large jam jar with tight-fitting lid*
  1 *teaspoon*
  1 *garlic crusher (or see page xvii)*
  1 *lemon squeezer*
  1 *plate*
  1 *large serving bowl*

Watercress and pepper salad
  1 *savoury chopping board*
  1 *sharp knife*
  1 *colander*
  1 *serving bowl*
  1 *small mixing bowl*
  1 *tablespoon*

Dessert
  1 *colander*
  1 *sweet chopping board* **or** a *plate*
  1 *sharp knife*
  1 *large serving bowl*
  1 *measuring jug*
  1 *tablespoon*
  1 *teaspoon*
  1 *potato peeler*
  1 *cheese platter and knife*

1 tin (14oz/400g) cannellini beans
9 tablespoons walnut oil
*3 tablespoons wine vinegar
*1 teaspoon sugar
1 clove garlic (optional)
1 orange
3oz/75g chopped walnuts

Watercress and pepper salad
*½ pint/300ml French dressing (see page 201)
3 mixed peppers, red, green and yellow
2–3 bunches watercress
4oz/100g sour cream

Garnishes
black and white grapes
fresh parsley
cherry tomatoes

Dessert

selection of summer fruits such as:
  2 green apples **or** pears
  1 large punnet strawberries
  1 large punnet raspberries
  2 ripe peaches **or** nectarines
  1lb/450g white seedless grapes
  3 kiwi fruits
  1 ripe honeydew melon
  2 bananas
¼ pint/150ml pure apple juice
¼ pint/150ml pure orange juice
*1–2 tablespoons caster sugar
1 tablespoon liqueur such as kirsch, Grand Marnier **or** calvados (optional)
1 pint/600ml single cream **or** 1 large tub vanilla ice cream
1 packet dessert biscuits of your choice
selection of cheese and biscuits
*8oz/225g butter **or** margarine

Check store cupboard

Countdown – Menu 18

If you want to prepare the whole menu, you will need 220 minutes (3 hours 40 minutes); this doesn't include the flexible break. If you are a slow cook, add 5–10 minutes to each course to ensure that you do not run out of time. Remember, the times given are only a guide as each cook will take different lengths of time to complete each task. Nearly all the dishes except the salads can be made in advance and frozen; some should be made a few days ahead, others only a few hours. The salads should be prepared 2 or 3 hours before the party, but not dressed.

Remember to prepare as much as possible before-hand so that there is less to do during the party. Don't forget you will need 2 cooked chickens; these can be bought ready-cooked or you can cook them yourself. If they are frozen, they must be defrosted at least 12 hours before preparing the dish.

Starter

PROBLEMS AND HANDY TIPS

Preparation time: 60 minutes
Cooking time: 12–15 minutes

Assemble all the ingredients and equipment you need for the starter. Set your timer for 60 minutes.
60 mins Take 1½lb/675g of fresh spinach, place it in a sink of cold water and soak for a few minutes.
58 mins Prepare the roulade tins by brushing a small amount of vegetable oil over the bottom and sides. Place 1 large sheet of greaseproof paper in each tin, folding it into the corners. Brush the paper with oil and set aside.
53 mins Finish washing the spinach. Discard any long stalks and brown or tough leaves. Place the spinach in a colander and allow to drain.
48 mins Fill the kettle and put it on to boil.
47 mins Place the drained spinach in a large saucepan and pour no more than ¼ pint/150ml

It is important to wash the spinach well, as it is often full of sand and grit.

Make sure you grease the corners and sides really well or you will have great difficulty removing the paper after the roulade has cooked.

Once the spinach starts to cook it will reduce dramatically, so only a small quantity of water is necessary.

of boiling water over it. Add a pinch of salt, place over a medium heat and cook for approximately 4–5 minutes. Preheat the oven to 200°C/400°F/ Gas mark 6.

45 mins Meanwhile, take 12oz/350g of button mushrooms, wash them well and remove the stalks. Chop the mushrooms, wash them well and place them in a medium-sized saucepan. Stir the spinach, pushing it down into the water.

Do not chop the mushrooms too finely as they give the filling a good texture.

40 mins Drain the spinach in a colander and run some cold water over it to stop it cooking. Press the spinach lightly with a wooden spoon to remove any excess water.

38 mins Put the spinach in a medium mixing bowl. Separate 6 eggs, putting the yolks into a bowl with the spinach and the whites into a separate large mixing bowl. Mix the spinach and egg yolks together.

See Handy Tip 2, page xvii for an easy way to separate eggs.

32 mins Take 1oz/25g (1 tablespoon) of butter or margarine and melt over a low heat or in a microwave oven. Pour the melted butter into the spinach mixture and season with salt, freshly ground pepper and a pinch of nutmeg.

Season the spinach well; once the roulades are cooked, there is no opportunity to do so.

29 mins Using either a balloon whisk or hand-held electric mixer, whisk the egg whites until they are stiff and able to hold their shape.

It is important that the egg whites are stiff and will stand in peaks before being added to the spinach mixture.

24 mins Take a metal spoon and carefully fold the egg whites into the spinach, keeping as much air in the mixture as possible. Pour it into the prepared tins and place in the preheated oven for approximately 12–16 minutes, or until the roulade is set.

Do not keep opening the oven door while the roulades are cooking or they will not be light and fluffy.

22 mins While the roulades are cooking, add 2oz/ 50g (2 tablespoons) of cooking margarine to the mushrooms in the saucepan and put over a low heat to cook.

20 mins Take 6oz/175g Gruyère cheese and grate it on to a plate. Set aside.

17 mins Check the mushrooms, If they have become soft and juicy, season with salt, pepper, a pinch of nutmeg and a pinch of mustard powder. Stir in 1 teaspoon of lemon juice, then turn the heat off.

Do not overcook the mushrooms. They are more delicious if left with a bit of texture.

15 mins Add 1oz/25g (1 tablespoon) of plain flour to the mushrooms. Put the saucepan back over a low heat and cook for 2 minutes, stirring all the time to remove the floury taste. Remove the saucepan from the heat and stir in the grated cheese and 6oz/175g (6 tablespoons) of the sour cream. Mix well. The mixture will be very thick at this stage. Set aside.

10 mins Take 2 sheets of greaseproof paper, each large enough for a roulade, and place them on a large chopping board or work surface. Check the roulades in the oven; when cooked, they should be firm but light and springy to the touch.

8 mins Once the roulades are cooked, take them out of the oven and place each one upside-down on a sheet of greaseproof paper. Carefully peel off the paper they cooked in, trying not to break the roulade.

5 mins Once all the paper has been removed, carefully spread the filling over the roulades, making sure you cover the whole surface.

3 mins Roll up the roulades, ensuring that the greaseproof paper underneath does not roll inside with the filling. Don't worry if some of the filling spills out – spoon it into a bowl and serve it separately. Wrap the greaseproof paper around the finished roulade to keep it together, leave to cool and then chill until required. Before serving, remove the greaseproof paper and cut the roulades into thin slices.

0 mins Wash up and clear away.

The roulades might need to be swapped around in the oven to allow them to cook evenly.

It is important to have the greaseproof paper ready in advance so that the cooked roulades can be placed straight on to it.

Any extra filling should be thinned with a little extra sour cream to make a sauce which can be served alongside the chilled roulades.

PROBLEMS AND HANDY TIPS

Main course
Cold roast beef with horseradish cream

Preparation time: 10 minutes
Cooking time: 60 minutes
Chilling time: 4 hours minimum

Use the following chart regardless of whether the meat is on or off the bone, or rolled.
Rare: allow 20 minutes per 1lb/450g, plus 15 minutes extra at the end of the cooking time.

MENU 18

Medium: allow 25 minutes per 1lb/450g, plus 20 minutes extra at the end of the cooking time.
Well done: allow 30 minutes per 1lb/450g, plus 30 minutes extra at the end of cooking time.

Assemble all the ingredients and equipment you need for the roast beef. Set your timer for 10 minutes. Preheat the oven to 220°C/425°F/Gas mark 7.

10 mins Take a roasting tin, add 1 tablespoon of dripping or fat, and place in the oven to melt.

8 mins Note the weight of the beef and calculate the correct roasting time based on the time chart.

6 mins Take the beef out of the packaging. Don't worry if there is a lot of fat surrounding it; this will help to keep the meat moist and basted while cooking, but it should be removed after cooking.

4 mins When the fat in the roasting tin has melted, take the tin out of the oven and place the beef in the centre of it. Season with a little salt and ground black pepper and place on the top shelf of the oven to cook.

0 mins Wash up and clear away.

Check the beef halfway through the cooking time and baste it. If it is becoming too brown on top, turn it over. When the beef is cooked, take it out of the oven and pour off the fat and sediment into a small bowl. Place the beef on a plate and allow to cool at room temperature. Take the bowl with the fat and sediment and carefully spoon all the fat into another bowl. Pour the remaining sediment over the cooked beef to keep it moist. When the meat is cool, cover it with cling film and place in the fridge to chill for a minimum of 4 hours.

Cold chicken in a tomato and basil sauce

Preparation time: 35 minutes
Cooking time: 10–15 minutes
Chilling time: 1 hour minimum

Assemble all the ingredients and equipment you need for the sauce. Turn to the additional recipes

Don't forget that the cooking times might vary slightly depending on how hot your oven is and what cut of beef you are cooking.

You can mix cooking oil with cooking margarine if you don't have any dripping.

If the meat doesn't have any fat around it, cover it in aluminium foil to prevent it burning.

See Cookery Terms, page 222, for a definition of 'baste'.

It is important to pour the sediment over the beef so it does not dry out.

PROBLEMS AND HANDY TIPS

on page 210 if you are going to cook the chicken yourself. Set your timer for 35 minutes.

35 mins Peel and chop 1 onion. Place it in a medium-sized saucepan with 1oz/25g (1 tablespoon) of cooking margarine and put over a medium to low heat to soften.

30 mins Add 1 tablespoon of tomato purée to the onion, followed by ½ glass of red wine, 2 heaped tablespoons of spicy tomato sauce and 1 teaspoon of brown sugar. Season with a pinch of salt and freshly ground black pepper.

25 mins Take a large bunch of fresh basil leaves, wash them well and shake off any excess water. Set a few leaves aside for garnish, but chop the remainder finely. Add the chopped basil to the other ingredients in the saucepan, put the lid half on and leave to cook on a low heat for 5–10 minutes.

20 minutes While the sauce is cooking take the chicken off the bone. First remove the skin and discard any fat. Now pull the legs away from the body and carefully ease off the meat. Cut or tear it into bite-size pieces. Place the chicken in a mixing bowl, making sure that the white and dark meat are well combined. Set aside. If preparing the meat takes longer than 10 minutes, don't worry: turn off the sauce while you complete the task.

10 mins Take the sauce off the heat and add 4 tablespoons of mayonnaise. Mix well and season with salt and ground black pepper. Add all the sauce to the prepared chicken and mix well. Place in a serving bowl, cover with cling film and chill until required.

0 mins Wash up and clear away.

Dessert

Preparation time: 35 minutes
Cooking time: None

The dessert can be made the day before and kept in the fridge until required. If the strawberries and

The onion can be roughly chopped as it will cook down before being added to the rest of the ingredients.

If you have poached the chicken yourself and would like to make a good stock, place the bones in the poaching liquid and simmer over a low heat for 60 minutes.

Check the seasoning before adding the sauce to the chicken. The meat will absorb the flavours as it chills.

PROBLEMS AND HANDY TIPS

raspberries are very soft, do not add them to the fruit salad until 1–2 hours before serving. The bananas should be added at the last minute to prevent them from discolouring.

Assemble all the ingredients and equipment you need for the dessert. Set your timer for 35 minutes.

35 mins Take all the fruit that needs to be washed, i.e. those that don't need peeling, wash them well and leave to drain.

The apples or pears do not need to be peeled as long as they are smooth and without blemishes.

30 mins Take the apples or pears and cut them into quarters. Remove the core from each quarter, cut the fruit into bite-size pieces and place in a large serving bowl.

25 mins Measure out ¼ pint/150ml of pure apple juice and ¼ pint/150ml of pure orange juice. Pour the juices over the apples or pears and stir well.

22 mins Dry the grapes on kitchen paper. If they are small and seedless, you can leave them whole. If they are large, cut them in half and remove any seeds. Add the grapes to the bowl.

Be warned, de-seeding the grapes is a slow job, so be patient.

18 mins Take the peaches or nectarines and peel them if the skin is rough or blemished. Cut the fruit in half, discard the stone, then slice the flesh into bite-sized pieces. Add to the fruit salad bowl and mix well.

13 mins Remove the stalks from the strawberries and cut the fruit, if very large, into halves or quarters. Add the strawberries and raspberries to the fruit bowl.

If you are making the fruit salad the day before and are worried that the strawberries and raspberries might become too soft, don't add them until a few hours before serving.

9 mins Take the melon and carefully cut it in half. Remove all the seeds using a teaspoon. Cut the melon into quarters then slide a sharp knife between the flesh and the skin. Cut the flesh into bite-sized cubes, add to the fruit bowl and mix well.

4 mins Take the kiwi fruits and peel them using a potato peeler or knife. Cut the flesh into thin slices; these can be left whole or cut in half, whichever you prefer. Take 1 tablespoon of caster sugar and sprinkle it over the fruit salad. Mix all the fruit together and check for sweetness. You might need to add an extra 1–2 tablespoons of caster sugar if the fruit is very tart. If you are going to add some liqueur, do so now and stir well. Cover the fruit bowl with cling film and place in the fridge to chill until required.

0 mins Wash up and clear away.

The bananas should be added just before serving the fruit salad or they will discolour and become soggy.

Do not make the fruit salad too sweet. Put the sugar bowl on the table so that your guests can sweeten the salad to their liking.

Relax

Have a break for as long as you like, but leave yourself at least 1 hour and 20 minutes to prepare the rest of the menu. The roulades, beef, chicken and fruit salad are all complete. You will have only the salads and last-minute tasks to do before the party.

Welcome back

Feeling better after your break?

Main course
New potatoes and Mixed bean salad

PROBLEMS AND HANDY TIPS

Preparation time: 40 minutes
Cooking time: 15–20 minutes

Assemble all the ingredients and equipment you need for the salads. Set your timer for 40 minutes.

40 mins Take 4lb/1.75kg of new potatoes, place them in a sink of warm water and wash well to remove all the soil. Put the potatoes in a large saucepan and cover with cold water. Add a few sprigs of fresh mint and a pinch of salt, place over a medium heat and bring to the boil. Reduce the heat and simmer for approximately 15–20 minutes.

If the potatoes have a lot of earth on them, leave them to soak in warm water for a few minutes. This will loosen the dirt and make it easier to wash them.

MENU 18

35 mins While the potatoes are cooking, prepare the mixed bean salad. Fill the kettle and put it on to boil. Take 1lb/450g of French beans, top and tail them, and place in a colander. Wash well under cold running water.

30 mins Transfer the beans to a medium-sized saucepan, add a pinch of salt and cover with boiling water. Put over a high heat and boil rapidly for 4–5 minutes, or until they are slightly soft but still crunchy.

It is important that the beans retain some 'bite'. It is better to undercook than overcook them.

27 mins Take 3 heads of red chicory, trim the root end, then slice the remainder thinly. Place in a colander, wash well and leave to drain. Take a bunch of spring onions, cut off the roots and remove the outer layer of skin. Chop thinly and place in a large bowl. Add the drained chicory and set aside.

If the chicory has a large white root, it is best to remove it as it can be bitter and unpleasant to eat.

22 mins Check the beans to see if they are cooked. If they are slightly soft but still have 'bite', turn off the heat and drain. Run the beans under cold water to stop them from cooking. Place them on a chopping board, cut them in half and then add them to the bowl with the onions and chicory.

The beans only need to be chopped if they are longer than bite-sized.

19 mins Check the potatoes by piercing them with a sharp knife. If the blade can be inserted easily, they are cooked and should be drained and run under cold water. Leave to cool in a colander.

The potatoes must be cooked but still hold their shape. Do not cook to the point where they fall apart.

16 mins Take 8oz/225g of beansprouts and add them to the salad bowl. Open a tin of cannellini beans, pour them into a fine sieve and discard the liquid. Wash the beans under cold water, shake dry and add to the other ingredients in the bowl. Mix the salad ingredients together well, cover with cling film and place in the fridge to chill.

10 mins To prepare the walnut dressing, place 9 tablespoons of walnut oil in a large jam jar. Add 3 tablespoons of wine vinegar, salt and ground black pepper and 1 teaspoon of sugar. Take 1 clove of garlic, if using, peel and crush it and add to the jar. Cut 1 orange in half and squeeze 1 half. Add the juice to the jam jar, screw the lid on tightly and

The dressing can also be made in a bowl if you do not have a jam jar with fitting lid.

Roll the orange under the palm of your hand on a work surface to release the flesh and increase the quantity of juice when squeezing.

166

shake well. Cut the other half of the orange into quarters, then slice thinly. Put on a plate and set aside to use as a garnish around the sides of the salad bowl. The chopped walnuts and dressing should be added to the salad just before serving.
2 mins Put the cooled potatoes in a serving bowl and cover with cling film. Place in the fridge to chill until required.
0 mins Wash up and clear away.

Watercress and pepper salad

PROBLEMS AND HANDY TIPS

Preparation time: 10 minutes
Cooking time: None

Assemble all the ingredients and equipment you need for the salad. Set your timer for 10 minutes. Turn to page 201 if you are going to make your own French dressing; if not, use a ready-made one.
10 mins Take 3 mixed peppers and cut them in half, discarding the stalk and seeds. Wash well under cold running water, then pat dry on kitchen paper. Chop the peppers finely, trying to keep all the pieces roughly bite-size. Place in a serving bowl and set aside.

Washing the peppers will remove any stray seeds.

4 mins Take the bunches of watercress, twist off the stalks and discard them. Wash well. If the watercress is ready to use, simply remove any long, thick stalks. Add to the peppers in the serving bowl and set aside to chill. The salad will be dressed a few minutes before serving.
0 mins Wash up and clear away.

If the watercress leaves and stalks are very large, it is a good idea to cut them up so that your guests can eat the salad with a fork.

Last-minute tasks

PROBLEMS AND HANDY TIPS

Set your timer for 30 minutes. This is how long you have before laying out the starter and serving.
30 mins Take the beef out of the fridge and slice it as thinly as possible. Arrange it on a plate, pour over all the juice to keep it moist, cover with cling film until you are ready to place it on a large

If you have a bread slicer with a very fine slicing blade, the beef can be carved with it; read the instructions well before using.

platter. Wash the mustard and cress under cold water, shake dry and set aside. Place the horse-radish cream in a small bowl ready to serve with the beef.

20 mins Take the roulades out of the fridge, calculate how many slices you will need, then cut them and place on individual plates. If you are going to serve French bread with the starter, place it in the oven to warm through. Put the butter on the table for your guests to help themselves.

Preheat the oven to 180°C/350°F/ Gas mark 5 for the French bread to warm through.

15 mins Take the potatoes out of the fridge and transfer them to a serving bowl. Wash the chives under cold running water and shake dry. Using a pair of kitchen scissors, snip some of the chives all over the potatoes.

Transfer the potatoes to the serving bowl very carefully as you do not want them to fall apart.

12 mins Take ½ pint/300ml French dressing and place it in a small mixing bowl. Add 4oz/100g of sour cream, mix well and set aside.

The dressing can also be mixed in a jam jar if you have another one available.

10 mins Take the mixed bean salad out of the fridge and transfer it to a serving dish, if necessary. Add 3oz/75g of chopped walnuts to the salad and set aside. The salad will be dressed a few minutes before serving.

Leave the walnuts on top of the salad; they can be tossed into it when you add the dressing.

6 mins Take the fruit salad out of the fridge and transfer it to a serving bowl if necessary. Add the strawberries and raspberries if they are not already included. Peel 2 bananas and slice them into the salad bowl. Mix well and chill until required.

The strawberries, raspberries and bananas can be added a few minutes before serving if you prefer.

1 min Take the French bread out of the oven and slice it; place it in a bread basket and put on the table for your guests to help themselves.

Watch points

PROBLEMS AND HANDY TIPS

Once the buffet has started, it is difficult to predict how long each course will take. The following instructions are given only as a guide.

If you are serving a cheese platter, it is a good idea to put the cheese out so that it has time to breathe. If the party is on a very warm day, put the cheese out only 1 hour before serving. Garnish the platter with a few small bunches of black and white grapes.

Serve the roulade on individual plates with the warm bread. The butter and any extra sauce can be placed on the table for your guests to help themselves.

Place the chicken on a large platter or in a bowl and garnish with a few basil leaves over the top.

The beef, which is already thinly sliced, should be placed on a large platter and garnished with freshly snipped cress all over the top. The horse-radish cream should be placed on the table for your guests to help themselves.

Mix the salad dressings and pour over the appropriate salads; toss well and serve.

Serve the potatoes with any extra fresh chives sprinkled over them.

The fruit salad should be stirred gently before serving. Place the cream or ice cream and dessert biscuits on the table for your guests to help themselves.

Leave the fruit salad and cream in the fridge until it is time to serve, especially if it is a very warm day.

Serve the cheese platter with biscuits and butter at the same time as the dessert for those who might prefer it instead of the fruit salad.

Remember that colour and freshness are very important in garnishes. Extra garnishes could include sliced or cherry tomatoes and sprigs of parsley.

Christmas roast menu

Difficult and time-consuming to prepare and cook
Cost level: expensive
Serves: 4

19

A 40-minute break is incorporated in this menu.

Main course

Roast turkey
Sausage-meat and apple stuffing
Sage and onion stuffing
Chipolata sausages and bacon rolls F*
Roast potatoes, parsnips, carrots and onions
Brussels sprouts with chestnuts
Bread sauce F*
Cranberry sauce and gravy

Preparation time = 146 minutes
Cooking time = 1½–2½ hours

Dessert

Christmas pudding with brandy butter
Mince pies F* with fresh cream

Preparation time = 38 minutes
Cooking time = 6 hours

Preparation time = 25 minutes
Cooking time = 20–25 minutes

Tea

Christmas cake

Preparation time = 45 minutes
Cooking time = 2½ hours

Drink

Chilled Champagne or sparkling wine would start and finish the meal in a festive manner. You might like to serve a full-bodied red or white wine with the main course

Here is a typical Christmas menu which you can adapt to suit your family's likes and dislikes. It is not necessary to cook every dish yourself. If time is short, you can buy a ready-made Christmas cake, pudding and mince pies. If you are going to make the cake and pudding yourself, this should be done a few months in advance as they both gain from maturing over a period of time.

As a starter, you could serve smoked salmon on fresh bread or toast; this always gets the festive meal off to a good start.

When buying the turkey and trimmings keep in mind the amount of space you will have in the oven as almost all the dishes cook at the same time.

Christmas meals are often difficult to cook because most of the dishes have to be prepared on the day. However, the countdown method alleviates much of the last-minute rush because you will prepare as much as possible in advance. This type of menu takes a lot of organization and planning to have all the dishes ready at the same time. Just keep calm, take things a step at a time and you'll have a wonderful day.

Roasting times for turkey

Cuts: Whole birds or pieces
Serving: 8oz–12oz/250–400g per person
Temperature: 180°C/350°F/Gas mark 4
Timing: *Small bird* (6–12lb/2–5½kg), allow 25 minutes per 1lb/450g
Medium bird (12–16lb/5½–7¼kg), allow 20 minutes per 1lb/450g
Large bird (16–25lb/7¼–11¼kg), allow 15–18 minutes per 1lb/450g

MENU 19

Equipment needed – Menu 19

Main course

2 large roasting tins
1 tablespoon
1 savoury wooden board
1 savoury wooden spoon
1 sharp chopping knife
1 mixing bowl
1 small bowl
1 teaspoon
a piece of string or a skewer
1 tin opener
1 round-ended knife
1 small saucepan with lid
1 medium saucepan with lid
wide roll of aluminium foil
kitchen roll

Dessert

Christmas pudding
2 pint/1.2 litre pudding basin
1 teaspoon
1 sweet wooden spoon
1 fine grater
1 sweet chopping board
1 sharp knife
1 lemon squeezer
2 small mixing bowls
1 fork
1 large saucepan with lid
1 tablespoon
string

Brandy butter
1 medium mixing bowl
1 sweet wooden spoon
1 tablespoon

Mince pies
1 mixing bowl
1 tablespoon
1 rolling pin or clean wine bottle
1 3¼ inch/8 cm pastry cutter
1 2¼ inch/6 cm pastry cutter
1 12-hole non-stick bun tin
1 teaspoon
1 small bowl
1 fork
1 pastry brush
1 flexible spatula
1 cooling rack

Shopping list – Menu 19

Main course

Turkey, stuffings, roast vegetables and extras
8oz/225g sausage-meat
*2 medium onions
1 eating apple
*salt and freshly ground black pepper
*2 tablespoons fresh breadcrumbs
*1 teaspoon dried mustard powder
*1 egg
1 packet sage and onion stuffing
1 small/medium (4–6lb/1.7–2.7kg) turkey
*2oz/50g (2 tablespoons) dripping or
   margarine and oil
*4 large potatoes
6 large carrots
4 large parsnips
4 rashers streaky bacon
4–8 chipolata sausages
1 bunch fresh parsley
Brussels sprouts with chestnuts
2lb/900g fresh Brussels sprouts
8oz/225g tinned chestnuts
*2oz/50g (2 tablespoons) butter or
   margarine
Cranberry sauce
½ pint/300ml water
*6oz/175g granulated sugar
8oz/225g fresh or frozen cranberries
Bread sauce
*1 small onion
*4 cloves
½ pint/300ml milk
*salt, pepper, nutmeg, mace
*1 small bay leaf
*2oz/50g (2 tablespoons) fresh breadcrumbs
*1oz/25g (1 tablespoon) butter or margarine
1 tablespoon fresh single cream
*1 tablespoon milk
Gravy
*2 heaped tablespoons plain flour
¾ pint/450ml fresh chicken stock or *1 stock
   cube
*1 glass red wine (optional)
*salt, pepper

Tea

Christmas cake
  8 inch/20 cm cake tin, 3 inch/7.5 cm deep
  1 pencil
  1 pair kitchen scissors
  1 small saucepan or bowl
  1 pastry brush
  1 fine sieve
  1 large mixing bowl
  1 sweet wooden spoon
  1 teaspoon
  2 medium mixing bowls
  1 tablespoon
  1 fine grater
  1 lemon squeezer
  1 sweet chopping board
  1 sharp knife
  1 small mixing bowl
  1 fork
  1 hand-held electric mixer or wooden spoon
  1 flexible spatula
  1 skewer
  1 cooling rack

*Check store cupboard

Dessert

Christmas pudding
  *a little melted butter or margarine
  *4oz/100g plain flour
  *½ level teaspoon each of mixed spice,
    nutmeg, cinnamon
  *6oz/175g fresh breadcrumbs
  6oz/175g finely shredded suet
  6oz/175g soft brown sugar
  2oz/50g chopped walnuts or blanched almonds
  12oz/350g dried mixed fruit
  2oz/50g dried chopped apricots
  1 orange
  *3 eggs
  *salt
  ½ teaspoon almond essence
  2 tablespoons brandy or sherry

Tea

Christmas cake
  *6oz/175g butter or margarine
  *8oz/225g plain flour
  ½ level teaspoon mixed spice
  *½ teaspoon each of cinnamon, grated nutmeg
  1 level teaspoon cocoa powder
  6oz/175g soft brown sugar
  1 tablespoon golden syrup
  1 orange, 1 lemon
  6oz/175g sultanas
  6oz/175g raisins
  8oz/225g dried mixed fruits, including
    apples, pears and peaches
  2oz/50g dried banana chips
  2oz/50g chopped walnuts or blanched almonds
  *4 eggs
  *salt
  (Use any combination of dried fruit and nuts,
    but make sure the total weight is 1½lb/600g.)

Brandy butter
  4oz/100g unsalted butter
  *4oz/100g caster sugar
  1–2 tablespoons brandy

Mince pies
  1 jar (12oz/350g) sweet mincemeat
  *2 tablespoons dry sherry
  8oz/225g shortcrust pastry, shop-bought or
    see recipe, page 203.
  *1–2 tablespoons plain flour
  *1 egg
  *2 tablespoons caster sugar

MENU 19

Countdown – Menu 19

If you want to prepare the whole menu, you will need 294 minutes (4 hours 54 minutes), which includes a 40-minute break. If you are a slow cook, add 5–10 minutes to each course to ensure that you do not run out of time. Remember, the times given are only a guide as each cook will take different lengths of time to complete each task. Try to prepare as much as possible in advance to allow you time to enjoy the day. Remember, the cake, pudding and mince pies can be made well ahead, and the stuffing, bacon rolls and Brussels sprouts can be partially made in advance. Read through the countdown carefully and decide what you are going to cook and when. Don't forget to calculate the turkey's cooking time in advance so that it has plenty of time to cook and rest. If you plan to eat at lunchtime, you will probably have to put the turkey on to cook early in the morning.

Tea
Christmas cake

> *Preparation time: 45 minutes*
> *Cooking time: 2½ hours*

Assemble all the ingredients and equipment you need for the Christmas cake. Set your timer for 45 minutes.

45 mins Prepare and line an 8 inch/20 cm cake tin (preferably loose-bottomed or spring-release). Place the tin on a sheet of greaseproof paper and draw around the base; cut out the shape just inside the pencil mark to ensure a tight fit. Cut a long strip of greaseproof paper for the sides, which should come 1 inch/2.5 cm above the top of the tin. Melt a little butter in a small saucepan or bowl, then use a pastry brush to coat the inside of the tin. Position the greaseproof paper around the sides and on the base, sticking down any places where

Take time to prepare the tin well, as it will make it easier to remove the finished cake later.

the paper overlaps. You can even grease the paper itself so that it peels off easily. Set the tin aside.

37 mins Measure out 8oz/225g of plain flour and sift it through a fine sieve into a mixing bowl. Add ½ level teaspoon of mixed spice, ½ level teaspoon each of cinnamon and ground nutmeg, and 1 level teaspoon of cocoa powder. Mix together and set aside.

Sifting the flour keeps the cake light and airy.

34 mins Place 6oz/175g of butter or margarine in a medium mixing bowl. Add 6oz/175g of soft brown sugar and 1 level tablespoon of golden syrup. Roll 1 lemon and 1 orange on a work surface to release the flesh, then wash and dry them well. Using a fine grater, grate all the rind into the bowl of butter, sugar and syrup. Set aside.

Rolling the fruit under the palm of your hands releases the flesh and increases the amount of juice you can squeeze out of the fruit.

28 mins Cut the lemon and orange in half and squeeze one half of each fruit. Set the juice aside to be used later.

25 mins Weigh out 6oz/175g of sultanas, 6oz/175g of raisins, 8oz/225g dried mixed fruit, 2oz/50g dried banana chips and 2oz/50g of chopped shelled walnuts or chopped blanched almonds. Chop the fruit and nuts, if necessary, so they are roughly the same size as the sultanas and raisins. Place in a medium mixing bowl and set aside. Preheat the oven to 170°C/325°F/Gas mark 3.

It is important to measure the ingredients accurately or the consistency of the cake will be wrong.

If the mixed fruit includes prunes, make sure that the stones are removed before adding the fruit to the mixture.

17 mins Break 4 eggs into a small bowl, add a pinch of salt and whisk with a fork. Set aside.

14 mins Using either a wooden spoon or electric mixer, beat the margarine, sugar, syrup and orange and lemon rind together until the mixture becomes pale, light and fluffy.

Using a hand-held electric mixer will save you time and energy.

10 mins Carefully beat a small amount of egg into the mixture, adding 1 tablespoon of the spiced flour with each addition of egg to prevent the mixture from curdling. Once all the egg is incorporated, sift all the remaining flour into the bowl and mix well with a wooden spoon or spatula.

If the mixture starts to curdle and separate, add a little extra plain flour and keep adding it until the mixture comes back together again.

5 mins Add the orange and lemon juice a little at a time, mixing well. Do not worry if the mixture starts to curdle at this stage. Once all the juice has been added, pour all the dried fruit into the mixture and stir well.

2 mins Carefully spoon the mixture into the prepared cake tin. Pack it down hard, smooth the surface and place in the centre of the pre-heated oven for 2 hours and 20–30 minutes.
0 mins Wash up and clear away.

To test if the cake is cooked take a fine skewer and insert it into the centre. If the skewer comes out clean and easily, the cake is cooked. It should also be firm to the touch and have shrunk away from the sides of the tin. Remove the cake from the oven and place it in the tin on a cooling rack for 15–20 minutes. Turn the tin upside-down so that the cake slips out, peel off the greaseproof paper and leave to cool on the rack. When the cake is completely cold, wrap it in greaseproof paper and then aluminium foil. Store in an airtight container until required. A Christmas cake can be served plain or covered in marzipan and decorated with royal icing.

Dessert
Christmas pudding

Preparation time: 30 minutes
Cooking time: 6 hours

The pudding should be made a few weeks in advance, then stored in a cool, dry place. Before serving it, you must steam it for 3 hours, which is included in the above cooking time. Assemble all the ingredients and equipment you need for the pudding. Set your timer for 30 minutes.
30 mins Grease a 2 pint/1.2 litre pudding basin with melted butter or margarine and set aside.
25 mins Measure out 4oz/100g plain flour and sift it into a large mixing bowl. Add ½ level teaspoon each of mixed spice, nutmeg and cinnamon, 6oz/175g of fresh breadcrumbs, 6oz/175g of finely shredded suet and 6oz/175g of soft brown sugar. Then add 2oz/50g of finely chopped walnuts or blanched almonds, 12oz/350g of dried mixed fruit

It is important to pack the mixture down into the tin or you will end up with holes in your cake once it is cooked.

Do not overcook the cake, or it will become dry and hard. It is better slightly soft and moist.

PROBLEMS AND HANDY TIPS

The pudding takes a total of 6 hours to cook: 3 hours now and a further 3 hours before serving.

It is important to measure the ingredients accurately or the consistency of the pudding will be wrong.

If the mixed fruit includes prunes, make sure that the stones are removed before adding the fruit to the mixture.

and 2oz/50g of chopped dried apricots. Mix well.

20 mins Take 1 orange and wash it well under cold running water. Grate the rind on a fine hole and place it in the flour mixture. Cut the orange in half and squeeze both halves. Strain the juice into a small bowl and set aside.

15 mins Break 3 eggs into a small bowl, add a pinch of salt, whisk with a fork and set aside. Quarter fill a large saucepan with water, put over a medium heat and bring to the boil.

12 mins Add ½ teaspoon of almond essence and 2 tablespoons of brandy or sherry to the flour mixture. Slowly mix in the beaten egg and stir well to incorporate all the ingredients. Slowly add the orange juice a little at a time, stirring continuously.

8 mins Place the mixture in the prepared pudding basin, push down firmly then cover with a double sheet of greaseproof paper. Cover this with a lid or a double thickness of aluminium foil. Tie tightly with string, making a loop across the top to act as a handle.

4 mins Put the basin in the saucepan of boiling water, adding more water if necessary to bring it 1 inch/2.5 cm below the top of the basin. Place the lid on the saucepan and steam for 3 hours. You will need to check the water level every hour and replenish it as the water evaporates.

0 mins Wash up and clear away.

Remember that the pudding should be stored in a cool, dry place until Christmas Day.

Make sure the mixture is firmly pressed down so that there are no air holes or gaps.

It is a good idea to put a pleat in the centre of the greaseproof paper to allow for the pudding to expand during cooking.

Make several loops for the handle as you do not want it to break as you are removing the pudding from the boiling water.

Brandy butter

PROBLEMS AND HANDY TIPS

Set your timer for 8 minutes.

8 mins Take 4oz/100g of unsalted butter and soften it at room temperature or in a microwave oven. Add 4oz/100g of caster sugar and beat well.

3 mins Add 1–2 tablespoons of brandy, according to your taste, and mix well. Place in a small serving bowl and chill until required.

0 mins Wash up and clear away.

If you are in a hurry and do not have a microwave oven, you can soften the butter in the oven on a low setting for a few minutes.

As an alternative to brandy, you can add some grated orange rind and 1 teaspoon of orange juice to the butter and sugar mixture.

Mince pies

Preparation time: 25 minutes
Cooking time: 20–25 minutes

Assemble all the ingredients and equipment you need for the mince pies. The quantities given make approximately 12 pies. If you are going to make the pastry yourself, turn to the recipe on page 203. It is a good idea to make the pastry in advance so that it can chill before cooking. Set your timer for 25 minutes.

If you are using frozen pastry, it will need to defrost at room temperature before being rolled out. This will take 1–2 hours.

25 mins Empty a jar of sweet mincemeat into a bowl, add 2 tablespoons of dry sherry and stir well.

20 mins Take the pastry out of the fridge if it has been chilling. Sprinkle flour over a clean work surface and roll out the pastry thinly. Using a large cutter 3¼ inch/8 cm in diameter, cut out 12 pie bases. Using a medium cutter 2¼ inch/6 cm in diameter, cut out 12 pie tops. If you cannot cut all the circles out of one piece of pastry, knead the pieces back together, then re-roll and cut out the number still needed. Preheat the oven to 200°C/400°F/Gas mark 6.

Check the cutters against the bun tin to ensure that the pastry circles you cut will be the correct size.

10 mins Carefully press each base into a non-stick bun tin, making sure that the pastry comes to the edge of each hole. Once all the bases are in place, spoon in enough mincemeat to three-quarters fill them.

Make sure the pastry is pressed firmly into the bottom of each bun tin before adding the mincemeat.

5 mins Break 1 egg into a bowl and whisk with a fork. Use a pastry brush to brush a little beaten egg round the rim of each case. Put the tops on the pies and pinch the rim to ensure a good seal. Brush the top of the pies with beaten egg and sprinkle with caster sugar. Place in the preheated oven for 20–25 minutes.

It is important to make a good seal around each pie or the filling will bubble out.

The beaten egg on top of the pies gives them a golden brown finish once they have been cooked.

0 mins Wash up and clear away.

When the mince pies are cooked, lever them out of the bun tin with a spatula and place on a rack to cool. If stored in an airtight tin, they will keep for up to one week.

Main course
Turkey and two stuffings

Preparation time: 45 minutes
Cooking time: 1½–2½ hours
  (for a 4–6lb/2–3kg turkey)

The sausage-meat and apple stuffing is placed under the skin of the bird and the sage and onion is used to fill the body. Assemble all the ingredients and equipment you need for the stuffings. Set your timer for 20 minutes.

20 mins Place 8oz/225g of sausage-meat in a mixing bowl. Peel and chop 1 onion as finely as possible, then add it to the sausage-meat and mix well with your clean hands or a wooden spoon.

The sausage-meat stuffing can also be made in a food processor, which will give a fine, smooth consistency.

14 mins Peel 1 apple and cut it into quarters; discard the core and slice the apple as finely as possible. Add to the sausage-meat and season with a little salt and ground black pepper. Add 2 table-spoons of fresh breadcrumbs, 1 teaspoon of dried mustard powder and 1 egg to bind the mixture together. Stir well and set aside.

It is important that the stuffing is well mixed and bound together or it will be difficult to stuff the turkey.

5 mins If you are going to use a sage and onion stuffing in the body of the bird, follow the instructions on the packet. Set aside to cool.

0 mins Wash up and clear away.

Instructions vary according to brand, so follow the packet carefully and check that the quantity will be sufficient for the number of guests you have.

Assemble all the ingredients and equipment you need to stuff the turkey. Reset your timer for 25 minutes. Preheat the oven to 180°C/350°F/Gas mark 4.

25 mins Take 1 large roasting tin and place 1 tablespoon of dripping or cooking margarine and vegetable oil in the bottom. Place in the oven to melt.

20 mins Carefully open up the front of the bird with a sharp knife so that you separate the skin from the breast meat. Using your fingers or a teaspoon, gently prise the skin away from the flesh without tearing it: this should be quite easy. Work your hand right over the top and sides of the bird, releasing the skin as you go. Stop once you get close to the rear end of the bird.

Stuffing the turkey under the skin prevents the breast from drying out and gives the bird extra flavour and moisture.

It is worth taking the time to stuff the turkey properly and ensure you do not leave out any bits. The meat is deliciously moist when the bird is stuffed in this way.

MENU 19

15 mins Once all the skin has been released, use your hands or a spoon to insert small amounts of sausage-meat stuffing all over the breast meat under the skin. When you have inserted it all and the breast is completely covered, press the skin down firmly.

10 mins Take the cooled sage and onion stuffing, shape it into a ball and push it into the tail-end cavity of the bird. Pull the skin together and secure with a skewer or piece of string to stop the stuffing leaking out.

5 mins Take the roasting tin out of the oven, put the stuffed turkey in it and place in the centre of the oven. Make a note of the time it goes in: you will need to cover the turkey with foil after 30 minutes.

0 mins Wash up and clear away.

Roast vegetables

Preparation time: 25 minutes
Cooking time: 1½–2 hours

Assemble all the ingredients and equipment you need for the vegetables. Set your timer for 25 minutes.

25 mins Take 1 large roasting tin, put 1 tablespoon of dripping or cooking margarine and vegetable oil in it and place in the oven underneath the turkey to melt.

22 mins Peel the potatoes, carrots and parsnips. Cut the potatoes into pieces of roughly the same size and place in a saucepan of cold water with a pinch of salt. Place over a medium heat and bring to the boil.

12 mins Top and tail the carrots and parsnips, and cut into halves or quarters if very large.

8 mins Take the roasting tin out of the oven and place the carrots and parsnips in it. Baste with the fat and season lightly with salt and pepper.

5 mins Check the potatoes. Boil them for 1 minute, then drain and add them to the tin with

You should find that the skin comes away from the breast meat easily. If not, wet your hands with a little water: the moisture often makes it easier. Make sure the turkey breast is evenly covered with stuffing or parts of the meat will dry out.

The sage and onion stuffing must be cool before it is used to stuff the turkey.

If you stuff the turkey in advance, you will need to keep it chilled until it is time to cook it.

PROBLEMS AND HANDY TIPS

It is important to keep all the vegetables roughly the same size so that they will cook evenly.

Do not boil the potatoes for more than 1–2 minutes or they will fall apart when roasted.

the carrots and parsnips. Baste with a little fat and place in the oven on the shelf above the turkey.

3 mins Peel and cut 1 onion into quarters and place in the tin with the turkey. Cover the whole turkey with aluminium foil, but not the complete tin. Return to the oven and continue to cook.

0 mins Wash up and clear away.

Brussels sprouts

PROBLEMS AND HANDY TIPS

Preparation time: 10 minutes
Cooking time: 8–10 minutes

10 mins Prepare 2lb/900g of Brussels sprouts by trimming a few outer leaves with a sharp knife. The sprouts should be tight, bright green and shiny, with no blemishes. Cut a small, shallow cross on the base of each sprout; do not cut too deeply or they will fall apart when cooking. Place the prepared sprouts in a saucepan or bowl and set aside. Cooking the sprouts is a last-minute task.

Cutting a cross in the sprouts helps them to cook more evenly.

Cranberry sauce

PROBLEMS AND HANDY TIPS

Preparation time: 8 minutes
Cooking time: 10–12 minutes

Assemble all the ingredients and equipment you need for the cranberry sauce. Set your timer for 8 minutes.

8 mins Put ½ pint/300ml of cold water into a saucepan, add 6oz/175g of granulated sugar and put over a medium heat to dissolve.

4 mins Wash the cranberries, if necessary, then add them to the pan. Cook rapidly for 2–3 minutes until the skins pop open, then reduce the heat and simmer gently for 10–12 minutes. Check the sweetness of the sauce, then cool, cover and place in the fridge until required. Cranberry sauce can be served hot or cold.

0 mins Wash up and clear away.

To save time, you can serve ready-made cranberry sauce.

If you are going to use frozen cranberries, you can place them straight in the saucepan with the sugar.

Do not make the cranberry sauce too sweet, as it accompanies a savoury dish. It is better slightly tart.

MENU 19

Bacon rolls

Preparation time: 8 minutes
Cooking time: 30–35 minutes

8 mins Take 4 slices of streaky bacon and cut off the rind with kitchen scissors or a sharp knife.

4 mins Place the bacon on a chopping board and stretch each piece by holding one end and running the back of a round-ended knife along it. Cut the bacon in half widthways. Roll up each piece of bacon and place on a plate, then cover and set aside.

0 mins Wash up and clear away.

It is important to stretch the bacon before rolling it up, because it shrinks as it cooks and the rolls become tight.

Relax

Have a 40-minute break or longer. This will depend on the cooking times for the turkey. You will need to leave 50 minutes to finish off all the last-minute tasks. If you are serving a Christmas pudding, you will need to steam it again for a further 3 hours. Check your timing as it might need to go on before your break.

Welcome back

Feeling better after your break? Check the turkey and vegetables in the oven. Baste them well and turn the vegetables over so that they can brown on all sides. The turkey should remain covered with the foil until 30 minutes before serving.

Last-minute tasks

Set your timer for 50 minutes. This is how long you have before you will sit down to eat the Christmas meal.

Bread sauce

Assemble all the ingredients and equipment you need for the bread sauce.

50 mins Peel 1 onion and press 4 cloves into it. Place the onion in a saucepan and add ½ pint/ 300ml milk. Season with pinches of nutmeg, mace, salt and white pepper, then add 1 bay leaf. Put over a medium heat and bring the milk to the boil, then turn the heat down and simmer for 10 minutes.

To save time, you can buy a packet of bread sauce mix. Make it up according to the instructions on the packet and ensure that it will be sufficient for the number of guests you are expecting.

45 mins Meanwhile, prepare 2oz/50g (2 tablespoons) of fresh breadcrumbs.

40 mins Fill the kettle and put it on to boil for the Brussels sprouts.

39 mins Remove the onion and bay leaf from the milk. Add all the breadcrumbs, 1oz/25g (1 tablespoon) of butter and 1 tablespoon of single cream. Mix well, season to taste and transfer to an ovenproof dish to cool.

34 mins If using fresh parsley to garnish on the vegetables, wash well, shake off any excess water and chop finely. Set aside.

The chopped parsley can be served over the roast vegetables to add colour.

30 mins Take the turkey out of the oven, remove the foil and carefully drain all the fat and juices from the tin into a bowl. Leave the bowl to stand. Add the bacon rolls and chipolata sausages to the roasting tin. Check the vegetables and turn them again if necessary. Put the turkey back in the oven to finish cooking.

You might need to get some help when draining the fat and juices from the turkey as the tin can be heavy and rather awkward.

Gravy

Make the gravy in a saucepan before the meat is completely cooked; this is easier than making it in the turkey tin and there is less risk of the bird getting cold.

25 mins Take the bowl containing the turkey fat and juices and use a tablespoon to transfer all the fat floating at the top to another bowl; leave the juices at the bottom. Place 2 tablespoons of turkey fat in a small saucepan.

The excess fat from the turkey can be kept in the fridge in a covered bowl and used as dripping for other roast meals.

MENU 19

20 mins Put the saucepan over a low heat until the fat bubbles. Remove from the heat and add 2 heaped tablespoons of plain flour; stir to form a thick roux. Put the roux back over the heat and cook for 2 minutes, stirring all the time. Remove from the heat and allow to cool.

See Cookery Terms, page 223, for an explanation of 'roux'.

If the mixture is very thin, add a little extra flour.

15 mins Pour ¾ pint/450ml of fresh stock into the roux mixture, or crumble in 1 chicken stock cube and add ¾ pint/450ml of cold water; stir continuously to ensure no lumps appear. Add 1 glass of red wine, if using, and all the juices from the turkey. Put the saucepan over a low heat and stir constantly as it thickens and comes to the boil. Simmer the gravy for several minutes to ensure that it doesn't have a floury flavour.

Add the liquid slowly so that you do not get any lumps: stop adding it if the mixture becomes lumpy. Beat the gravy hard until it becomes smooth again, then continue adding the liquid.

If the gravy has a thin film of fat on top, see Handy Tip 8, page xviii, for an easy way to remove it.

10 mins Season with a little salt and ground black pepper, then turn off the heat.

8 mins Take the ovenproof bowl of bread sauce and pour 1 tablespoon of milk on top of it. Place in the bottom of the oven to warm through.

Adding the milk to the bread sauce prevents it from drying out.

6 mins Put the gravy back over a low heat and slowly bring to the boil.

2 mins Take the cranberry sauce out of the fridge and put it on the table for your guests to help themselves.

1 min Check the turkey, bacon rolls, sausages and vegetables; this will give you an idea of how much time you have left before serving.

0 mins Wash up and clear away.

Cook the Brussels sprouts only when you are sure how much time you have left, as they should be firm rather than soggy. Cover the sprouts with boiling water and cook on a medium heat for 8–10 minutes. The time will vary depending on the size of the sprouts. When cooked, drain and put the sprouts back in the saucepan. Add 8oz/225g of tinned chestnuts and 2oz/50g (2 tablespoons) butter or margarine. Put back over the heat and sauté for 2 minutes. Serve at once, piping hot.

If you want to use fresh chestnuts, cut a small slit in their skins, place in a saucepan of cold water and bring to the boil. Simmer for 10 minutes. Take off the heat and plunge into cold water. The skins should come off easily once cool.

Watch points

Once the meal has started, it is difficult to predict how long each course will take. The following instructions are given only as a guide.

Take the turkey out of the oven 5–10 minutes before you want to carve it. This allows the meat to relax and makes carving easier. Check the gravy and turn it off if it is boiling. Put the main course plates and serving dishes in to warm if you have the facility. Turn the oven down to 150°C/300°F/Gas mark 2.

Don't forget all the accompaniments that go with the meal. Place them in individual serving dishes and garnish the roasted vegetables with chopped parsley.

Put the mince pies in a warm oven to heat through while you are eating the main course. The Christmas pudding will continue to steam until you are ready to serve it.

Serve the main course.

To serve the Christmas pudding, turn it out on to a serving dish, decorate with holly leaves and spoon over 2 tablespoons of brandy. Apply a lighted match to the pudding and watch it flambée. When the flames have subsided, slice the pudding and serve with brandy butter. Don't forget to offer the mince pies served with cream.

Make sure there is plenty of water in the saucepan for the pudding to continue steaming.

Checklist to ensure you haven't forgotten anything: roast turkey, two stuffings, roast potatoes, carrots, parsnips and onions, Brussels sprouts with chestnuts, bacon rolls, chipolata sausages, bread sauce, cranberry sauce, gravy.

Roasting times for meats
Beef

Cuts:	Topside, top rump, silverside, rib or sirloin.
Serving:	4–6oz/100–150g off the bone or 6–12oz/150–300g on the bone per person.
Temperature:	220°C/425°F/Gas mark 7.
Timing:	**Rare:** allow 20 minutes per 1lb/ 450g, plus 15 minutes extra at the end of the cooking time.
	Medium: allow 25 minutes per

1lb/450g, plus 20 minutes extra at the end of the cooking time. **Well done:** allow 30 minutes per 1lb/450g plus 30 minutes extra at end of the cooking time.

Use this time chart regardless of whether the meat is on the bone, off the bone or rolled.

Accompaniments: Roast potatoes, parsnips, carrots, onions, green vegetables, Yorkshire pudding, horseradish sauce or cream, English mustard, gravy.

Lamb

Cuts: Leg, shoulder, fillet end, best end of neck, stuffed, boned breast.

Serving: 8–12oz/250–400g per person, on the bone.

Temperature: 220°C/425°F/Gas mark 7.

Timing: **Rare to medium** – 25 minutes per lb/450g, plus 25 minutes extra at the end of the cooking time. **Well done** – 30 minutes per lb/450g, plus 30 minutes extra at the end of the cooking time.

Accompaniments: Roast potatoes, parsnips, carrots, onions, green vegetables, gravy, mint sauce, redcurrant jelly.

Pork

Cuts: Leg, loin, fillet end, knuckle end.

Serving: 8–12oz/250–400g per person, joints on the bone; 4–6 oz per person, joints off the bone.

Temperature: 200°C/400°F/Gas mark 6.

Timing: 30–35 minutes per lb/450g, plus 35 minutes extra at the end of

the cooking time. Pork must
always be served well cooked,
never rare.

Accompaniments: Roast potatoes, parsnips,
carrots, onions, green
vegetables, sage and onion
stuffing, apple sauce, cranberry
sauce, gravy.

Chicken

Cuts:	Whole birds or pieces.
Serving:	A medium chicken weighing 3–3½lb/1.25–1.5kg will feed 4–6 people.
Temperature:	200°C/400°F/Gas mark 6.
Timing:	80–90 minutes for a medium-sized chicken.
Accompaniments:	Roast potatoes, parsnips, carrots, onions, green vegetables, bacon rolls, cocktail sausages, pork sausage-meat stuffing, bread sauce, gravy.

Duck

Cuts:	Whole birds
Serving:	16–20oz/500–600g per person.
Temperature:	180°C/350°F/Gas mark 4.
Timing:	25 minutes per 1lb/450g.
Accompaniments:	Roast potatoes, parsnips, carrots, onions, green vegetables, sage and onion stuffing, orange and parsley stuffing, apple sauce, gravy.

Crème de la crème menu

Difficult to prepare and cook
Cost level: expensive
Serves: 4

A 40-minute break is incorporated in this menu.

<u>Starter</u>	Lamb's liver terrine[F*] with melba toast	*Preparation time = 50 minutes* *Cooking time = 1½–2 hours*
<u>Main course</u>	Crispy roast duck à l'orange with a red wine sauce Roast baby new potatoes Mange-tout or French beans	*Preparation time = 60 minutes* *Cooking time = 2 hours*
<u>Dessert</u>	Hot mocha soufflé with wafer biscuits and cream	*Preparation time = 35 minutes* *Cooking time = 20–25 minutes*
<u>Drink</u>	Full-bodied red wine	

This menu is difficult and time-consuming to prepare and cook. You will need to be well organized to have everything ready on time. The liver terrine should be made in advance, at least the day before, and chilled. Serve it with melba toast (see recipe, page 209) or hot fresh bread. The duck is delicious and very rich, so do not give your guests too much. The roast new potatoes make a pleasant change from the boiled variety. Don't overcook the green vegetables – keep them crisp and full of flavour. The dessert must be cooked just before you serve it, so you will need to be well organized and have everything ready, including your guests! The best plan is to have a break between the main course and the dessert so you can prepare the soufflé. Serve it with wafer biscuits and single cream.

Equipment needed – Menu 20
Starter

1 savoury chopping board
1 pair kitchen scissors
1 round-edged knife
1 small loaf tin, approx. 1lb/450g capacity
1 sharp knife or food processor with fine blade
1 savoury wooden spoon
1 mixing bowl
1 fine grater
1 lemon squeezer
1 tablespoon
1 large roasting tin
1 round-edged knife
kitchen paper

Main course

1 large roasting tin with a wire rack that sits inside the tin
1 fork or skewer
1 sharp knife
1 savoury chopping board
1 lemon squeezer
1 small roasting tin
1 tablespoon
1 small saucepan
1 medium saucepan with lid
1 savoury wooden spoon
1 measuring jug
1 wine glass
1 teaspoon
1 colander
1 carving knife
2 bowls
kitchen paper

Dessert

1 tablespoon
1 small saucepan or bowl
1 ovenproof soufflé dish, 3½ inch/9 cm deep and 7 inch/18 cm in diameter
1 pastry brush
1 double saucepan or 1 heatproof bowl that fits tightly inside a large saucepan
1 large mixing bowl
1 small mixing bowl
1 balloon whisk or hand-held electric mixer
1 sweet wooden spoon
1 teaspoon
1 flexible spatula

Shopping list – Menu 20
Starter

4oz/100g streaky bacon
12oz/350g fresh lambs' livers
1 spring onion
2oz/50g (2 tablespoons) sausage-meat
*1 egg
2oz/50g (2 tablespoons) fresh breadcrumbs
*salt and freshly ground black pepper
1 lime
1 tablespoon dry sherry
1 tablespoon crème fraîche
margarine for greasing
small bunch fresh parsley to garnish
melba toast (see recipe, page 209) or 1 long French loaf

Main course

1 large duck, approx. 6lb/2½–3kg, or 2 small ducks, with giblets
2 oranges
*salt, pepper
1–1½lb/450–600g baby new potatoes
*2oz/50g (2 tablespoons) cooking margarine
Red wine sauce
*2 tablespoons fat from the duck
*2 heaped tablespoons plain flour
½ pint/300ml fresh chicken stock or *1 stock cube
*1 glass red wine
2 teaspoons redcurrant jelly
*salt, pepper, mustard powder
2lb/900g mange-tout or French beans

Dessert

*1oz/25g (1 tablespoon) butter or margarine
*3oz/75g caster sugar
*6oz/175g plain dark chocolate
*4 eggs
*1 tablespoon coffee essence or 3 teaspoons instant coffee granules
1 tablespoon brandy (optional)
1 tablespoon icing sugar
1 packet wafer biscuits of your choice
½ pint/300ml single cream (optional)

Check store cupboard

189

MENU 20

Countdown – Menu 20

If you want to prepare the whole menu, you will need 185 minutes (3 hours 5 minutes), which includes a 40-minute break. If you are a slow cook, add 5–10 minutes to each course to ensure that you do not run out of time. Remember, the times given are only a guide as each cook will take different lengths of time to complete each task. The liver terrine should be made in advance to allow it time to cook and chill. The main course should be prepared and cooked on the night. The hot soufflé is made between courses, so make sure you are well organized beforehand.

Starter

Preparation time: 35 minutes
Cooking time: 1½–2 hours

Assemble all the ingredients and equipment you need for the starter. If you have a food processor with a fine blade, follow the countdown instructions and blend the mixture each time you add a new ingredient. This will save time and give you a very smooth pâté. Set your timer for 35 minutes.

35 mins Take 4oz/100g of streaky bacon and discard the rind. Place the rashers on a chopping board and stretch them by running the back of a round-ended knife along them. Use the stretched bacon to line a loaf tin. For the best result, place the rashers across the width of the tin, not the length, making sure that there are no gaps. You might need to cut one or two rashers in half to make a good covering. Set aside.

25 mins Take 12oz/350g of lambs' livers, discard any connective tissue and gristle and roughly chop them. Place in a mixing bowl or food processor and blend. Set aside.

20 mins Take 1 spring onion, remove the root and outer layer, then chop very finely. Add to the mixing bowl with the livers.

It is important to line the loaf tin well as the bacon prevents the pâté from oozing out.

16 mins Add 2oz/50g (2 tablespoons) of sausage-meat and 1 whole egg, then mix well. Stir in 1oz/25g (1 tablespoon) of fresh breadcrumbs (1 slice of fresh bread finely chopped). Season the mixture with a pinch of salt and some freshly ground black pepper. Preheat the oven to 180°C/350°F/Gas mark 4.

12 mins Wash and dry 1 lime. Using the fine side of a grater, grate the rind into the mixing bowl. Cut the lime in half, squeeze 1 half and add the juice to the mixture. The remaining half should be sliced thinly and used to garnish the cooked terrine.

After drying the lime, it is a good idea to roll it on a work surface under the palm of your hand; this loosens the skin and makes it easier to squeeze.

7 mins Add 1 tablespoon of dry sherry, if using, and 1 tablespoon of crème fraîche. Stir well.

The sherry adds extra flavour to the terrine, but you do not have to use it.

5 mins Take the lined tin and carefully spoon in the meat mixture. Press it down using the back of a tablespoon and make sure it is tightly packed into the corners. Do not overfill the tin: leave a ½-inch/1 cm gap at the top.

Make sure the meat mixture is packed tightly into the tin as this will make it easier to turn out. If you have any mixture left over, place it in a separate loaf or cake tin and cook at the same time as the terrine.

2 mins Take a double sheet of aluminium foil, grease it lightly with margarine and place it over the top of the loaf tin, pressing to secure it. Place the tin in a large roasting tin and add enough cold water to come halfway up the sides of the loaf tin. Place the two tins in the preheated oven and cook for 1½–2 hours. The time will vary, depending on the oven and size of your loaf tin.

Do not overfill the water-bath: there should be no danger of water getting into the terrine. The terrine must cook for a minimum of 1½ hours.

0 mins Wash up and clear away.

Set your timer for 60 minutes: at that point you will need to check that there is still enough water in the water-bath. Reset the timer for 30–45 minutes. Once the terrine is cooked, allow it to cool, then chill it in the fridge until required.

Make the melba toast now, if you like (see recipe, page 209). It can be stored in an airtight container until required.

Dessert

PROBLEMS AND HANDY TIPS

Preparation time: 20 minutes

To make the hot soufflé a little easier, prepare a

MENU 20

few things in advance so that there is less to do at the last minute. You will have to put the soufflé together after you have eaten the main course, so allow 15 minutes to finish preparing it, then 20–25 minutes for it to cook. Your guests won't mind a break between courses at this stage of the meal. Set your timer for 20 minutes.

20 mins Melt ½oz/12g (½ tablespoon) of butter or margarine in a small saucepan or bowl, then use a pastry brush to brush it on the inside of your soufflé dish. Make sure all the edges are well covered. Add 1oz/25g (1 tablespoon) of caster sugar, then shake the dish around so that the butter is covered by the sugar. Set aside.

15 mins Weigh out 6oz/175g of plain chocolate, break it into pieces and place in a heatproof bowl or the top of a double saucepan. Half fill a large saucepan (or the bottom half of a double sauce-pan) with warm water, ensuring that it comes no more than halfway up the sides of the bowl once it is inside the saucepan. Place the pan over a medium heat and bring to the boil.

12 mins While the chocolate is melting, separate 4 eggs: place the whites in a large mixing bowl and the yolks in a smaller bowl. Add 2oz/50g (2 table-spoons) of caster sugar to the yolks and beat with a balloon whisk or hand-held electric mixer for a few minutes, until the mixture becomes pale.

7 mins Stir the chocolate. If it has melted, turn off the heat and remove the bowl from the pan. (Do this using oven gloves or a tea towel as the bowl will be very hot.) Add the remaining ½oz/12g (½ tablespoon) of butter to the melted chocolate and stir well until melted.

3 mins Add 1 tablespoon of coffee essence (or 3 teaspoons of instant coffee granules dissolved in 1 tablespoon of boiling water) to the egg and sugar mixture and stir well. If using brandy, add 1 tablespoon of it to the bowl and mix well. Set aside.

0 mins This is as far as you can go with the soufflé preparation. Wash up and clear away.

Prepare as much as possible now to save the panic at the last minute.

Roll the soufflé dish around so that the caster sugar coats the dish evenly. Discard any excess sugar by tapping the dish.

Make sure the water does not boil over into the melting chocolate.

See Handy Tip 2, page xvii for an easy way to separate eggs.

The butter gives the chocolate a rich, silky look.

Leave the bowl of chocolate in a warm place to prevent it from hardening.

Main course

Preparation time: 20 minutes
Cooking time: 2 hours

Assemble all the ingredients and equipment you need for the main course. Roast duck requires 20 minutes per lb plus 10 minutes extra. If you are using two birds, calculate the cooking time by the largest bird. A 6 lb/2½ kg duck would take just over 2 hours (120 minutes) to cook. Set your timer for 20 minutes. Preheat the oven to 220°C/425°F/Gas mark 7.

20 mins Check inside the bird and remove the packet of giblets, if present. Wash the duck under cold running water and pat dry with a clean tea towel or kitchen paper. Place it on a wire rack inside a roasting tin and prick the skin all over with a fork or skewer. Place the giblets in the bottom of the roasting tin if they will add flavour to the sauce.

15 mins Take 2 oranges and roll them on a work surface under the palm of your hand to release the flesh. Cut the oranges in half, squeeze 3 halves and pour the juice all over the duck. Cut the remaining half of orange in half and place inside the neck cavity of the duck. Lightly sprinkle the skin with salt, then place the duck in a preheated oven to cook. Make a note of the time the bird goes in, and calculate when it should come out.

10 mins While the duck is cooking, wash the baby new potatoes and then dry them with kitchen paper or a clean tea towel. Place them in a small roasting tin, add 2oz/50g (2 tablespoons) of cooking margarine, season with salt and ground black pepper and set aside. The potatoes will take 1–1½ hours to cook, so work out what time they will need to go in the oven to be ready at the same time as the duck.

0 mins Wash up and clear away.

Relax

Have a 40-minute break. When you return you will have to make the sauce for the duck, cook the

A duck is a very fatty bird so it is important to place it on a wire rack so that it doesn't sit and cook in the fat. This way all the fat can drain away into the tin.

The skin is pricked to help the fat to escape from the bird and run into the tin.

Rolling the orange under the palm of your hand releases the flesh and makes it easier to squeeze.

The salt on the skin of the duck will help to make it crisp and crunchy during the cooking time.

It is important to dry the potatoes well before putting them into the tin or they can become soggy.

Cover the potatoes with a clean tea towel or cling film while you go for your break. They will be put in the oven to cook when you return.

vegetables, turn out and garnish the terrine, and put the soufflé together.

Welcome back

Feeling better after your break?

Last-minute tasks

Set your timer for 40 minutes. This is how long you have before sitting down to eat the starter.

40 mins Check the duck in the oven and baste if necessary. (Ducks are very fatty birds, so basting is not essential.) Turn the oven down to 200°C/ 400°F/Gas mark 6. Place the new potatoes in the oven on the shelf below the duck. They will need 1–1½ hours, depending on how large they are.

See Cookery Terms, page 222, for a definition of 'baste'.

If the potatoes are very small, they will take only 1 hour to cook.

Switch the duck and potatoes around in the oven if the duck starts to brown too quickly.

Red wine sauce

Make the sauce in a saucepan rather than the roasting tin. You can still use all the juices from the meat, but there is less risk of the meat over-cooking or going cold.

35 mins Take the duck out of the oven and carefully drain all the fat and juices into a bowl. Put the duck back into the oven and continue to cook. Using a tablespoon, carefully spoon all the fat into a bowl, leaving the sediment at the bottom of the first bowl.

It is important to remove as much fat as possible from the sediment so that you don't have a greasy sauce.

The excess fat from the duck can be kept in the fridge in a covered bowl and used as dripping for other roast menus.

30 mins Place 2 generous tablespoons of duck fat in a small saucepan and put over a low heat until the fat bubbles. Remove from the heat and add 2 heaped tablespoons of plain flour, stirring to form a smooth, thick roux. Put the roux over a low heat and cook for 2 minutes, stirring constantly. Remove from the heat and allow to cool.

See Cookery Terms, page 223, for an explanation of 'roux'.

25 mins Measure out ½ pint/300ml of fresh chicken stock or dissolve 1 chicken stock cube in

½ pint/300ml of boiling water. Add to the roux, stirring constantly to make sure no lumps appear. Add 1 glass of red wine, 2 teaspoons of redcurrant jelly and all the juices from the duck. Put the saucepan back over a low heat and bring to the boil, stirring constantly as it thickens. Simmer the sauce for several minutes to ensure that it does not have a floury flavour. Season with salt, ground black pepper and a pinch of mustard powder, then turn off the heat.

20 mins Top and tail the mange-tout or French beans, wash them in a colander, then place in a saucepan and set aside.

10 mins Take the terrine out of the fridge and remove the foil cover. Place a plate on top of the tin and quickly turn the whole thing upside-down and give it a firm shake. The terrine should fall out on to the plate. If it doesn't, run a round-ended knife around the edge of the tin to loosen the bacon and try again. Take the half of lime set aside earlier, slice it thinly and use to garnish the terrine. Add a few sprigs of parsley to finish the decoration.

5 mins Fill the kettle and put it on to boil for the vegetables.

4 mins Place the melba toast in a basket or bowl on the table. If serving fresh bread, put it in the oven to warm. Place some butter on the table for your guests to help themselves.

2 mins Pour the boiling water over the vegetables, add a pinch of salt and bring to the boil over a medium heat.

0 mins Wash up and clear away.

Watch points

Once the meal has started, it is difficult to predict how long each course will take. The following instructions are given only as a guide. Don't forget you will have to put the soufflé together after you have eaten the main course.

Before sitting down to eat the starter, check the vegetables and turn them down or even off if you

Add the liquid very slowly so that you do not get any lumps: stop adding the liquid if the sauce becomes lumpy. Beat it hard until it becomes smooth again, then continue to add the liquid.

If the sauce still has a thin film of fat on the top, allow it to settle, then place a double piece of kitchen paper on top of it. The fat will be absorbed by the paper and can then be discarded. Repeat until all the fat has been removed.

When the terrine is turned out, you might find that it has a thin layer of fat which has come from the bacon. Remove it with a tablespoon or some kitchen paper, then garnish.

Do not start cooking the vegetables until you know you are only 5–10 minutes away from serving them.

PROBLEMS AND HANDY TIPS

are worried that they might overcook. Check the duck and new potatoes in the oven and, again, if you are worried that they might overcook, turn the oven down to 110°C/225°F/Gas mark ¼.

If you have the facility to warm the main course plates and serving dishes, put them in to warm now.

Serve the terrine with the melba toast or warmed bread.

Take the duck out of the oven. Drain all the fat and juices from it into a small bowl. Carefully spoon all the duck fat into another bowl, so you are left with just the juices in the original bowl. Add all the juices to the red wine sauce, place over a low heat and slowly bring to the boil.

Check the vegetables. When they are cooked, drain off the water and place them in a serving dish on the table. Put the roast potatoes in a serving dish on the table or back into the oven to keep warm while you carve. Carve the duck. Pour the heated sauce into a sauce boat and place on the table. Serve the main course.

The potatoes are ready when they have shrunk in size and are soft when pierced through the centre with a sharp knife.

Take the duck out of the oven 5 minutes before serving. This allows the meat to relax and makes carving much easier.

Remember to keep the vegetables crisp. French beans and mange-tout are always better when they have a little 'bite'.

Hot mocha soufflé

PROBLEMS AND HANDY TIPS

Preparation time: 15 minutes
Cooking time: 20–25 minutes

Collect all the bowls of ingredients which have already been prepared. Follow the countdown carefully and put the soufflé straight into the oven. Once it has risen and cooked, it must be eaten immediately. Preheat the oven to 200°C/400°F/Gas mark 6. Set your timer for 15 minutes.

15 mins Take the bowl with the egg yolk mixture and add it to the melted chocolate; stir well as the chocolate thickens. Set aside.

12 mins Take the bowl of egg whites and beat them, using either an electric mixer or a balloon whisk, until they are stiff and stand in peaks.

8 mins Check that the oven shelf is in the centre of the oven with no shelves above it. Carefully fold

If the chocolate has become too thick or even hard, you will need to warm it through again. Place the bowl in a saucepan of hot water for a few minutes so the chocolate can melt.

Fold and lift the mixture to incorporate as much air as

the chocolate mixture into the egg whites using a tablespoon or flexible spatula, lifting the mixture as much as possible to incorporate lots of air. **Do not beat the mixture.** When the mixture is a uniform colour, pour it into the prepared soufflé dish.

1 min Place in the preheated oven for 20–25 minutes.

0 mins Clear away the mixing bowls and anything left from the main course.

The cooked soufflé should be well risen and firm to the touch. If it wobbles, it will need to cook for a further 5 minutes. Dust with icing sugar as soon as it comes out of the oven and serve with wafer biscuits and single cream.

possible; this makes for a much lighter soufflé.

A few minutes before the soufflé is cooked, put the bowls, cream and wafer biscuits on the table so that you can serve it immediately. The icing sugar will start to melt on top of the soufflé – this is meant to happen.

Appendix

Additional recipes

Basic white sauce
Serves: 4

Equipment

1 small saucepan with lid
1 tablespoon
1 savoury wooden spoon
1 measuring jug
1 balloon whisk
1 fine sieve

Ingredients

*1oz/25g (1 tablespoon) cooking margarine
*1oz/25g (1 tablespoon) plain flour
*1 pint/600ml milk
*salt, pepper, nutmeg
*dried mustard powder

Variations
4oz/100g Cheddar cheese
   or
4oz/100g button mushrooms,
*1 pinch nutmeg and a *dash of lemon juice,
   or
1 small bunch fresh herbs (eg. parsley,
   coriander, basil, fennel or tarragon)

Check store cupboard

Countdown method

Preparation time: 15 minutes
Cooking time: 10 minutes

Assemble all the ingredients and equipment you need for the sauce. Set your timer for 15 minutes.
15 mins Place 1oz/25g (1 tablespoon) of cooking margarine in a small saucepan and put over a low heat to melt.
12 mins Remove the saucepan from the heat, add 1oz/25g (1 tablespoon) plain flour and stir to form a smooth paste. (This mixture is called a 'roux'.) Put the roux back over the heat and cook for 2 minutes to remove the starchy flavour. Remove from the heat and allow to cool.
8 mins Measure out 1 pint/600ml of milk, add it gradually to the roux and stir with a balloon whisk or wooden spoon, making sure that no lumps

PROBLEMS AND HANDY TIPS

If the margarine and flour paste is too thick, add a small amount of extra margarine to form a softer paste.

If at any point the sauce starts to become lumpy, stop adding the milk. Take a balloon whisk and beat the sauce well until all the lumps have disappeared. Then

appear. Stop once you have added three-quarters of the milk. Put the pan back over a low heat and bring to the boil, stirring constantly as the sauce thickens. If it becomes very thick, add the remaining milk until it reaches the right consistency.

2 mins When the sauce is boiling, turn down the heat and simmer for 2 minutes. Season with salt, pepper and a pinch of mustard powder. Use immediately or leave to stand with a lid on. Don't forget to reheat it before use.

0 mins Wash up and clear away.

continue to add the milk, stirring the sauce constantly.
Do not add all the milk straight away in case the sauce becomes too thin.

If the sauce is lumpy, wait until it has thickened and simmered for 2 minutes, then sieve it. Discard the lumps and serve.

Variations
Cheese sauce

Grate 4oz/100g of Cheddar sauce and add it to the white sauce after it has thickened and simmered for 2 minutes. Do not cook the cheese or it will become stringy. Season well and serve with cauliflower or a vegetable of your choice.

If the sauce is not going to be served straight away, add the grated cheese once it has been reheated or it will become stringy.

Mushroom sauce

Wash 4oz/100g of button mushrooms under cold running water, drain well and pat dry on kitchen paper. Slice the mushrooms thinly, place in a saucepan with 1½oz/37g (1½ tablespoons) cooking margarine and cook for 2–3 minutes. Take the saucepan off the heat and add 1½oz/37g (1½ tablespoons) of plain flour. Then follow the countdown method for the white sauce. Season with a pinch of nutmeg and a dash of lemon juice and serve.

Mushroom sauce needs slightly more flour and margarine as the mushrooms absorb the fat. The nutmeg and lemon juice enhance the flavour of the mushrooms.

Herb sauce

Finely chop some fresh herbs, such as parsley, coriander, basil, fennel or tarragon, and add to the basic white sauce. They will add colour and flavour.

The herbs should be washed well and finely chopped before adding them to the sauce at the end of the cooking time.

Additional recipes

Hollandaise sauce
Serves: 4

Equipment

1 small saucepan
1 tablespoon
1 double saucepan or 1 heatproof bowl that fits
    inside a large saucepan
1 small bowl
1 balloon whisk
1 sharp knife
1 savoury chopping board
1 teaspoon

Ingredients

*3 tablespoons white wine vinegar
*2 large eggs
*5oz/125g butter
*salt and ground white pepper
*2 teaspoons lemon juice

*Check store cupboard

Countdown method

Preparation time: 15 minutes
Cooking time: 15 minutes

This classic, rich French sauce is always served warm. It usually accompanies young or steamed vegetables such as new potatoes or asparagus. It is also delicious with hot salmon or shellfish. Assemble all the ingredients and equipment you need for the sauce; it is essential to be very well organized to prevent the sauce from separating or curling. Set your timer for 15 minutes.

15 mins Put 3 tablespoons of white wine vinegar into a small saucepan and place over a low heat. Bring to the boil and keep boiling until reduced to approximately 2 tablespoons.

12 mins Take a large saucepan or the bottom part of a double saucepan and fill it half full of cold water. Place over a low heat and bring almost to the boil.

8 mins Take 2 large eggs and separate them. You will not use the whites, so place them in a small bowl, cover with cling film and store in the fridge. Place the egg yolks in a heatproof bowl or the top section of a double saucepan and beat them with a balloon whisk. Add a small amount of the reduced vinegar, whisking constantly.

5 mins Take 5oz/125g of butter and cut it up into

PROBLEMS AND HANDY TIPS

Make sure the vinegar has reduced before using it.

Do not put too much water in the saucepan as it must not splash over into the sauce. Do not allow the water to boil.

See Handy Tip 2, page xvii for an easy way to separate eggs.

small pieces. Place the egg yolks and vinegar over the hot water in the saucepan, making sure the bowl does not actually touch the water. (The water should simmer but not boil.) Whisking constantly, add half the butter and allow it to melt. When the mixture becomes smooth and forms a thick cream, slowly add the remaining butter. If at any time the sauce starts to get hot, remove from the bowl and allow it to cool before continuing.

1 min Season with a little salt and ground white pepper and add 2 teaspoons of lemon juice. Taste and adjust the seasoning. Serve lukewarm.

0 mins Wash up and clear away.

Never allow the mixture to get too hot; if in doubt, remove from the heat and leave to cool.

If the sauce starts to separate or curdle, take it off the heat and quickly stir in an ice cube. If you are lucky, this will bring the sauce back together.

French dressing
Serves: 10–12

Equipment
1 measuring jug
1 large deep mixing bowl **or** large jug
1 balloon whisk **or** tablespoon
1 sharp knife
1 garlic crusher (or see Handy Tip 1, page xvii)
1 teaspoon
1 bottle **or** jar with a tight-fitting lid

Ingredients
*1 pint/600ml olive oil
*7fl oz/200ml white wine vinegar
*2 cloves garlic (optional)
*1 teaspoon of white **or** brown sugar
*1 teaspoon lemon juice
*2 teaspoons French mustard
*mustard powder
*1 teaspoon salt
*freshly ground black pepper

Check store cupboard

Countdown method

PROBLEMS AND HANDY TIPS

Preparation time: 12 minutes
Cooking time: None

This is a basic French dressing recipe, so it will need testing and adapting before you feel happy with the taste: everyone likes different strengths and flavours. The dressing is best made in advance as this gives all the ingredients, especially the garlic, time to mature. It will keep for 6 weeks in a bottle with a tight-fitting lid at room temperature. Always shake the bottle well before using.

Additional recipes

Assemble all the ingredients and equipment you need for the dressing. Set your timer for 12 minutes.

12 mins Measure out 1 pint/600ml of olive oil and place it in a large mixing bowl or jug. Measure out 7fl oz/200ml of white wine vinegar and add to the oil. Mix well using a balloon whisk or tablespoon.

7 mins If using garlic, peel and crush it into the bowl. Add 1 teaspoon of white or brown sugar, 1 teaspoon of lemon juice, 2 teaspoons of French mustard, a pinch of dried mustard powder, 1 teaspoon of salt and a little black pepper to taste. Mix well and taste the dressing. Adjust the strength according to your taste.

0 mins Wash up and clear away.

Experiment with this dressing: you will find your own ingredients to make the dressing suit your taste.

Variations

- Replace the olive oil with extra-virgin olive oil or walnut oil.
- Replace the white wine vinegar with red wine vinegar, cider vinegar, garlic vinegar, tarragon vinegar or lemon juice to taste.
- Add 2 tablespoons of natural yoghurt, sour cream, mayonnaise, evaporated milk or condensed milk to ¼ pint/150ml of French dressing.
- Add any of the following, but do not mix too many flavours: horseradish sauce or freshly grated horseradish, freshly grated ginger, honey, freshly squeezed orange juice, poppy seeds or caraway seeds.
- The following fresh herbs can also be added to the dressing for colour and flavour: chopped chives, parsley, coriander, basil, fennel, mint or tarragon.

Some oils can be rather stubborn when mixing with vinegar, so always mix the two thoroughly.

See Handy Tip 1, page xvii for an easy way to crush garlic without a garlic crusher.

Season the dressing well before putting it aside or serving it.

Basic shortcrust pastry F*

Serves: 4

Equipment

1 fine sieve
1 large mixing bowl
1 sharp knife
1 tablespoon

Ingredients

*8oz/225g plain flour
*salt
*2oz/50g (2 tablespoons) margarine
2oz/50g (2 tablespoons) lard
*3–4 tablespoons cold water
*2 tablespoons flour for rolling

*Check store cupboard

Countdown method

PROBLEMS AND HANDY TIPS

Preparation time: 15 minutes

The pastry is best chilled before use; it can also be frozen but must be defrosted at room temperature for 2–3 hours. Assemble all the ingredients and equipment you need for the pastry. Set your timer for 15 minutes.

15 mins Measure out 8oz/225g of plain flour and sift it into a large mixing bowl. Add a pinch of salt, 2oz/50g (2 tablespoons) of margarine and 2oz/50g (2 tablespoons) of lard. Using a sharp knife, cut the fat into the flour.

It is important to sift the flour really well as this keeps the pastry nice and light.

12 mins Using your fingertips, rub the fat into the flour until it resembles fine breadcrumbs. Do not allow the fat to melt or become too sticky.

7 mins Make a well in the centre of the mixture and stir in 3–4 tablespoons of cold water a little at a time until the mixture starts to form a firm dough. (You may not need to add all the water.) Use your hands to bring the pastry together.

If you have very warm hands run them under cold water before starting to rub the fat into the flour. If the pastry is becoming very sticky due to the heat of your hands, use 2 round-ended knives instead.

5 mins Place the pastry on a floured work surface and knead lightly for a couple of minutes. Wrap the pastry in cling film and put it in the fridge to chill.

0 mins Wash up and clear away.

Do not use too much flour on your board or the pastry will become dry and brittle.

If the pastry is too soft and sticky, add a little extra plain flour and knead again to make a firm ball.

See page 33 for instructions on rolling out the pastry, lining and filling a flan ring, oven temperatures and cooking times.

Additional recipes

Rich shortcrust pastry F*

Serves: 4

Equipment

1 fine sieve
1 large mixing bowl
1 sharp knife
2 small bowls
1 tablespoon
1 teaspoon

Ingredients

*8oz/225g plain flour
*salt
*4oz/100g margarine or butter
2oz/50g (2 tablespoons) lard
*1 egg
*2 tablespoons cold water
1 teaspoon lemon juice
*2 tablespoons extra flour for rolling

*Check store cupboard

Countdown method

PROBLEMS AND HANDY TIPS

Preparation time: 20 minutes

The pastry should be chilled before use; it can also be frozen but must be defrosted at room temperature for 2–3 hours. Assemble all the ingredients and equipment you need for the pastry. Set your timer for 20 minutes.

20 mins Measure out 8oz/225g of plain flour and sift it into a large mixing bowl with a pinch of salt. Measure out 4oz/100g of margarine or butter and 2oz/50g (2 tablespoons) of lard. Using a sharp knife, cut the fat into the bowl of flour.

It is important to sift the flour well as this keeps the pastry light.

15 mins Using your fingertips, rub the fat into the flour until it resembles fine breadcrumbs. Do not allow the fat to melt or become too sticky.

10 mins Separate 1 egg and mix the yolk with 2 tablespoons of cold water and 1 teaspoon of lemon juice.

If you have very warm hands, rub them under cold water before starting to rub the fat into the flour. If the pastry is becoming sticky due to the heat of your hands, use 2 round-ended knives to work in the fat instead.

7 mins Make a well in the centre of the flour and add the yolk mixture a little at a time, stirring constantly. Once the mixture starts to form a firm ball, stop adding the liquid. Use your hands to bring the pastry together.

2 mins Place the pastry on a floured work surface

Do not use too much flour on your board or the pastry will become dry and brittle.

and knead lightly for a couple of minutes. Wrap the pastry in cling film and put it in the fridge to chill. **0 mins** Wash up and clear away.

See page 33 for instructions on rolling out the pastry, lining and filling a flan ring, oven temperatures and cooking times.

If the finished pastry is too soft and sticky, add a little extra plain flour to bring it back to a firm ball of pastry.

Sweet rich shortcrust pastry

If making shortcrust pastry for a sweet dish, follow the countdown method for rich shortcrust pastry, but add 1oz/25g (1 tablespoon) of caster sugar after you have rubbed the fat into the flour. Mix well, then continue following the countdown instructions for rich shortcrust pastry.

Basic pizza dough ^{F*}
Serves: 4

Equipment

1 fine sieve
1 large mixing bowl
1 tablespoon
1 sharp knife
1 teaspoon
1 measuring jug
1 small saucepan **or** bowl
2 round-ended knives
1 or 2 baking trays
1 rolling pin **or** clean wine bottle

Ingredients

*8oz/225g plain flour
*salt
*1oz/25g (1 tablespoon) butter or margarine
¼oz/6g fresh yeast **or** 1 level teaspoon dried
   yeast and 1 teaspoon caster sugar
*5 tablespoons milk
*6 tablespoons water
*oil **or** margarine for greasing
*2 tablespoons flour for rolling

*Check store cupboard

Countdown method

PROBLEMS AND HANDY TIPS

Preparation time: 20 minutes

This quantity of dough will make one large deep pizza or two medium-sized thin pizzas. This will also depend on the side of your baking tins. Assemble all the ingredients and equipment you

Additional recipes

need for the pizza base. Set your timer for 20 minutes.

20 mins Measure out 8oz/225g plain flour and sift it into a mixing bowl. Add a pinch of salt and 1oz/25g (1 tablespoon) of butter or margarine. Cut the fat into small pieces, then rub it into the flour using your fingertips. Make a well in the centre of the mixture.

15 mins Check the instructions on the yeast packet and prepare as directed. Mix fresh yeast to a smooth paste with 1 teaspoon of warm water; mix dried yeast with 1 teaspoon of sugar and 1 teaspoon of water. Set aside.

12 mins Measure out 5 tablespoons of milk and 5 tablespoons of water to make ¼ pint/150ml of liquid in total. Heat the milk and water in a microwave oven or a small saucepan until it is lukewarm: you should be able to put your finger in it.

8 mins Pour the warmed liquid and yeast into the well in the flour, then stir gently until the mixture starts to bind. Using your clean hands or 2 round-ended knives, bring the dough together. If it is too sticky and will not bind, add a little extra plain flour until it comes together.

4 mins Place the dough on a clean work surface and knead well for a few minutes until it forms a smooth, elastic ball. Place the dough in a large bowl, cover with a damp tea towel and put in a warm place, such as an airing cupboard. The dough should rise and double in size after about 20–30 minutes.

0 mins Wash up and clear away.

Once the dough has increased in bulk, take it out of the bowl and place on a floured work surface. Knock it back to form a smooth ball again, then divide it in half if you are going to make 2 pizzas. Take 1 or 2 baking trays and lightly grease them with a little oil or margarine. Roll the dough out to the size, shape and thickness you want for your pizzas.

Use two round-ended knives to cut the fat into the flour with criss-cross action. This method is very good if you have very warm hands or would rather not get sticky hands.

If yeast gets too hot, it loses its rising properties.

Measure out the liquid as accurately as possible or you will end up with a very stiff or sticky dough.

If the milk becomes too hot, you will have to wait until it has cooled before adding it to the flour mixture.

The bowl can be lightly greased with a little oil to stop the dough from sticking to it.

To 'knock back' the dough means to work it firmly under your hands on a floured work surface.

It is always a good idea to grease the baking tins so that the cooked pizza can be easily removed.

See page 50 for suggested toppings and how to put the pizzas together. Cook in a hot oven preheated to 220°C/425°F/Gas mark 7 for approximately 25–30 minutes. Cooking times will vary depending on the size and thickness of your pizzas.

Choux pastry F*

Serves: 24

Equipment

1 measuring jug
1 medium saucepan
1 fine sieve
1 savoury or sweet wooden spoon or 1 hand-held
    electric mixer
1 small mixing bowl
1 fork
2 large baking trays
1 piping bag with small plain or fluted nozzle or
    1 teaspoon
1 small ovenproof container
1 spatula
1 skewer

Ingredients

*½ pint/300ml water
*4oz/100g butter or margarine
*5oz/125g plain flour
*4 eggs
*salt

*Check store cupboard

Countdown method

Preparation time: 30 minutes
Cooking time: 20–25 minutes

Assemble all the ingredients and equipment you need for the choux pastry. Remember this recipe serves 24 as it accompanies the cocktail or drinks party menu. Set your timer for 30 minutes.

30 mins Measure out ½ pint/300ml of water and place in a medium saucepan. Add 4oz/100g butter or margarine, place over a medium heat and bring slowly to the boil.

25 mins Meanwhile, measure out 5oz/125g of plain flour and sift it into a bowl.

23 mins Once the water is boiling and the butter has melted, remove the saucepan from the heat.

PROBLEMS AND HANDY TIPS

If you have a hand-held electric mixer, use it in the second stage of making the choux pastry, i.e. when you start adding the eggs to the mixture. This will save time and energy.

Additional recipes

Quickly pour in all the flour and stir vigorously with a wooden spoon until the mixture becomes smooth and there are no lumps to be seen. Set aside to cool.

20 mins Break 4 eggs into a mixing bowl, add a pinch of salt and whisk with a fork. Preheat the oven to 200°C/400°F/Gas mark 6.

18 mins Using either a wooden spoon or an electric mixer, slowly incorporate a small amount of beaten egg to the flour and water mixture. Make sure the mixture comes together each time before adding more egg. When finished, it should be thick and glossy and drawn away from the sides of the saucepan.

13 mins If making buns for the recipe on page 152, take 2 large baking trays and wet them with water. This helps the buns to rise.

12 mins Take a clean piping bag fitted with a small plain or fluted nozzle, if you have one. Fill it with the choux mixture and carefully pipe small circles on the trays. If you don't have a piping bag, put the teaspoonfuls of mixture on the trays. Make sure you leave about 1 inch/2.5 cm between the buns so they have room to rise and spread out.

4 mins When the baking trays are full, place them in the preheated oven to cook for 20–30 minutes. Put a small, ovenproof container filled with water in the bottom of the oven. This increases the amount of steam and helps the choux buns to rise.

0 mins Wash up and clear away.

Check the buns after 20–25 minutes. If they are well risen and golden brown, take them out of the oven and loosen them from the trays with a spatula. Make a small hole in the side of each bun with a skewer: this allows the steam to escape and leaves a hole which makes it easy to insert the filling if you are using a piping bag. Remove the container of water from the oven, then put the choux buns back in for 3–5 minutes to dry out. Transfer them to a wire rack to cool.

It is important that the flour is poured into the water quickly and stirred rapidly or it will become lumpy.
Stand the saucepan in a sink of cold water to help the mixture cool more quickly. The eggs cannot be added to the choux mixture until it is cool.

The harder the mixture is beaten, the better the choux pastry.

The damp baking trays play a very important part in helping the choux buns to rise. The more steam that is created, the bigger and better the buns will be.

Do not take the buns out of the oven until they are well risen, firm to the touch and golden brown. If they are taken out too early, they will collapse and be soggy.

The choux buns should be filled only a few hours before being served or they will become soggy.

Unfilled choux buns freeze extremely well; place them in an airtight plastic bag or plastic container.

This recipe is also suitable for desserts such as éclairs and profiteroles.

Melba toast

Serves: 4

Equipment	**Ingredients**
1 grill and grill pan	6 medium slices of fresh brown or white bread
1 bread board and plate	
1 bread knife	
1 baking tray	

Countdown method

PROBLEMS AND HANDY TIPS

Preparation time: 15 minutes
Cooking time: 15 minutes

Melba toast will keep crisp and fresh for a few days in an airtight tin or container, so you can make it in advance. Assemble all the ingredients and equipment you need for the melba toast. Set your timer for 15 minutes. Preheat the oven to 180°C/350°F/Gas mark 4.

15 mins Place the bread under a low grill or in a toaster on a low setting: it should heat through but not brown.

Make sure the bread doesn't brown. It must be only lightly toasted.

10 mins Place the toast on a chopping board and cut off the crusts using a sharp knife. Placing your hand over a piece of toast, slice through the toast horizontally using a sawing motion (1 piece of toast becomes 2 thin slices). Repeat until all the toast is sliced in half.

Don't worry if the bread falls apart while you are trying to saw it through the middle: it will be all right once it has cooked and dried out.

3 mins Place the bread, toasted side down, on a baking tray and place in a preheated oven for 15 minutes to dry out. Check the toast after 7–8 minutes as you might need to turn it over. The slices should curl up and become golden brown when ready.

If you like your melba toast really crisp, leave it in the oven a little longer than suggested.

1 min Remove the toast from the oven and leave to cool. Place in a basket to serve, or store it in an airtight tin or container until required.

0 mins Wash up and clear away.

Additional recipes

Poached chicken and chicken stock ^{F*}

Serves: 4

Equipment

1 large saucepan with lid
1 savoury chopping board
1 sharp knife
1 savoury wooden spoon
1 tablespoon
1 plate or roasting tin
1 fine sieve
1 or 2 bowls or freezer containers

Ingredients

1 medium to large whole chicken
*1 onion
*1 carrot
*6 peppercorns
*1 teaspoon of salt
*2 bay leaves

*Check store cupboard

Countdown method

PROBLEMS AND HANDY TIPS

Preparation time: 15 minutes
Cooking time: 60 minutes

Assemble all the ingredients and equipment you need for poaching the chicken. Set your timer for 15 minutes.

15 mins Wash the chicken under cold running water, then place in a large saucepan. Add enough cold water to cover the breast of the bird. Put the lid half on the saucepan, place over a medium heat and bring slowly to the boil.

Do not overfill the saucepan or the liquid will bubble out and the breast of the chicken will overcook.
Half covering the saucepan creates enough steam to cook the chicken breast, but also allows excess steam to escape.

10 mins Take 1 onion and 1 carrot, peel and chop them roughly and add to the saucepan with the chicken. Add 6 peppercorns, 1 teaspoon of salt and 2 bay leaves. Stir well.

5 mins Leave the chicken half covered to cook for approximately 60 minutes. (The time will vary, depending on the size of the chicken and the size of the saucepan.) Once the water is boiling, turn the heat down to the lowest setting and continue to cook. Do not allow the chicken to boil rapidly or it will become tough and rubbery.

Extra vegetables and herbs, such as celery, parsnips and parsley, can be added to the pan for extra flavour.

Chicken should never be undercooked. When in doubt, always cook it for a little longer than recommended.

0 mins Wash up and clear away.

To check whether the chicken is cooked, use a

spoon or knife to prise the meat away from the bone. If the legs come away from the body easily and there is no red in the meat, the chicken is cooked. If you are in doubt, it is always better to cook the chicken a little longer.

Once you are sure the chicken is cooked, transfer it to a plate or roasting tin and allow it to cool before taking the meat off the bones.

To make a good chicken stock, put all the bones back in the saucepan of liquid, place over a low heat and bring to the boil. Simmer for 50–60 minutes. Allow to cool, then strain the liquid through a fine sieve. Place the stock in a bowl, cover with cling film and chill. If you prefer, the stock can be frozen in a freezerproof container with lid for up to 3 months. Defrost the stock 8 hours before using it.

A good chicken stock will become a jelly once it has been chilled.

If there is a lot of stock, it is a good idea to divide it between two or more containers so that it can be used for separate sauces, soups or gravies.

Vegetable chart

See Handy Tip 11, page xviii, for a general rule on how to cook all vegetables.

Trim off the long stalk in line with the body and soak the artichokes in cold salty water for 1 hour. Remove the artichokes from the cold water and strip away the tough outer leaves. Bring a large saucepan of salt water to the boil and plunge the artichokes into water and cook for 35–40 minutes, or until the leaves pull away easily. Drain the artichokes upside-down to remove any excess water. Serve hot and whole on a starter plate with some finger bowls. Allow your guests to pull of the leaves and dip them in either a Hollandaise sauce (see page 200 for a recipe), melted butter or a cold vinaigrette. When you reach the heart, remove the choke or hair, and eat the heart with a knife and fork.

Artichoke, globe
Allow 1 whole artichoke per person.
Available all year.
Serve hot or cold.

Wash the asparagus thoroughly under cold running water. Take care not to damage the delicate tips. Trim off the bases, cutting all the stalks to roughly the same length. Place the asparagus in a saucepan large enough to lie them flat. Pour on enough boiling water to cover them. Add a pinch of salt and simmer for 15 minutes or until tender. The cooking time will depend on the size of the stalks. Drain the asparagus and serve with a Hollandaise sauce, melted butter or vinaigrette.

Asparagus
1lb (450g) serves 3–4 people.
Serve hot or cold.

Wash the aubergines well under cold running water and cut them into ½ inch/1 cm slices. Lay them on a plate or board and sprinkle liberally with salt. (This is called degorging and it draws out the bitter taste that is sometimes found in aubergines.) Allow the aubergines to soak in the salt for 20 minutes before turning them over and repeating the process on the other side. Wash all the salt off before cooking. Aubergines can either be fried in

Aubergines (egg plant)
Allow 6–8oz (175–225g) per person.
Available all year.
Serve hot or cold.

margarine and oil, deep fried, or cooked in the oven. Serve as a vegetable, in a ratatouille, cut in half and stuffed, or as a starter dip.

Top and tail the beans and keep them whole if they are not too large. Place the prepared beans in a saucepan, add a pinch of salt and pour on just enough boiling water to cover them. Cook for 10–15 minutes. This will vary depending on how large and thick the beans are. Serve them hot with a small amount of butter or cold in a salad with a vinaigrette.

Beans, French
Allow 4–8oz (100–225g) per person.
Available all year.
Serve hot or cold.

Top and tail the beans and remove the string down one side. Slice into diagonal 1 inch/2.5 cm strips. Place in a saucepan, add a pinch of salt and pour just enough boiling water over the beans to cover them. Cook for 12–15 minutes. The cooking time will vary depending on how large the beans are. Drain and serve hot with a small amount of butter or cold in a salad with a vinaigrette.

Beans, Runner
Allow 4–8oz (100–225g) per person.
Available July to October.
Serve hot or cold.

Twist off and discard all the leaves. Wash thoroughly and place in a saucepan. Fill the saucepan with cold water and add a pinch of salt. Allow to come to the boil and then simmer for approximately 2 hours. The cooking time will vary depending on the size of the beetroot. When they are soft all the way through, drain the water and peel and slice them into thin pieces. Serve hot with a white sauce or cold, diced or sliced with a salad dressing.

Beetroot
Allow 4–6oz (100–175g) per person.
Available all year.
Serve hot or cold.

Remove the beans from their shells and place them in a saucepan. Add a pinch of salt and pour over just enough boiling water to cover them. Cook for 20–30 minutes until the beans are soft. Serve hot with some butter, a parsley sauce or cold in a salad with a dressing.

Broad beans
Allow 8oz (225g) per person.
Available April to August.

Discard the coarse outer leaves and cut the stems off about 2 inch/5 cm from the head. If the heads are very large cut them in half. Wash

Broccoli
Allow 6–8oz (175–225g) per person.
Available all year.
Serve hot or cold.

Vegetable chart

the broccoli well and place it in a saucepan. Add a pinch of salt and pour just enough boiling water over the broccoli to cover it. Cook for 8–10 minutes. This time will depend on how large the pieces of broccoli are. Drain well and serve either with hot butter and toasted almonds or a Hollandaise sauce. Broccoli can also be served cold in a salad.

Remove any damaged outer leaves and discard. Trim a small amount off the stalk and make a cross in the base of each stalk. Wash the sprouts and place them in a saucepan. Add a pinch of salt and pour over just enough boiling water to cover them. Cook for 10–12 minutes or until the sprouts are soft but still holding their shape. Drain and serve hot with a small amount of butter or, at Christmas, with some chestnuts.

Brussels sprouts
Allow 4–6oz (100–175g) per person.
Available September to April, best when cold and frosty.
Serve hot.

Discard any damaged, coarse outer leaves. Cut the cabbage into quarters. Remove the centre stalk and shred the cabbage. Use raw, as it is, for a salad. To cook, place the shredded cabbage in a saucepan and pour just enough boiling water over it to cover. Add a pinch of salt and cook briskly for 8–10 minutes until soft but still crunchy. When cooking red cabbage add 1 tablespoon of wine vinegar to the water. Drain the cabbage and serve hot with a small amount of butter and a little grated nutmeg, if you like.

Cabbage, white or red
Allow 4oz (100g) per person: 1 large cabbage will feed 4 easily.
Available all year.
Serve hot or cold.

New carrots: remove the feathery leaves at the top. If the carrots are very young, it might not be necessary to peel them at all. Cut them into even-sized pieces and cook them for approximately 10 minutes.
Old carrots: peel and top and tail them. Cut them into even-sized pieces either sliced or diced. Place them in a saucepan with just enough cold water to cover them. Add a pinch of salt and cook for 10–15 minutes. The cooking time will depend on the size and age of the carrots. Drain and serve hot with a

Carrots
Allow 4–6oz (100–175g) per person.
Available all year.
Serve hot or raw.

little butter or parsley to add colour. Carrots can also be served cold in a salad, either diced or grated. They must be peeled first.

Cut the cauliflower into sprigs or florets. If there are any large sprigs, cut them in half so that all the pieces are roughly the same size. Wash the sprigs in cold water, place them in a saucepan and add a pinch of salt. Pour boiling water over them to just cover. Cook for 8–10 minutes. The cooking time will vary greatly depending on the size of the sprigs. Serve hot on its own, or with a white or cheese sauce poured all over it.

Cauliflower
Allow 1 medium-sized cauliflower to serve 4.
Available all year, best from June to October.
Serve hot or raw with dips.

Cut a small amount off the top and bottom of the celery bundle to separate the stalks. Wash each stalk well under cold running water. Depending what you are going to use the celery for, either cut it into even-sized lengths to use raw for dips or leave it in long lengths to serve in a jug of water on the table with cheese. To cook, pour boiling water over the celery, add a pinch of salt and cook for approximately 20–30 minutes. The cooking time will vary depending on how large the celery pieces are. Alternatively, par-boil the celery before putting it into the oven to bake for 1–1½ hours at 180°C/350°F/Gas mark 4. Serve with a hot white or herb sauce.

Celery
Allow 2–3 sticks per person.
Available all year.
Serve hot or raw.

Trim off any damaged leaves and, using a sharp knife, cut the chicory into thin slices. Wash well and drain. Use in a salad or as a base for a starter. Chicory can also be cooked in boiling water with a little lemon juice for 12–15 minutes. Serve hot, tossed in butter or with a white or cheese sauce.

Chicory
Allow 1–2 heads per person.
Available September to June.
Serve hot or raw.

Remove the outside leaves from the cob so that all the yellow corn is visible. Take a saucepan large enough to hold the cobs and fill it with water. Add a pinch of salt and bring the water to the boil. Plunge the cobs into the water and cook for 20–25 minutes. This cooking time will vary greatly de-

Corn-on-the-cob
Allow 1 cob per person.
Available February–May and June–November.
Serve hot.

Vegetable chart

pending on the size of the cobs and their age. Test that the corn is soft with a sharp knife. Always serve hot with melted butter.

Wash the courgettes well under cold running water. Top and tail and cut them either in half down the centre or into thin slices. Sprinkle liberally with salt and leave them to stand for 10 minutes. (This is called degorging and removes the bitter taste often found in these vegetables.) Make sure you wash all the salt off before cooking. Cook halved or stuffed courgettes in an ovenproof dish in the oven at 180°C/350°F/Gas mark 4, for 30–40 minutes. Alternatively add a knob of cooking margarine to a saucepan or frying pan and cook sliced courgettes briskly on the hob for 5–8 minutes, until they become soft but still can hold their shape. Courgettes can also be served raw, thinly sliced in a salad, but they must be young to taste sweet.

Courgettes (Zucchini)
Allow 4oz (100g) per person.
Available all year.
Serve hot or raw.

Wash the cucumber well if you are going to use the skin, or peel the cucumber and trim the top and bottom. Slice the cucumber very thinly or dice it for a salad. Grate the cucumber if you are going to use it for a sauce. Cucumber can also be cooked. Add 1 oz/25g (1 tablespoon) of cooking margarine to a saucepan or frying pan and cook briskly for 15–20 minutes. Season well before serving.

Cucumber
Allow 4oz (100g) per person.
Available all year.
Serve hot or raw.

Fennel is a vegetable and a herb which can be eaten cooked or raw. It has a strong flavour of aniseed and has become increasingly popular in recent years. Remove the feathery green tips at the top; these can be used whole or chopped as a garnish. To cook the fennel bulb, slice it into quarters or eighths (if very large), discarding any tough outer leaves. Steam or plunge into boiling water and cook for approximately 8–10 minutes, or until tender but still slightly firm. Cooking times will vary depending on the size of the fennel head. Serve as an accompaniment with fish or meat dishes.

Fennel (finocchio)
Allow 1 large heard to serve 4.
Available all year round from specialist shops and large supermarkets.
Serve hot or raw.

For salads, fennel can be used blanched or raw. To blanch it, finely slice the fennel head, discarding any tough outer leaves. Plunge into boiling water for 1–2 minutes. Drain through a colander, then hold under cold running water to stop it cooking; drain well. To serve raw, discard any tough outer leaves and chop finely.

Cut off the base stalk and separate the leaves, discarding any coarse old brown ones. Wash well and drain. Shred into small pieces. Place in a saucepan, add a pinch of salt and pour just enough boiling water over the leaves to cover. Cook for 8–10 minutes, depending on the age of the greens. Serve tossed in butter with a little nutmeg.

Greens (Spring)
Allow 6–8oz (175–225g)) per person.
Available February–June.
Serve hot.

Trim off the root, discard any damaged outside leaves and as much green top as necessary. Slice the leek in half and then into semi-circles. Wash extremely well to get rid of grit and sand. Place in a saucepan with a pinch of salt and pour just enough boiling water over them to cover. Cook for 8–10 minutes until soft but still squeaky. Leeks can also be cooked in the oven in an ovenproof dish with a small amount of cooking margarine at 180°C/350°F/Gas mark 4 for approximately 1 hour. Serve hot with a white or cheese sauce or cold with a vinaigrette.

Leeks
Allow 8oz (225g) per person.
Available August–May.
Serve hot or cold.

Remove and discard any coarse outer leaves. Wash the lettuce well under cold running water and leave to drain well. Lettuce is usually used raw in salads and starters and served with a dressing. It can be cooked to make a lettuce soup; the lettuce is added to a saucepan with a small amount of cooking margarine and cooked briskly until it reduces. It is often puréed with the rest of the soup.

Lettuce
Allow 1 round soft lettuce for 2 people. Iceberg will go further.

Top and tail the mange-tout, wash them well, and place them in a saucepan with a pinch of salt. Pour just enough boiling water over them to cover. Cook for 5–8 minutes but no longer as they are best served crunchy. Serve hot, tossed in butter and

Mange-tout
Allow 6–8oz (175–225g) per person.
Available all year but at a price.
Serve hot or cold.

Vegetable chart

seasoned well with ground black pepper. They can also be served cold in a salad or as part of a vegetable dish.

Peel the marrow well, making sure you get through the thick skin. Cut it in half down the centre and remove the core and pips. These should come out quite easily using either a knife or spoon. Either stuff the marrow or cut it into 1 inch/2.5 cm strips. Cook stuffed marrow in the oven at 200°C/400°F/ Gas mark 6 for approximately 60 minutes. Sliced marrow should be cooked in a saucepan with a small amount of cooking margarine; this is a mixture of frying and steaming. Marrow is often served in a ratatouille or in a casserole with tomatoes. It can be served hot or cold.

Marrow
Allow 6oz (175g) per person.
Available July–October
Serve hot or cold.

Wash mushrooms well to remove any soil and trim the stalks. There is no need to peel cultivated mushrooms. Slice or cut into quarters depending how you are going to use them. Mushrooms can either be fried in a small amount of margarine, baked in the oven, grilled or deep-fried. They only take a few minutes to cook. Once dark juice starts to run out of them, they are cooked. (Add lemon juice and nutmeg to mushrooms for extra flavour.) They can also be stuffed and cooked in the oven, or served raw in salads.

Mushrooms
Allow 2–3oz (50–75g) per person.
Available all year.
Serve hot, cold or raw.

Peel off and discard the outer skin. Slice or chop, depending on how the onion is going to be used. Fry onions in a small amount of cooking margarine for approximately 5–8 minutes or roast in the oven with meat for approximately 1–1½ hours. Onion rings can be deep fried for 3–4 minutes or grilled. Onions can be served hot, cold or raw in salads.

Onions
Allow 6oz (175g) per person.
Available all year.
Serve hot, cold or raw.

Trim off the root. Discard any dirty, damaged outer leaves. Chop spring onions into fine slices and either serve them raw in a salad or cook them rapidly in a Chinese wok.

Onions (spring)
Allow 1 bunch for 4 people.
Available in summer.
Serve hot or raw.

Peel the parsnips and trim them at the top and bottom. Cut into chunks or thin strips, depending on how you are going to cook and serve them. Parsnips can be placed in a saucepan of cold water with a pinch of salt, slowly brought up to the boil and allowed to simmer for 20–30 minutes, depending on their size. They are delicious mashed with potatoes to make a purée or roasted alongside a joint of meat in the oven.

Parsnips
Allow 6oz (175g) per person.
Available September–May.
Serve hot.

Most peas are cooked straight from the freezer. Cook frozen peas in boiling water with a pinch of salt and sugar for approximately 4–5 minutes, until they go wrinkly and soft. If you do come across fresh peas in pods, shell them and wash them well. Pour boiling water all over them and cook them with a little salt for 10–15 minutes. The cooking time will vary depending on the size and age of the peas. They are served hot with a knob of butter or cold in salads and rice dishes.

Peas
Allow 8oz (225g) per person.
Available frozen all year. Fresh from March–December.
Serve hot or cold.

Old potatoes: peel the potatoes and place them in a saucepan of cold water with a pinch of salt. Allow the water to come to the boil and then simmer for 20–30 minutes, depending on the size of the potatoes. Alternatively par-boil the potatoes and then roast them in the oven alongside a joint of meat; cut into sticks and deep fry them to make chips; or slice them thinly and sauté (fry) them in a frying pan with a small amount of cooking margarine. To cook baked potatoes, scrub the skins well and place the unpeeled potatoes in the oven for around 1–1½ hours at 200°C/400°F/Gas mark 6. Boiled old potatoes can also be used to make into potato salad.

Potatoes (old)
Allow 2 potatoes per person, on average.
Available all year.
Serve hot or cold.

New potatoes: Wash the potatoes well, but do not peel them. Put them in a saucepan of cold water with a pinch of salt and (if you like the flavour and it is available) a sprig of fresh mint. Bring the water slowly to the boil and simmer for approximately 15–20 minutes, depending on the size of the potatoes. Serve them (skins on) with butter or a

Potatoes (new)
Allow 3 to 4 potatoes per person.
Available spring to summer.
Serve hot or cold.

Vegetable chart

sauce. New potatoes are delicious eaten cold, either as they are or in a salad with a dressing.

There is a wide variety of new and exciting salad leaves readily available in supermarkets. This means you can change a boring green salad into an interesting dish of numerous colours and tastes. Any combination of leaves can be used, but try to mix bitter and sweet flavours as well as colours; fresh herbs chopped into a salad also add colour and flavour. Don't forget that extras can be added to fill out a salad, e.g. cucumber, tomatoes, beetroot, celery, chicory, peppers, avocado, artichokes, fennel, apples, celery, carrots, raisins, nuts and hard-boiled eggs. Always serve a salad with a good salad dressing; see page 201 for instructions on making your own.

Salad leaves
Iceberg, cos, little gem, lambs' lettuce (mâche or corn salad), rocket, frisée, watercress, young spinach, Chinese cabbage (leaves), young kale, curly endive. Available all year.
Serve raw.

Remove and discard coarse stems and any discoloured leaves. Wash the spinach thoroughly under cold running water and allow it to drain well. Place the spinach in a saucepan with a pinch of salt. Pour boiling water over the spinach. Cook for 5–8 minutes, until the spinach is soft. Drain well, as spinach tends to hold water. Serve as it is or tossed in garlic, ginger and butter or sour cream. Spinach can also be served raw in salads, but make sure it is well washed and young, otherwise it might be tough.

Spinach
Allow 8oz (225g) per person. Available all year. Also frozen.
Serve hot, cold or raw.

Peel the swede and cut into even-sized chunks. Discard any root or top. Place the pieces of swede in a saucepan of cold water with a pinch of salt. Allow the water to come to the boil then simmer for 20–25 minutes until the swedes are soft. Drain well, serve with butter and nutmeg, or mash well to a smooth purée and mix with butter and nutmeg.

Swedes
Allow 4–6oz (100–175g) per person.
Available September–June.
Serve hot.

Cut the peppers in half and remove the seeds, core and stalk. Wash the peppers well under cold running water. This will also help to wash out any stubborn seeds. If you are going to stuff a pepper you should only remove the core, stalk and

Sweet peppers
Allow 4oz (100g) per person.
Available all year.
Serve hot, cold or raw.

seeds so that it remains whole. (Large peppers can be cut in half and then stuffed.) Slice the peppers as required. Peppers can either be sautéed, blanched or baked in the oven. They can also be served raw in a salad.

This is bought either frozen or canned. It can be served hot or cold. Follow the cooking instructions on the packaging.

Sweet corn

Wash the tomatoes well, unless you are going to remove the skins. Tomatoes can be cooked in a variety of ways: grilled, fried, baked, stuffed or raw in salads. Make sure you remove the core if you are cutting the tomatoes up. Serve hot or cold.

Tomatoes
Allow 1–2 per person.
Available all year.

Peel and discard any top leaves or roots and cut the turnip into even-sized chunks. Place these in a saucepan of cold water with a pinch of salt and slowly bring to the boil. Allow to simmer for 25–30 minutes. The cooking time will vary depending on the size of the turnips. Serve with butter and nutmeg or mash to a smooth purée, season well and add a small amount of butter and nutmeg.

Turnips
Allow 4–6oz (100–175g) per person.
Available all year.
Serve hot.

Glossary of cookery terms

I have tried to keep complicated cookery terms to a minimum. Those with which you may be unfamiliar are listed below.

Bain-marie This is a water bath – a container of water in which delicate dishes, such as egg custard, must sit when cooking in the oven so they don't get too hot. The water surrounding the dish stops it from overheating. I use a roasting tin as it is big enough to hold a dish and plenty of water. A double saucepan, which is used on top of the hob, works on the same principle.

Baste To spoon hot fat or liquid over meat or vegetables to prevent them from drying out.

Beat To stir hard with either a wooden spoon, a balloon whisk or an electric mixer.

Blanch To plunge fruit or vegetables into boiling water for 1–2 minutes in order to start the cooking process. Vegetables are often blanched before being frozen.

Blend To mix either liquid or solid ingredients together.

Boil To allow the food to bubble rapidly on a medium to high heat.

Bouquet garni This is a small bunch of herbs and aromatic plants traditionally tied into a bundle and used to enhance the flavour of stews and soups. Nowadays, bouquet garni can be bought from supermarkets in the form of sachets containing powdered herbs.

Bring to the boil To allow food to reach a high temperature where it bubbles.

Casserole A glass, ceramic or cast-iron dish with a tight-fitting lid used to cook meat or vegetables slowly in a sauce in the oven.

Chop To cut food into small pieces without worrying about precision.

Coat To cover food with flour, egg, milk or breadcrumbs in order to protect it while cooking or add flavour.

Consistency The texture and thickness of a sauce or gravy.

Cook down To allow the ingredients to cook and shrink in size.

Cool To take the food away from the heat and leave it to stand for at least 5 minutes to cool down.

Cream To mix ingredients together (often fat and sugar) to make a light, creamy consistency.

Crudités Raw vegetables, such as carrots, celery, peppers, cucumber and cauliflower, which are cut into sticks or sprigs, then used for dunking in prepared dips.

Curdle To cause ingredients to separate; this can happen with sauces and mayonnaise.

Decorate To make a sweet dish look appetizing, pretty and colourful. (The decoration does not have to be edible, but must be easy to remove if it isn't.)

Degorge To sprinkle vegetables (such as courgettes and aubergines) liberally with salt to remove the bitter flavour often found in them.

Drain or strain To pass through a colander or sieve to remove water, or to separate solid food from a liquid. Sometimes the liquid is kept for a sauce or gravy, so it is strained into a bowl or measuring jug.

Flake To break up into small pieces.

Fold To mix gently and carefully, lifting the mixture all the time, trying to incorporate as much air as possible.

Fry To cook food in a hot fat or oil in a frying pan on top of the stove.

Garnish This is the same as decoration but is used when referring to savoury foods. Garnishes should always be edible, as they are often put into the food, i.e. parsley in a soup or watercress around a plate of meat or fish.

Glaze To give a dish a shiny finish, using beaten egg or milk. This is usually done to pastry.

Grill To cook directly under or over a heat source, or to brown the top of a dish to make it look appetizing (always use a heatproof dish).

Hold its shape A mixture that will stand up in peaks in the mixing bowl and stay there for several minutes (e.g. egg whites when whisked).

Leave a trail To test whisked mixture for readiness, lift some of it up with a spoon and watch the mark left in the top of the mixture. If the mark remains for a few seconds, the mixture has left a trail and is ready to be used.

Marinade A seasoned liquid (usually made the day before cooking) in which meat, fish or vegetables are soaked to add flavour to a dish.

Par-boil To place meat or vegetables in cold water, bring them slowly to the boil and partially cook them for 2–3 minutes.

Pith This is the white part of a citrus fruit that lies directly underneath the coloured skin. It is there to protect the fruit but is bitter in taste and should be avoided when grating the rind of the fruit as it can spoil the taste of a dish.

Plunge To immerse meat or vegetables quickly in a boiling liquid.

Poach To cook meat, fish or vegetables very slowly in a liquid, either in the oven or on top of the hob. The liquid is often used to make a sauce to accompany the dish afterwards.

Purée To sieve or liquidize a fruit or vegetable to create a smooth, thick mixture.

Reduce To boil a liquid rapidly to evaporate some of the water: this increases the strength of flavour, particularly for a special gravy or sauce.

Roast To cook meat or vegetables in a hot oven in a roasting tin with fat or dripping.

Roux This is a mixture of fat and plain flour, which forms the basis of most sauces. It should always be cooked for a few minutes to remove the starchy flavour, then allowed to cool before the liquid is added.

Sauté To fry food quickly over a high heat with as little fat as possible.

Scald To bring a liquid almost to boiling point but no further. As soon as the liquid starts to bubble, it should be removed from the heat. This is often done to milk before adding it to a custard or sauce.

Glossary of cookery terms

Seal To fry food quickly, usually meat or fish, in order to keep in the juices. The food is then casseroled or stewed slowly, which allows all the flavours to be retained in the dish.

Season To add salt and pepper to a dish, to suit your taste. Sometimes you will need to add extra ingredients such as nutmeg, herbs and mustard powder. The recipe will give you details.

Seasoned flour This is a mixture of plain flour, salt and ground pepper. It is used to coat meat, fish and sometimes vegetables before they are fried or sautéed, as it helps to seal in the juices and also adds extra flavour.

Short A word used to describe dry, brittle pastry which tends to crack easily when being rolled out or when used to line tins. A pastry becomes short when not enough liquid is added to it.

Sieve To remove lumps from food to give it a smooth consistency, e.g. flour or fruit purées.

Simmer To cook food very slowly on the lowest heat possible.

Slice To cut meat, vegetables or fruit into pieces or strips.

Soak To immerse in a liquid for minutes or hours, depending on the recipe.

Stew To cook meat, vegetables or fruit in a liquid either on the hob or in a moderate oven to tenderize them.

Stock A flavoured liquid. Stock can be home-made, bought fresh from a supermarket or made by adding boiling water to a flavoured stock cube. Stock is used in casseroles, stews, sauces and gravy.

Tart This means that a fruit is rather bitter or sour and will probably need sweetening with extra sugar.

Whip To beat well with a balloon whisk or electric mixer. If you over-whip cream it will curdle, so be very careful.

Whisk *See* Whip.

Zest This is the coloured outer rind of citrus fruits such as oranges and lemons. Zest is often used in dishes to add colour, texture and flavouring. It is usually grated on a fine grater straight into the dish.

Index

Index

carrots
  buttered 133
  Christmas roast 170
  how to cook 214
  Vichy 116
cashew nuts, lemon chicken with 64
casseroles
  chicken casserole with peanut and
    ginger sauce 105
  definition 222
  pork chop casserole with apple and sage 74
  removing fat from xviii
cauliflower, how to prepare and cook 215
celery
  how to prepare and cook 215
  mixed cheese and croûton salad 116
cheese
  bacon and onion rosti 7
  choux buns stuffed with Gruyère cheese
    142
  cottage cheese and cucumber dip 44
  feta cheese 37, 116
  grape and melon cheese sticks 142
  mixed cheese and croûton salad 116
  mixed cheese platter with biscuits 155
  potato and spinach layer 116
  sauce, recipe 199
  smoked salmon and cream cheese
    croissants 44
  tomatoes with mozzarella and basil 13
cheesecake, chocolate 82
chestnuts, Brussels sprouts with 170
chick peas: hummus dip 29
chicken
  casserole with peanut and ginger sauce
    105
  cold chicken in tomato and basil sauce
    155
  lemon chicken with cashew nuts 64
  marinated chicken legs 82
  poached chicken 216
  roasting times 192
  spicy chicken drumsticks 44
  stock 210
chicory
  how to prepare and cook 215
  tomato, avocado and chicory salad 29
china and crockery xi, xx
Chinese stir-fry menu 64
chipolata sausages 170

chocolate
  and banana cream 21
  cheesecake 82
  hot mocha soufflé 188
  mousse au chocolat 105
chop, to 222
chopping boards xix
choux buns stuffed with Gruyère cheese 142
choux pastry, basic recipe 207
Christmas cake 170
Christmas pudding 170
Christmas roast menu 170
ciabatta bread 37
cider 74
coat, to 222
cocktail party menu 142
coffee
  hot mocha soufflé 188
coleslaw 82
consistency 222
cook down, to 222
corn-on-the-cob, how to cook 215
cornflour, how to use xix
cottage cheese and cucumber dip 44
courgettes
  chilled ratatouille 125
  how to prepare and cook 216
cranberry sauce 170
cream, to 222
cream
  cheese and smoked salmon croissants 44
  crème brulée 116
  crème fraîche 125
  sour 1, 29
croissants, filled 44
crudités 29, 44, 142
  definition 222
cucumber
  and cottage cheese dip 44
  how to prepare and cook 216
  raita 96
curdle, to 222
curry menu (Indian) 96
custard tarts 44
cutlery xi, xx, xxi

dahl soup 96
decorate, to 222
deep-freeze stores xii
degorge, to 222

Index

Index

Index